Praise for
GET A FINANCIAL LIFE:

"A highly readable and substantial guide to the grown-up worlds of money and business. Backed up by bibliographies, source lists, and useful phone numbers, this book could be tucked into one of those ubiquitous backpacks to guide novices through the thickets of apartment rentals, mortgage applications, taxes and more. Its strength is in explaining both the principles and the practicalities involved in each chunk of the landscape."

—Deborah Stead, *The New York Times*

"A daring book aimed at Generation Xers unafraid of a blunt author who will tell them what to do fast. . . . A life's worth of smart financial advice."

—Linda Stern, *Newsweek*

"With all those new choices, personal financial decision making is getting more and more complicated, even for the computer generation. Beth Kobliner's book provides a much-needed and sensible guide."

—Paul A. Volcker, Former Chairman, Federal Reserve Board

"One of the best guides to help young people get a handle on money matters."

—Burton G. Malkiel,
Chemical Bank Chairman's
Professor of Economics,
Princeton University; author,
A Random Walk Down Wall Street

"I have six children who will soon need 'a financial life.' This is the kind of basic, readable book they should have."

—Stuart Varney, *CNN Business News*

"Laying a solid financial foundation is one of the most important and rewarding tasks facing young people today. In *Get a Financial Life*, Beth Kobliner has created a great guide that will make the job much easier and a lot more fun."

—Dean Shepherd, Anchor, CNBC

"Shaw said youth is wasted on the young. I suspect the Kobliner financial wisdoms will work out well at all our ages."

— Paul A. Samuelson, Institute
Professor Emeritus, MIT;
Nobel Laureate in Economics

"A broad-ranging primer. . . . The quality of information is uniformly high, and there isn't a single chapter that doesn't contain useful but not obvious advice alongside a clear and well-presented blueprint."

— Ken Kurson, *Worth*

"Informative, laden with sound advice, and attractively packaged with charts and lists, this small book is ideal for anyone needing a primer on personal finance. All the 'basics' are here: setting goals; checking and savings accounts; investing; buying a home; insurance; slashing taxes. Especially useful for younger readers is its long-range perspective."

— Guy Halverson,
The Christian Science Monitor

"Beth Kobliner has written one of the best personal finance books currently available. *Get a Financial Life* is 'must' reading for young adults—and has a lot of solid information for the 40 and over crowd as well."

— *The Midwest Book Review*

"If getting a financial life is terrifying, Kobliner eases readers into it gently. . . . Financial books generally aren't light reading, but this one is easily digestible."

— Suzanne Sullivan, *Kiplinger's*

"Contrary to rumor, young people do care about finance. After all, many are paying off college loans and worry that Social Security won't be around when they retire. *Get a Financial Life* offers sensible advice written for people just starting out in their work life."

— Chris Farrell, *Sound Money,*
Public Radio International

"If you're young—and you follow the rules in this book—you won't worry whether there's Social Security down the road."

— Ray Brady, Economics Correspondent,
CBS Evening News

"Wake up, Generation X! Beth Kobliner is telling you it's time to smell the latte. In *Get a Financial Life,* Kobliner serves a rich, smooth brew of common sense on everything from paying off your student loan to saving for (gasp) your own kid's college education. The advice is thoughtful, precise and up-to-date. But the simple, step-by-step explanations make getting a financial life easier than steaming the perfect froth on a cappuccino."

—Saul Hansell, Business Reporter,
The New York Times

"An eminently digestible resource suited to the attention span of the MTV Generation. Buying this book right now is probably one of the best—and cheapest—investments a Gen Xer can make."

—Stacy Morrison, *Time Out New York*

Here's What the Experts Said About Individual Chapters of *Get A Financial Life:*

Chapter 3 (Debt):

"The 'Debt and the Material World' chapter provides straightforward solutions to the problems of personal debt that plague many young people today."

—Durant Abernethy, President,
National Foundation for
Consumer Credit

Chapter 4 (Banking):

"It's tough to get ahead, and Beth Kobliner has some very solid advice in her banking chapter that will help you make every dollar count. Who has time to learn the *hard* way?"

—Fritz Elmendorf, Vice President,
Consumer Bankers Association

Chapter 5 (Investing):

"Kobliner's easy, can-do writing style and command of the investment material make this book essential reading for all those who find investments hopelessly complex."

—Lewis J. Altfest, Ph.D., CFA,
President, L. J. Altfest & Co.

Chapter 6 (Retirement):

"Kobliner's discussion of do-it-yourself retirement plans is top-notch— clear, concise, and comprehensive."

> —Karen Ferguson, Director,
> Pension Rights Center;
> coauthor, *Pensions in Crisis*

Chapter 7 (Housing):

"There are very few sources of *practical,* step-by-step advice for young households getting started in the housing market. Beth Kobliner's book fills this gap in an accessible, accurate, and valuable way."

> —John Tuccillo, Vice President and
> Chief Economist, National
> Association of Realtors

Chapter 8 (Insurance):

"Many authors explain basic principles of personal insurance, but Beth Kobliner also provides practical and usable advice for young people, and she does it all in a clear, readable style."

> —Eric A. Wiening, CPCU, ARM, AU,
> Assistant Vice President, American
> Institute for Chartered Property
> Casualty Underwriters

Chapter 9 (Taxes):

"Beth Kobliner's book provides a road map for avoiding tax potholes on your travels throughout your financial life."

> —Jeff J. Saccacio, Partner,
> Coopers & Lybrand L.L.P.

PERSONAL FINANCE IN YOUR TWENTIES AND THIRTIES

BETH KOBLINER

GET A
FINANCIAL
LIFE

A FIRESIDE BOOK

Published by Simon & Schuster

New York   London   Toronto

Sydney   Singapore

FIRESIDE
Rockefeller Center
1230 Avenue of the Americas
New York, NY 10020

FIRESIDE and colophon are registered trademarks
of Simon & Schuster, Inc.

Designed by Katy Riegel

Manufactured in the United States of America

10   9   8   7   6   5   4   3   2   1

Library of Congress Cataloging-in-Publication Data

Kobliner, Beth.
      Get a financial life : personal finance in your twenties and thirties /
Beth Kobliner.
            p.   cm.
      "A Fireside Book." Includes bibliographical references and index.
      1. Finance, Personal.   2. Young adults—Finance, Personal.   I. Title.
HG179.K59   2000
332.024'0562—dc21   00-029719
                                                                            CIP
ISBN   0-684-81213-4
            0-684-87261-7

Figure 5-1, page 123, from *Stocks, Bonds, Bills and Inflation*® *1999 Yearbook,*
© 1999 Ibbotson Associates, Inc. Based on copyrighted works by Ibbotson and
Sinquefield. All rights reserved. Used with permission.

To my parents, Harold and Shirley Kobliner,
who taught me how to handle money,
and to Sylvia Porter,
who gave me the opportunity to write about it

SPECIAL ACKNOWLEDGMENTS

This expanded and updated version of *Get a Financial Life* has been an enormous team effort. Beginning on page 301, I've listed the more than 600 sources to whom I turned for expertise in both the original and current editions of the book. This special section, however, acknowledges those people who have made contributions above and beyond the call of duty.

First, the financial experts who have given generously of their time in helping me prepare both versions of *Get a Financial Life*. Special thanks go to managing director of financial planning solutions at PricewaterhouseCoopers Kent Allison; investment advisors Lew and Karen Altfest; vice president and chief economist of Fannie Mae David Berson; quantitative modeling consultant Ed Chang; student loan advisor and president of Campus Consultants Kalman Chany; fee-only insurance consultant Glenn Daily; Professor of Bank Management at the University of Virginia Richard DeMong; vice president of communications of the Consumer Bankers Association Fritz Elmendorf; fee-only financial planner Steven Enright; director of the Pension Rights Center Karen Ferguson; pension expert extraordinaire Martin Fleisher; vice president at HSH Associates Keith Gumbinger; executive director of the Women's Institute for a Secure Retirement Cindy Hounsell; life insurance actuary with the Consumer Federation of America James Hunt; tax advisor and senior tax partner at Goldstein Golub Kessler & Co. Stuart Kessler; principal of the Vanguard Group Brian Mattes; credit card guru and president of RAM Research Group Robert McKinley; banking expert and chairman of Moebs Services Michael Moebs; partner at Grant Thornton Tom Ochsenschlager; national director of large employee group services at Ernst & Young Glenn Pape; director of consumer affairs at the Insurance Information Institute Jeanne Salvatore; tax attorney Martin M. Shenkman; vice president of Financial Planning Group at David L. Babson & Co. William Speciale; and assistant vice president of American Institute for CPCU and Insurance Institute of America Eric A. Wiening.

I also owe a debt of gratitude to the following people, whose expertise was invaluable in putting together this new edition of the book: media relations associate at Lipper Inc. Camilla Altamura; president of RBA Insurance Strategies Roy Assad; senior manager at Deloitte & Touche John Battaglia; director of technology and marketing communications at Fannie Mae Raschelle Burton; director of research at Bankrate.com Karen Christie; editor-in-chief and publisher of No-Load Fund Investor Sheldon Jacobs; communications director at Unum Provident James Johnson; executive vice president and general counsel at Bank Lease Consultants Randall McCathren; public affairs manager at the USA Group Bob Murray; public affairs officer of the IRS Don Roberts; and managing director of the Vanguard Core Management Group Gus Sauter. And I greatly appreciate the assistance given by these experts while I was preparing the first edition of *Get a Financial Life*: investment advisor Jack Bonné; former public affairs officer of the IRS Wilson Fadely; tax partner at Deloitte & Touche Jerry Gattegno; tax expert and professor of law at Vanderbilt University L. Harold Levinson; former banking expert at Bank Rate Monitor Gail Liberman; president of Wholesale Insurance Network (WIN) Keith Maurer; former principal at Furash & Co. Edward L. Neumann; vice president of underwriting at Norwest Mortgage Sharon Ridenour; tax attorney Diane Rivers; and former research analyst with the Center for Study of Responsive Law Janice Shields.

My former coworkers at *Money* were incredibly generous with their time and help when I was writing the first edition of *Get a Financial Life*. They included Caroline Donnelly, Richard Eisenberg, Judy Feldman, Carla Fried, Eric Gelman, Jordan Goodman, Bonnie Hilton Green, Holly Ketron, Lani Luciano, Kelly Smith, and Patti

Straus. I would especially like to thank Gary Belsky and Walter Updegrave for their incredibly valuable feedback on the original edition. My gratitude also goes to Tyler Mathisen of CNBC and Frank Lalli, the former managing editor of *Money*, who has been a mentor to me.

Many friends and colleagues also offered valuable input at various stages. They include Rick Allen, Robin Alssid, Richard Burgheim, Larry Burke, Eileen Choi, Fran Claro, Joe Claro, Paul Cohen, Jon Cowan, James Gates, Lynn Goldner, Ken Garfinkle, Beth Hassrick, Glenn Hodes, Jennifer Jaeck, Jonathan Karp, Sam Kerstein, Skye Ketron, John Kildahl, Janet Klosklo, Michelle Kosch, Steve Kotsen, Michael Kantor, Harold Kobliner, Kenneth Kobliner, Miriam Diamond Kobliner, Perry Kobliner, Shirley Kobliner, Kathy Landau, Megan McCrudden, Carmen Morais, Vanessa O'Connell, Max Phillips, Parker Reilly, Ruby Reilly, Mark Safire, William Safire, Rebecca Scott, Rebecca Belle Shaw, Adam Benjamin Shaw, Anne Morgan Spalter, Michael Spalter, and Dave Zinczenko.

I would also like to single out Anne Fentress, Andrew Bradfield, David Witt, Nicole Chong, and particularly Adam Feldman, who have logged literally hundreds of hours helping me ensure that every detail in the new edition has been meticulously researched, re-researched, checked, and rechecked.

I am also especially indebted to Danielle Claro, whose insight, humor, and remarkable editing skills were a godsend.

I owe gratitude to Simon & Schuster, notably to Sarah Pinckney Whitmire, my editor on the original version, as well as Bob Asahina, Doris Cooper, Airié Dekidjiev, Sue Fleming-Holland, Seth Gershel, Mark Gompertz, Christine Lloreda, Jennifer Love, Rachel Rader, and Trish Todd. I would like to thank Gordon Kato, who believed in this book from the beginning, and Lisa Bankoff, Abigail Rose, and Suzanne Gluck of ICM.

I want to thank Rebecca Belle and Adam Benjamin for their incredible patience and understanding during late nights and worked weekends.

And most of all, I would like to thank my husband, David, who continues to offer complete, unwavering love and devotion. He is my inspiration.

CONTENTS

4. Basic Banking

*Learn How to Get the Most from Your Bank for the
Least Amount of Money*

5. All You Really Need to Know About Investing

For New Investors, the Feeling Is Mutual (Funds)

6. Living the Good Life in 2030

*Think It's Crazy to Worry Now About Retirement
Then? It's Crazy Not To*

7. Oh, Give Me a Home 175

Advice on Getting an Apartment or House of Your Own

8. Insurance: What You Need and What You Don't 213

Finding the Right Policies and Forgoing Coverage You Can Do Without

9. How to Make Your Life Less Taxing

INTRODUCTION

A lot has happened since 1996, when I wrote the first edition of *Get a Financial Life*.

The Internet has revolutionized the way many people interact with the world. The economy has experienced the greatest period of prosperity it has ever known. In the last three years of the 1990s alone, stock values doubled, and just about any stock with a "dot com" after its name has seemed like a winning lottery ticket.

Despite these changes, the premise of the original edition of *Get a Financial Life* still holds: Many people in my generation—those now in their twenties and thirties—do not expect to live as well as their parents. In inflation-adjusted dollars, people 25 to 34 years old today still earn lower incomes on average than our counterparts in the 1970s. And we are carrying more personal debt (like credit cards and student loans) than any other generation has at our age.

The good news is that there has never been a better time to get your financial life in order. If you're drowning in credit card debt, there are dozens of low-rate cards aggressively competing for your business. If you're hoping to buy a home in the next few years, there are more low down-payment loans to choose from than ever before. If you're eager to start investing—even with very little money—new tax-favored savings plans are available to help you make the most of whatever you can afford to set aside. And the Internet has made it exponentially easier to find everything from low-interest-rate auto loans to high-interest-rate savings options.

This book will show you how to make the most of your money, whether you earn $20,000 or $200,000, whether you're single or attached, whether you're financially adept or financially confused. You will learn how to save even if you're barely making ends meet. You'll get straightforward advice on how to select the right stock mutual funds. You'll pick up tax strategies that could save you hundreds of dollars a year. You'll discover how to reduce outrageous bank fees and carefully evaluate your online banking options. You'll find strategies for handling your student loans. You will get unbiased advice on what kinds of life, health, and auto insurance you need, and what kinds you should avoid.

This book will provide answers to specific questions, including: Should I contribute to my company's 401(k) plan? How do I determine whether I should buy or rent a home? Where's the best place to save? When does it make sense to start investing? How can I find out what's in my credit report? Should I buy or lease a car? What tax credits can I claim? How can the Internet help me shop for a home loan? Should I get a Roth IRA? Do I need a stockbroker?

If the thought of reading an entire book on personal finance seems daunting, relax. Chapter 1 offers a summary of some of the most important steps you'll need to take, and "Financial Cramming" review sections at the end of each chapter highlight key concepts so you can be sure that you've nailed them.

By the way, all of the information in this second edition of *Get a Financial Life* has been meticulously re-researched and updated, but not everything needed to be rewritten; I have decided *not* to change anything just for change's sake. The bottom line of *Get a Financial Life* hasn't changed a bit. Once you get started, you'll see that achieving your financial goals can be a lot easier than you think—that is, if you take advantage of the biggest benefit you still have on your side: time.

CRIB NOTES

A "Cheat Sheet" for Time-Pressed Readers

I F T H E I D E A of reading a whole book on personal finance leaves you cold, this is the chapter for you. The advice below cuts to the chase and sets you on the road to a solid financial life. So if you don't have the patience to read the entire book right now, adopting one or two of these strategies will still put you ahead of the game.

Of course, as someone's mother once said, cheaters only cheat themselves. And while this chapter is a good launching point, ignoring the remaining eight chapters is a little like relying on the *Cliffs Notes* version of *Moby Dick:* You'll get the basic plot line but never understand it in any real depth. Still, the following crib notes should give you a rundown on the basics. I've tried to list them in rough order of importance, but your priorities may depend on your own situation.

1.   Insure yourself against financial ruin.

It's not surprising that people don't like to talk about insurance. It's expensive, confusing, and mostly about sickness and death. But if you're interested in getting adequate medical care in case of a serious accident or illness, and would prefer not to bankrupt yourself and your family in the process, there really is no higher financial priority than health insurance.

If you work for a company that offers employees health insurance, you're lucky; participating in your employer's group plan will almost always cost you much less than buying a policy on your own, and the coverage you get is likely to be more comprehensive than any individual policy you could afford. However, in an effort to reduce their costs, many companies have shifted to what is known as **managed care,** which means you may be limited in your choice of doctors and treatments. If you're given more than one type of health insurance plan to choose from through your employer, make sure you consider not only price but also the type of coverage you will receive. If, for example, you're thinking about joining a type of plan called a **health maintenance organization (HMO),** inquire about exactly what is covered, ask about the procedure for seeing specialists, and find out what happens if you want to visit a doctor outside the HMO. Although HMOs are generally less expensive than other plans, if you come down with a serious illness and want to see a specialist outside your HMO network, you may have to foot the entire bill yourself. Before you sign up for any health insurance plan, talk to coworkers about their experiences with the various options.

If the company you work for does not offer health insurance, you'll have to pay for it yourself. If you recently graduated from college, see if you can extend coverage from your parents' plan for a few years. If you're job hunting, at the very least get temporary coverage. If you're employed but your company doesn't offer you insurance, see if there are any organizations you can join (a trade association, for example) that will allow you to purchase health insurance at a group rate. This can be much less expensive than purchasing individual coverage. Since plans vary dramatically from state to state, your best bet is to call the major insurers and HMOs in your area and see what they have to offer. Also try Quotesmith (800-556-9393; www.quotesmith.com), InsWeb (www.insweb.com), and your local Blue Cross/Blue Shield company (www.bluecares.com) for quotes. And if you're having trouble getting insurance because of a preexisting medical condition, your state insurance department should be able to provide you with the names of companies that will cover you. (See page 220 for the phone number of your state's office.)

Another type of protection you may want to consider is life insurance, but only if you have children or someone else is financially dependent on you. If you don't have dependents, you don't need life insurance. If you do, the type you should buy is called **term insurance,** which is relatively inexpensive. Get quotes from agents at USAA (800-531-8000; www.usaa.com) and Ameritas (800-552-3553; www.ameritas.com). You should also consult Web sites that will let you compare quotes from different firms side by side, like Term4sale (www.term4sale.com) and Quotesmith (800-556-9393; www.quotesmith.com). One warning: If you deal with a life insurance agent, be prepared to hear a big pitch for a type of policy known as **cash value life insurance.** Ignore it. It's more profitable for the agent, but it's probably not a good deal for you.

Depending on your financial situation, you may also want to consider protecting your earning power with disability insurance. A disability policy will pay you an income (typically 60% to 70% of your current salary) if you're injured or very sick and are unable to work for an extended period of time. Depending on the state in which you're employed, you may already be covered by a mandatory disability insurance program and/or by insurance provided voluntarily by your employer as part of your standard employee benefits package. Even if you are, it's a good idea to find out how much coverage you have, whether it's possible to buy more, and what it would cost you. If disability insurance is not available to you through your employer's plan, look into purchasing some on your own. Companies that specialize in disability insurance are Unum (800-843-3426; www.unum.com) and Northwestern Mutual Life Insurance (800-672-4341; www.northwesternmutual.com).

For additional tips on purchasing all types of insurance, see Chapter 8.

2.   Pay off your debt the smart way.

More often than not, the smartest financial move you can make is to take any savings you have (above and beyond money you need for essentials like rent, food, and health insurance) and pay off your

high-rate loans. The reason is simple: You can "earn" more by paying off a loan than you can by saving and investing. Paying off a
credit card that has a 17% interest rate is equivalent to earning 17%
on an investment, *guaranteed*—an extremely attractive rate of
return. (Actually it's even better than that; it's the equivalent of earning 17% *after taxes*.) If you want a full explanation of this concept,
turn to page 51. Otherwise, take my word for it.

If you can't pay off your high-rate debt immediately, take steps
to reduce the interest rate you pay. As a short-term strategy, you
can switch to a new credit card and take advantage of the super-
low introductory rates (known as "teaser rates") that many credit
card companies offer to new customers. But these rates only last
for a few months and then spike up to much higher rates. In the
long run, it probably makes more sense to apply for a card with
a long-lasting low rate, but you'll need an excellent credit rating
to qualify. For lists of low-rate credit card issuers, visit the Web
sites of Bankrate.com (www.bankrate.com), Consumer Action
(www.consumer-action.org), and CardWeb (www.cardweb.com).
(If you don't have access to the Internet, call 800-344-7714 or
send a request and check or money order for $5 to CardTrak, P.O.
Box 1700, Frederick, MD 21702.)

If you have several different types of debt—say, a credit card balance on a card with a 17% interest rate, a car loan with a 10% rate,
and a student loan at 8%—pay off the loan with the highest interest rate first. One strategy to consider is stretching out your student
loan payments over 15 or 20 years instead of 10 years through a
process known as **loan consolidation.** (To see if you're eligible, call
the company that handles your loan.) This will reduce your monthly
student loan payment and leave you with extra cash. Use this money
to pay off your credit card balance faster. Once you've gotten rid of
your credit card debt, start paying off your auto loan faster. After
you wipe out that loan too, increase your student loan payments to
at least their initial levels.

The only time it doesn't make sense to kill your debt is when the
interest rate you're being charged is *lower* than the rate you can
receive on an investment. If, for example, you have a special student
loan with a 3% rate, you'd be better off maintaining your usual

payment schedule on the loan and putting your cash into an investment that pays an after-tax rate greater than 3%.

For detailed information on credit cards, auto loans, student loans, home equity loans, and credit reports, see Chapter 3.

3. Start contributing to a tax-favored retirement savings plan.

Next to flossing, saving money in a retirement plan is the smartest habit to acquire when you're young. If you're lucky enough to work for a company that offers a retirement savings plan like a 401(k), you should take advantage of it.

There are several reasons to participate in a 401(k). For starters, many employers will match a portion of the amount you put into such a plan. That means the company will contribute a set amount—say, 50 cents—for every dollar you contribute, up to a specified dollar amount. That's an immediate 50% return on your money! (In fact, if your company offers such a fabulous matching deal, you should probably contribute to the plan even before paying off your credit card debt.) In addition, the federal government allows you to delay paying taxes on the money you contribute to a 401(k) until you withdraw that money. That translates into an immediate tax break of hundreds of dollars each year. If, for example, you contribute $1,000 to a 401(k), you will reduce your taxable income by $1,000. If you're in the 28% tax bracket, that's a savings of $280. (You are in this tax bracket in 2000 if you are single and your taxable income is between $26,250 and $63,550, or if you are married and you and your spouse's combined taxable income is between $43,850 and $105,950.)

Be forewarned that you're likely to come across people who'll tell you you're too young to lock up your money in a retirement savings plan. Ignore them. While it's true that you won't be able to withdraw your money until you reach age $59^{1}/_{2}$ without paying a 10% penalty, many plans allow employees to borrow against their retirement savings at favorable rates. What's more, your money will grow tax-free in a retirement plan for years. The benefits of tax-free growth could easily outweigh the penalty you'd have to pay for making an early withdrawal. And if you switch jobs, you may be able to move your 401(k) money into your new employer's plan.

The easiest way to start contributing is to contact your employee benefits office and ask to have a set percentage of each paycheck automatically transferred into your company plan. Try to contribute the maximum allowed by law. If you can't afford to stash away this much, at least contribute the maximum amount for which you're eligible to receive matching funds.

If you aren't lucky enough to work for an employer that offers a 401(k) or a similar company retirement plan (and possibly even if you are), you should start investing in an **individual retirement account (IRA)**. The most you can contribute to an IRA is $2,000 annually; if at all possible, contribute this amount every year. There are two main kinds of IRA: traditional **deductible IRAs** and **Roth IRAs**. Deductible IRAs, like 401(k)s, give you an immediate tax break and let you delay paying taxes on your money until you withdraw it. Roth IRAs work the other way around: You don't get an upfront tax break, but the money you invest grows tax-free forever; you won't have to pay federal income tax when you withdraw that money at retirement.

IRAs don't have all the advantages of 401(k)s, so putting money in an IRA is somewhat less pressing than enrolling in your company-sponsored plan. For starters, with an IRA you don't have the benefit of an employee matching program. Also, you can't borrow money from an IRA before you reach age $59^{1}/_{2}$ the way you can with most 401(k)s; if you need to get at your money, you'll probably have to pay the 10% penalty. (There are exceptions to this rule if you're withdrawing the money from an IRA for certain educational or homebuying expenses.) Even if you have to pay the penalty for making an early withdrawal from your IRA, you'll often still come out ahead.

If your employer *does* offer a 401(k) with matching, you should contribute to that plan before thinking about an IRA. Once you've hit the maximum your employer will match, you should contribute to an IRA as well.

For answers to commonly asked questions about tax-favored

retirement savings plans, including which kind of IRA to choose, see Chapter 6.

4. Reduce your monthly banking fees.

Chances are you don't give your bank too much thought. But by becoming aware of bank charges, you may be able to save hundreds of dollars a year.

Two of the most burdensome bank fees are checking charges and automated teller machine (ATM) fees. To reduce these charges, and possibly eliminate them entirely, shop around for a bank that waives them for customers who maintain a specified minimum balance. Some banks require you to maintain the minimum in a checking account only; others waive monthly checking charges as long as the combined balances in your checking and savings accounts (and other bank savings options) meet the minimum requirement. Either way, look for a bank with a low minimum. While some banks require you to keep as much as $10,000 in the bank to get free checking and ATM use, others require you to keep just $100. Even if you have enough money to meet the higher minimum balance requirements, it still makes sense to find a bank with low balance requirements. That way you won't have to tie up large sums of cash in a bank account that pays a pitifully low interest rate.

Before you switch banks, ask whether yours will waive its minimum balance requirement if you sign up for **direct deposit** (which means that your entire paycheck would be automatically deposited into your checking or savings account each pay period); some banks will. You should also find out if you're eligible to join any credit unions, which are special not-for-profit banks that tend to have lower minimum balance requirements and lower fees all around. (For help in finding a credit union, contact the Credit Union National Association at 800-358-5710 or www.cuna.org.) Or look into opening a checking account at one of the growing number of banks that operate only over the Internet, many of which require no minimum balance for checking.

For more tips on banking smart, see Chapter 4.

5. Build an emergency cushion with an automatic savings plan.

If you find it impossible to save any money, you're not alone. But once you've gotten rid of your high-rate debt and taken care of Crib Notes 1, 2, 3, and 4, it's time to start saving. A relatively painless way to do it is to enroll in an automatic savings plan. These plans allow you to have money automatically withdrawn from each paycheck and funneled into a bank account or mutual fund. (See Crib Note 6 for a brief discussion of mutual funds.)

Once you've met the minimum balance requirement for free checking at your bank, you're ready to invest in a special type of mutual fund called a **money market fund.** Money market funds are considered nearly as safe as bank savings accounts and tend to pay higher interest rates. To find a money market fund, check out Web sites like Bankrate.com and Money.com, which offer lists of the highest interest rates currently being offered. Another strategy is to open a money market fund at the same low-cost mutual fund company where you plan to purchase all of your mutual funds in the future. (For my suggestions on specific low-cost mutual fund companies that offer money market funds, see Crib Note 6.) Find out if the fund company and your employer will allow you to have the amount you want to invest automatically deducted from your paycheck and deposited into the fund. If not, the next best option is to have the mutual fund company automatically siphon the cash out of your checking account once or twice a month and deposit it into the fund.

No matter what type of automatic savings plan you choose, your goal should be to save at least three months' worth of living expenses in a money market fund before you even think about the more aggressive investments discussed in Crib Note 6. To figure out what three months' worth of living expenses amount to, use the worksheet in Chapter 2. For virtually everything you need to know about money market funds, see Chapter 5.

6. Begin investing in stock and bond mutual funds.

Once you have your three-month savings cushion in place in a money market fund, it's time to get a bit more aggressive with your investments. The advantage of stocks and bonds over money market funds is that they've historically tended to earn higher rates of return for investors over long periods of time, and many experts predict that they will continue to do so in the future. You may need these higher returns to stay ahead of inflation. (For a discussion of inflation and why you'll need to worry about it, see Chapter 5.)

The downside of stocks and bonds is that they're riskier than money market funds. You can lose money by investing in them. Only you can decide how much risk you're willing to take for the chance to earn higher returns over time, but one reasonable approach might be to put about half your holdings into stocks, one-third into bonds, and the rest in money market funds.

If you do decide to put some of your money in stocks and bonds, I recommend that you do so by investing in stock mutual funds and bond mutual funds. A **mutual fund** is a type of investment that pools together the money of thousands of people. It's headed by a fund manager, who invests the entire sum in a variety of stocks, bonds, and/or money market instruments. (To find out exactly what these are, you'll need to read Chapter 5.) I recommend that you consider only **no-load mutual funds** with low expenses. A load is a fee that some mutual fund companies charge each time you put money in or take money out of a fund. Avoid investing in load funds; they don't perform any better on average than no-load funds, so there's no point in paying the extra fees. Expenses are the annual fees charged by the fund and can take a serious bite out of your investment returns if you're not careful.

Although stock funds are considered somewhat riskier than bond funds, they have also performed somewhat better over the years. If you decide to invest in a stock fund, I recommend you consider a type known as a **stock index fund**. Two companies that offer index funds are Vanguard (800-662-7447; www.vanguard.com) and T. Rowe Price (800-638-5660, www.troweprice.com). Vanguard has the lowest fees and the largest selection of index funds, but you'll generally need at least $3,000 to open an account there. T. Rowe Price allows investors to get started by putting in just $50 a month.

Bonds are typically less risky than stocks but riskier than money market funds. Holding bonds as well as stocks will help to diversify your investments, thus reducing your overall risk. Companies that offer no-load bond funds with low expenses include Vanguard (800-662-7447; www.vanguard.com), Galaxy Funds (877-289-4252; www.galaxyfunds.com), and USAA (800-531-8181; www.usaa .com). While there are several different types of bond funds, a reasonable approach would be to choose an **intermediate-term bond fund** that invests in government securities or highly rated corporations.

To learn more about bond funds, stock funds, and investing in general—you guessed it—you'll have to read Chapter 5.

7. Think about buying a house or apartment.

At a certain point in life, you may start to feel that you should buy a home. Deciding that it makes sense to purchase a place of your own involves more than simply comparing your monthly rent with the monthly mortgage payments you'd make as an owner. A range of financial factors, including the tax break you'll get from buying, the fees you'll pay when you buy, and how long you plan to live in the new home, should enter into your decision. For a discussion of some of these factors and information on where you can get software to help analyze your own situation, turn to Chapter 7.

Just a few years ago, the biggest obstacle to buying a home was coming up with the down payment. Today there are several options available, especially if you have good credit. Start by calling your state housing office to see if it offers any low down payment mortgage options for which you're eligible. The advantage of these state programs is that they typically charge a lower interest rate than you can get on a bank mortgage. (For the phone number of your state housing office, see page 192.)

Your next step is to get information on Fannie Mae and Freddie Mac, two companies that were established by the government to help banks and mortgage companies expand their mortgage offerings to all types of borrowers. Fannie and Freddie offer several low down payment loan programs (as low as 3%). When you shop around, ask lenders if they participate in Fannie's "Flexible 97" and

"Community Home Buyer's Program," or in Freddie's "Affordable Gold" and "Alt 97." They'll know what you mean. For several free booklets from Fannie Mae on purchasing a home, call 800-688-HOME (www.fanniemae.com).

If you don't qualify for one of these programs, a third alternative is the Federal Housing Administration (FHA) loan program. FHA loans require only a 3% down payment, and they're usually easier to qualify for, but the deal you get may not be quite as good. Contact a lender or your local Housing and Urban Development office (www.hud.gov) for more information on FHA loans.

If you don't qualify for any of these programs, don't give up. There are many lenders out there that offer creative options. For more housing-related tips for buyers and renters, see Chapter 7.

8.   Get smart about taxes.

Nobody likes paying taxes. One way to reduce the portion of your paycheck that goes to Uncle Sam is to take as many tax deductions as you are eligible for. Deductions are specific expenses that the government allows you to subtract from your income before calculating the amount of tax you're required to pay. Taking advantage of these tax deductions is a lot easier than it may sound.

The government allows you to take advantage of deductions in either of two distinct ways. The easiest approach is to take the **standard deduction,** which is simply a fixed dollar amount ($4,400 for singles, or $7,350 for couples, in 2000) that you subtract from your income. Although all taxpayers are permitted to take the standard deduction, depending on your circumstances, you may wind up paying less if you **itemize** your deductions instead. Itemizing means listing separately the specific items that are deductible under the current tax laws and then subtracting their total cost from your income.

If you choose to itemize your deductions, you'll have to fill out a tax form called a 1040 (also known as the long form) rather than the simpler 1040A (the short form) or the 1040EZ (the really short form). You'll then have to list your deductions on an attachment to Form 1040 called Schedule A. Among the types of expenses you may be allowed to deduct are state and local taxes you've paid, donations you've made to a charity, and certain moving, job-hunting, business travel, and education expenses.

The only way to find out if you can save money on your taxes by itemizing instead of taking the standard deduction is to fill out a copy of Schedule A and see if the amount you're allowed to deduct is greater than the standard deduction. Even if you find that you won't save money by itemizing this year, this exercise will help get you better acquainted with some common types of deductions and may help you plan things in a way that could reduce your tax bite next year.

There are some deductions you can take whether you itemize or not, like contributions to a deductible IRA or interest payments on your student loans. If you have children or educational expenses, you may also qualify for valuable tax credits, which subtract money directly from the amount you owe the IRS.

To get tax forms and a general instruction book from the IRS, call 800-TAX-FORM (or go to its Web site at www.irs.gov) and ask for Tax Publication 17, *Your Federal Income Tax*. Also consider using your computer to help you prepare your taxes. The Web site TurboTax (www.turbotax.com) provides you with the forms and instructions you'll need, performs all the necessary calculations, and prints out completed forms you can send to the IRS. It will also let you send your return straight to the IRS electronically. For about $35 you can purchase tax software that performs the same tasks; two programs worth considering are TurboTax (or MacInTax for Macs) and TaxCut.

For specific ways to cut your tax bill, see Chapter 9.

TAKING STOCK OF YOUR FINANCIAL LIFE

Figuring Out Where You Are and Where You Want to Go

YOU MAY KNOW someone who obsesses over every dollar he spends, keeping track of every charge he makes and balancing his checkbook to the penny. He tracks his spending on personal finance software, never misses a credit card payment, and always files his taxes in early January.

You're a bit different. You know you should be keeping better tabs on where your money goes, but somehow your paycheck seems to disappear after you cover the basics like rent and food. But you're young, you say. You have plenty of time. Once you make more money, you'll start thinking about getting your finances in order and planning for the future.

The truth is, you don't have to spend your life huddled over a calculator, sifting through receipts. But now is the time to start paying attention to your money. Although your paycheck will increase as you get older (we hope), your financial commitments will also grow.

The good news is that if you start paying attention to your finances today, you can develop some habits that will help you for the rest of your financial life. For example, by regularly saving a small amount now, you will be rewarded with a very big payoff later on. If you're 25 years old and you put as little as $5 a day into a savings program offered by your employer, you could well be a millionaire by age 65. (Of course, a million dollars forty years from now is likely to be worth a lot less than it's worth today, but you get the idea.) The point is, you need to start right away. This chapter will help you get organized so you can begin.

PUTTING A PRICE TAG ON YOUR GOALS

Most of us have one or two specific financial dreams that we would love to realize within the next few years. You may want to buy a car by the time you're 25. You may long to own a house by age 30. You may hope to have a feeling of financial security by age 35. Or you may simply want to move out of your parents' place as soon as possible.

The first step toward turning your financial fantasy into an achievable goal is calculating the dollar value of your dream. If you're not sure what that figure is, use the following guidelines:

- **A home.** The median-priced home for first-time homebuyers in 1999 was $113,300. To qualify for a home loan, you usually need to make a down payment of between 3% and 20% of the total price; you'll also need to pay about 1% to 4% to the bank for "closing costs." So for a $100,000 home, you would need to have saved somewhere between $4,000 and $24,000. Of course, these figures could be higher or lower depending on where you live. There are some "no down payment" mortgages available as well. (For details, see Chapter 7.)

- **A new car.** Expect to make a down payment of 10% to 20% on a new automobile. To buy a $20,000 car, you will need to have from $2,000 to $4,000 in cash.

- **A financial emergency cushion.** Generally, an acceptable financial cushion is equal to at least three months' worth of living expenses. This amount will probably guard against a total and immediate disruption of your life if, for example, you lose your job. Although saving for a home, a car, or any other tangible item seems like a lot more fun, accumulating enough for a financial emergency cushion is a necessity.

LEARNING HOW TO REACH YOUR GOALS

Once you've determined what your goals are, you're ready to work toward achieving them. Use the table in Figure 2-1 to help. It gives you a rough idea of how much you'll need to put aside each month to end up with a specific dollar amount in a set number of years. The table assumes that inflation will be 3% and the money you put away will earn a rate of return of 5% before taxes. (Of course, no one can know what will happen to inflation and interest rates in the future, but these are considered reasonable estimates.) It also assumes that your combined federal, state, and local tax rate is 33% for the next 10 years.* The table factors in tax rates because you will have to pay taxes each year on the earnings you receive on certain investments. (For details on figuring out your tax rate, see Chapter 9.)

If you tend to be a good saver, you may not be fazed by the amount you'll need to save each month. If you're like most people, though, you'll probably have to save more than you think you can spare. Don't get discouraged. The next part of this chapter will help you figure out how to get this money from your current income. Even though you may ultimately decide you have to adjust your planned goal—or the amount of time it takes for you to reach it— at least you'll be on your way toward making it happen.

---

* Here's how I got the 33%: If in 2000 you are single and earn between $26,250 and $63,550 per year, or are married and together earn between $43,850 and $105,950, your federal tax rate is 28%. Depending on where you live, your state and local taxes might be about 5%; 28% plus 5% is 33%. One thing to keep in mind: If you itemize your tax deductions, you get to deduct the state taxes you pay. This will have the effect of reducing your rate somewhat. (See Chapter 9 for details.)

Figure 2-1

HOW MUCH DO YOU NEED TO SAVE EACH MONTH TO MEET YOUR GOALS?

Look across the top row and find the dollar amount that corresponds to your goal. Now look down the far-left column and locate the number of years in which you hope to achieve your goal. The point at which your goal and the number of years intersect is the amount you need to save each month.*

	YOUR GOAL										
Years to Reach Your Goal	$1,000	$2,000	$3,000	$5,000	$7,000	$10,000	$20,000	$30,000	$50,000	$70,000	$100,000
1	$84	$169	$253	$421	$590	$843	$1,686	$2,529	$4,214	$5,900	$8,429
2	43	85	128	213	299	427	854	1,280	2,134	2,988	4,268
3	29	58	86	144	202	288	576	864	1,441	2,017	2,882
4	22	44	66	109	153	219	438	657	1,094	1,532	2,188
5	18	35	53	89	124	177	355	532	886	1,241	1,773
6	15	30	45	75	105	150	299	449	748	1,047	1,495
7	13	26	39	65	91	130	260	389	649	908	1,298
8	11	23	34	57	80	115	230	345	575	804	1,149
9	10	21	31	52	72	103	207	310	517	724	1,034
10	9	19	28	47	66	94	188	283	471	659	942

Sources: Ernst & Young; PricewaterhouseCoopers

* The goals listed across the top row of the table are in constant dollars. So if your goal is to buy a car in five years, that's equivalent to a $20,000 car today, you need to set aside $355 every month to end up with a sum that has the same purchasing power $20,000 currently has. In other words, you don't have to worry about inflation eroding the value of the $20,000; the table factors it in for you. The amount you need to put into your account every month is simply the figure listed in the table (in this example, $355).

FIGURING OUT WHERE
YOUR MONEY GOES

Saving isn't easy for most people, and putting aside a fixed amount each month seems like an impossible task. But the fact is, you probably *can* save—even if you feel like you're barely making ends meet now. The key is getting a handle on your current spending habits and then reevaluating your priorities. This section will help you do the necessary financial soul searching it often takes to help achieve specific goals.

The first step is to keep a detailed spending diary for two weeks so that you can get a better sense of your regular cash expenditures. Get a little notebook and write down everything you spend money on. This sounds like a tedious exercise, but you'll find it's a very useful way to track your cash flow. Once you've done that, you're ready to fill out the worksheet in Figure 2-2. The point of the worksheet is to help you see where your money goes and then set priorities.

Keep in mind when you fill out the worksheet that it's not necessary to be exact. Use your pay stubs and bank statements to come up with reasonable estimates in the income section. For the outflow section, look at your pay stubs, spending diary, checkbook, and credit card statements. Don't forget that this worksheet is helping you examine your *monthly* expenses. For large expenses (like tuition, travel, and furniture), come up with a monthly estimate. For expenses that vary from month to month (like car repairs and clothing), take an average from four or five months' worth of entries in your checkbook. (If you make most major purchases with a credit card, use your credit card statements too.) If possible, choose a month from each season so you can calculate a more accurate average.

Once you have completed the worksheet, subtract your total outflow from your total income. If you come up with a negative number, that means you're spending more than you're taking in, and you're going to have to cut back. To do this, you will need to think about your priorities and make some tough choices. Would you be

Figure 2-2

WORKSHEET:
A MONTH IN YOUR FINANCIAL LIFE

INCOME (what you take in each month):

Salary and bonuses (before tax)   _____

Pay from extra jobs (before tax)   _____

Investment income, such as interest, earnings,
   and dividends (before tax)   _____

Scholarships   _____

Other   _____

TOTAL INCOME PER MONTH (BEFORE TAX)   _____

OUTFLOW (what you pay out each month):

Federal, state, and local income tax and FICA
   (get this figure from your pay stubs)   _____

Tax on investment income*   _____

Mortgage or rent   _____

IRA and 401(k) contributions   _____

Groceries   _____

Gas and electricity   _____

Telephone   _____

Eating out (including morning coffee, snacks,
   and lunches out)   _____

Clothes   _____

Student loan payments   _____

Car loan payments   _____

Car expenses (gas, repairs, maintenance)   _____

Public transportation (bus, train, taxi costs)   _____

Health insurance premiums   _____

Homeowners/renters insurance premiums   _____

Auto insurance premiums   ————————

Disability insurance premiums   ————————

Life insurance premiums   ————————

Home expenses (furnishings, maintenance)   ————————

Laundry, dry cleaning   ————————

Tuition   ————————

Child care   ————————

Medical and dental expenses not covered by
  insurance   ————————

Bank fees   ————————

Hobbies   ————————

Night life   ————————

Movies, theater, cable TV   ————————

Internet access fee   ————————

Computer software, CDs, cassettes   ————————

Gifts   ————————

Vacation   ————————

Magazines, newspapers, books   ————————

Personal care (haircuts, toiletries, cosmetics)   ————————

Health club fees   ————————

Membership fees, charitable contributions   ————————

Pets, pet care   ————————

Miscellaneous   ————————

   TOTAL OUTFLOW PER MONTH   ————————

TOTAL MONTHLY INCOME   ————————

minus   TOTAL MONTHLY OUTFLOW   ————————

equals your   MONTHLY CASH FLOW   ————————

* To estimate the tax on the investment income, multiply the amount of interest you received for the month by your tax bracket. If you don't know your tax bracket, multiply the interest by 0.33 to get a rough idea.

THE ART OF NEGOTIATION:
WHEN A SPENDER MARRIES A SAVER

Anne and Marc moved in together in June and started to plan a March wedding. Anne's parents said they'd be willing to contribute $10,000 for the event, so the couple figured out that they'd need to pitch in $5,000 of their own to have the wedding of their dreams. The problem was coming up with the cash. Anne, who is frugal and likes being debt-free, felt that with some careful planning, they could accumulate the money. After all, they each earned about $35,000. Marc, however, thought that raising that kind of cash was out of the question. He already *owed* more than $3,000 to various credit card companies and didn't see how he could possibly save the money. Why couldn't they just wait and see how much cash they received as wedding presents and then charge the rest? After two weeks of discussion (actually, arguments), they decided to list their income and expenses and see if they could work out the problem. By writing things down, Marc quickly realized that if he cut out expensive lunches (he spent four times as much as Anne did) and put off buying clothes for work until the spring (he spent twice as much as she did on suits), he could come up with a good chunk of change. He also was forced to acknowledge the fact that having Anne as a roommate would actually make saving much easier; it cut his rent, utilities, and basic phone charges in half. The compromise: Anne and Marc would each set aside $150 every two weeks in a joint bank account earmarked for wedding expenses only.

able to save $150 a month by cooking at home rather than eating out every other night? Do you spend as much on clothes as you do on rent? Are you spending too much money on gifts, especially around holiday time? Are you subscribing to more magazines than you can actually read? Is your car costing more than it's worth? These are some of the questions to consider.

With these questions in mind, go back over the entire outflow section. Consider where you can cut back—and by how much. Once you've done that, star the items that you feel are absolute necessities. (For most of us, that includes mortgage or rent, groceries, utilities, student loan payments, and health insurance premiums—although even here, many of us can cut back if we need to.) Subtract your outflow on necessities from your total income. The answer (which is positive, hopefully) is the amount of discretionary income you have left. Some of that money should be set aside to meet your goals, and the rest is for items that are not necessities. At this point, it should become clear whether you need to adjust the size of your goal or the number of years in which you can realistically hope to attain it.

FINANCIAL RULES OF THUMB

To help you evaluate whether your spending and saving habits are right on track, wildly off base, or somewhere in between, I've listed a few financial rules. Like an ideal weight or relationship, these rules of thumb will give you financial ideals to strive for. Realistically, they aren't always possible to attain, but it's good to set high goals. Use the worksheet you filled out to help with your calculations.

- **The Debt Rule: Your total debt (not including your mortgage) should be less than 20% of your annual take-home pay.** To see if you meet this standard, list all the money you owe, including unpaid balances on your student loans, your credit cards, your car loan, and any other lines of credit, and add these amounts together. If the total exceeds 20% of your annual take-home pay, see Chapter 3 for tips on reducing your debt. Of course, anyone with student loans probably fails the debt-rule test. (The $10,000 in student loans I had when I graduated from college represented more than 60% of my take-home pay!) Fortunately, mortgage lenders tend to be more forgiving of borrowers with student loans than of those with lots of credit card debt. For this reason, you may want to exclude your student loans from this calculation. Just make sure the total of all your other loans, especially credit card balances, falls well below this 20% mark.

- **The Housing Rule: Spend no more than 30% of your monthly take-home pay on rent or mortgage payments.** This rule may or may not apply depending on where you live. If you live in a small town or a city like St. Louis or Cleveland, this may sound reasonable. But if you live in New York City, San Francisco, or Miami, for example, you probably won't meet this guideline unless you share a place with roommates or you don't mind living in a closet.

- **The Savings Rule: Save at least 10% of your take-home pay each month.** It's critical to think of your savings as a fixed monthly expense that's part of your budget, just like car payments and rent. While there's no magical reason to save exactly 10%, it's a good target to shoot for. Include in that

HEY, BIG SPENDER

Because of the way our tax system works, the cost of buying something is higher than you think. Here's why: Say you find a great jacket for $70, and you buy it. If you are in the 30% tax bracket, you actually had to earn $100 in order to pay for the jacket. That's because $100 taxed at 30% is $70. Keep this in mind on your next shopping spree.

10% the money you set aside to meet your short-term goals as well as the funds you put in a company retirement plan. If you can save more, you should. In fact, some hard-core financial planners recommend that you save 10% in retirement savings plans alone, plus another 5% outside of your retirement plan. See Chapters 4, 5, and 6 for details on where and how to save.

GETTING YOUR FINANCIAL LIFE IN ORDER

It's easier to gain control of your finances if you're organized. Here are some tips:

- **Set up a financial filing system.** To get your paperwork organized, you need a place to put items like credit card statements and bank statements. The easiest way to do this is with file folders and an inexpensive cardboard filing cabinet. Ideally, you should file paperwork as soon as you receive it. Since almost no one who has a life really does that, set up an "in box" in which you stash away stuff that needs to be filed, and then do all your filing once a month. Here's a rundown of the folders you'll need:

  —*Auto Loans.* Save loan agreements that list the terms of your loan.

  —*Auto (Other).* Keep your purchase agreement, your certificate of title, and any warranty you may have. Also hold on to warranties and receipts from repair work.

  —*Bank Statements.* Also include canceled checks in this file. Pull out checks for items that may be deductible on your taxes or related to home improvements, and stick them in the proper folders.

  —*Brokerage Accounts.* If you have any, keep statements that show purchases and sales of investments. You'll also need to hold on to stock or bond certificates.

—*Credit Cards.* Set up a different folder for each card you have. Throw your credit card receipts into these folders. When you get statements, make sure they match your receipts. Once you've done that, pluck out receipts for those purchases that may be tax-deductible and put them in the folder for tax-deductible items.

—*Home Improvements.* Keeping track of these expenses could pay off if you ever decide to sell your home.

—*Home (Purchase).* Hang on to your closing statement and all the other documents related to the purchase.

—*Insurance.* You'll need separate folders for auto, home, rental, life, health, and disability insurance. Keep your policies, descriptive literature, copies of any claims that you make, and statements of reimbursements.

—*Individual Retirement Accounts (IRAs).* See Chapters 6 and 9 for details.

—*Mortgage Interest Payments.* If you own a home, hold on to statements related to these payments.

—*Mutual Funds.* File your year-end transaction statements.

—*Pension Plan/Retirement Plan Statements.* Keep all "summary plan descriptions" you receive from your employer, and save quarterly statements from your retirement savings plan. Also hang on to documents relating to other employee benefits, such as profit-sharing plans.

—*Personal Documents.* Store important documents such as your passport, Social Security card, and marriage certificate here.

—*Property Tax/Real Estate Tax.* These payments are tax-deductible, so hold on to statements related to them.

—*Salary.* Keep your weekly pay stubs, your year-end pay stub, and any written information you receive regarding your bonus.

—*Student Loans.* Save your original loan agreement and your monthly statements.

—*Tax-Deductible Items.* If you don't have many deductible expenses, use this as a catch-all folder. Otherwise, you may want to set up separate folders for each specific type of deduction you can take. (See Chapter 9 for details on these deductions.)

—*Tax Returns.* Each January you receive "W-2s" from your employer and "1099s" from a variety of sources including employers, banks, and mutual fund companies. Save them in this file. Also hold on to copies of your tax returns, your tax-related forms, and any supporting documentation. Create a new folder for each year.

—*Warranties, Rebates, Receipts, Online Order Forms.* Hold on to these for all major purchases. The receipts will help you if you ever need to verify to an insurance company that a particular item was stolen or ruined in a fire. When you order items online, print out copies of the order forms to serve as receipts until the item arrives.

• **Know what to save and what to throw away.** Some people are pack rats who habitually save every scrap of paper. (I am the worst offender.) The fact is, you don't need to keep all receipts and bills. In general, you'll want to hold on to receipts related to tax-deductible expenses or those that are necessary to take advantage of a warranty. You'll also want to keep receipts of major purchases for insurance purposes. Below is a detailed list of what you need to save and what you can toss.

Throw out now:

—*Old phone bills* (unless you intend to deduct a portion of your phone bill on your taxes)

—*Supermarket receipts*

—*Old utility bills*

Throw out after one year:

—*Canceled checks* (except those you need for tax or insurance purposes)

—*Store receipts, online order forms, and credit card statements* (except those you need for tax or insurance purposes or for proof of purchase necessary for a warranty)

Throw out after three years:

—*Bank statements* (which you may need to produce if you're audited)

Save forever:

—*Birth certificate*

—*College transcripts*

—*Credit card agreement* (for as long as you have the card)

—*Diplomas*

—*Divorce decree and property agreement*

—*Home improvement receipts* if you own your home (see Chapter 9)

—*Home inventory* (see Chapter 8)

—*Insurance policies*

—*Loan agreements*

—*Marriage certificate*

—*Passport* (current one)

—*Pension plan and retirement plan documents*

—*Receipts for major purchases* (to use as proof in case of a fire or burglary)

—*Social Security card*

—*Stock purchase agreements*

—*Tax returns, additional tax forms, and supporting documentation.* (Actually, you can probably throw out the supporting documentation, like receipts, three years after you file your return. See Chapter 9 for details.)

— *Warranties* (for as long as they last)

— *Work performance reviews, memos on job performance*

— *Year-end pay stubs and bonus statements*

— *Year-end transaction statements from mutual fund companies*

- **Consider using a computer to help.** One way to track your spending, as well as get a clearer sense of your total financial picture, is to use personal finance software. If you and your partner fight about money, a computer budgeting program can be especially helpful because it offers an organized, objective way of seeing how your money is actually being spent. One of the main features of these programs is a checkbook management spreadsheet that automatically balances your checkbook. The programs make it easy for you to calculate what portion of your income goes to various categories, such as "housing," "clothes," and "telephone." At the end of a few months, you can see how much you spent in each category, and you might learn something useful. For example, you might discover that you eat out twice as much in the winter as you do in the summer, you use three times as much electricity in the summer as you do in the winter, or you spend three times as much on clothes as you do on anything else.

  Good personal finance programs can also help you with basic financial planning. Many include worksheets that enable you to figure out quickly what your monthly payments would be on a given loan or how much you'd need to save each year at a given interest rate to achieve a specific goal. Most allow you to print checks from your computer. You may also want to consider paying your bills electronically; most personal finance programs have arrangements with banks and bill-paying services that allow you to pay via the Internet. (For details on other ways to pay your bills electronically, see Chapter 4.)

At the time of this writing, the two leading personal finance software packages are Quicken and Microsoft Money, basic versions of which cost about $40. But the world of personal finance software is changing rapidly; for the latest on which programs work best, consult a recent issue of *PC Magazine* (www.pcmag.com) that rates personal finance software.

If your financial life is fairly simple or if you're not comfortable using a computer, you probably shouldn't bother with this type of software; it could bog you down rather than help you out.

FINANCIAL CRAMMING

- To calculate how much you need to save each month to reach specific financial goals, look at Figure 2-1 on page 36. Although it's based on several assumptions about inflation, your tax bracket, and the rate you'll be able to earn on investments, it will still give you a rough idea of how much money you'll need to set aside.

- Keep a spending diary for two weeks. By forcing yourself to write down everything you spend money on, you will get a better sense of why your cash seems to disappear each month.

- Consider these guidelines when evaluating your financial fitness: Spend no more than 30% of your monthly take-home pay on housing and dedicate at least 10% of your take-home pay to savings. Also, don't allow your total debt (not including your mortgage) to exceed 20% of your annual take-home pay.

- Gain control of your finances by setting up a filing system and developing regular bill-paying habits. And take a look at personal finance software like Quicken and Microsoft Money, which can help you keep track of your spending.

DEBT AND THE MATERIAL WORLD

Finding the Best Loans and Getting Yourself Out of Hock

SUPPOSE YOU'RE 30 years old and you owe $3,500 on your credit card. The interest rate on your card is 17%. If you regularly make the minimum payment required by the credit card issuer, when will you be debt-free? (Drum roll, please.) The answer is . . . when you are 63 years old. By then, you would have paid $7,324 in interest, plus the original amount you borrowed.

The point of this chilling example is clear: Carrying a lot of credit card debt—or for that matter, lots of any type of debt—can be hazardous to your financial health for a very long time. Unfortunately, debt is a problem many of us are intimate with. The amount of money that Americans owe on their credit cards has more than doubled in the past decade alone.

Whether you're trying to dig your way out of debt or simply looking for a low-cost loan, this chapter will provide tips on managing your credit card debt, shopping for student loan repayment plans, locating attractive auto loans, and weighing the benefits of home equity loans. It will also provide you with an inside look at how your credit habits affect your credit report, the report card of your financial life.

TWO POINTERS FOR ANYONE
WITH DEBT

Before I plunge into the nitty-gritty details of credit cards, student loans, and auto loans, there are two basic principles you should know:

- **If you have savings, pay off your high-rate debt.** In most cases, the very best investment you can make is to pay off your credit cards and auto loans. This is because the interest rates on such debt are higher than the rates you can expect to receive from most investments. Paying off a loan with a 16% interest rate, for instance, is in effect paying yourself a guaranteed 16% rate of return, *tax-free*. That's a rate even Wall Street big shots would be thrilled to get.

   For a better understanding of why it pays to pay off your debt, consider the following example. Say you have a choice between paying off a $1,000 loan and keeping $1,000 in a bank savings account. The loan has an annual interest rate of 16%, and the bank savings account pays a rate of 2% after taxes. If you keep the $1,000 in the bank for a year, you will earn $20 in interest on it while paying $160 in interest on the loan, ending up with a $140 loss. But if you forget about the savings account and instead pay off the loan immediately, you will earn no interest and will also pay no interest. Clearly it's better to break even than to pay $140 in interest.

- **Transfer debt from high-interest-rate loans to lower-rate loans.** The process of transferring debt from high-rate loans to lower-rate loans is known as **refinancing**. Obviously it's better to pay 8% to borrow money than it is to pay 18%. If, for example, you currently have credit card debt that you can't pay off entirely, apply for a low-rate credit card that allows you to transfer your current debt to it. If you have auto loans, you may also be able to lower the rates you're paying by refinancing.

CREDIT CARDS

Whether you're a sensible user or big-time abuser of credit cards, there are steps you can take to reduce your costs. This section will show what they are.

How to Find the Right Card for You

Despite what the ads say, whether your card has a Visa seal or MasterCard logo is not that important. These are just membership organizations. It's the bank or company that *issues* the card—such as Citibank or MBNA—that matters. Issuers control the rates, fees, and other factors that are critical to you.

Look for a credit card that best suits your personal spending habits. If you usually carry a balance from month to month, get the lowest interest rate you can. But if you always pay off your balance in full, the rate doesn't matter. Your priority is to find a card that doesn't charge an annual fee and does provide a **grace period,** which is a period of time lenders give you before they start charging interest. If you pay off your entire balance each month, you may also want to consider special "reward" cards that offer frequent-flyer mileage or credits toward a car for every dollar you charge. If you have a troubled credit history or have a tough time controlling your credit card spending, you may want to consider a secured card or a debit card. (More on these options later.)

Although there are hundreds of different credit cards available, most of us need no more than two. Limiting your access to credit is a smart move whether you're a binge shopper or a model of self-control. That's because lenders with the most attractive rates tend to reject prospective borrowers based on their *potential* to run up a lot of debt.

How to Get a Low-Rate Credit Card

If you don't have enough cash to pay off your credit card balance immediately, you'll want to get the lowest-rate card possible and transfer your debt to it. The way it generally works is that the low-rate issuer provides you with checks that you can use to pay off the balances on high-rate cards. The details of how this system works vary from card to card, so you need to read the fine print before you sign up. Some low-rate issuers, for example, offer you a 25-day grace period before interest accumulates on the money you borrow; others tack on transfer fees and start charging interest the moment the checks are cashed.

There are two kinds of low-rate cards: cards with temporary low introductory rates known as **teasers**, and cards with low rates that last.

Teaser rates (sometimes called "promotional rates") generally last for six months or less. After that period, the rate usually increases dramatically. But while the low teaser rate lasts, it can save you a lot of money. Transferring a $2,000 balance from a 16% card to one with a 7% teaser rate, for example, would save you $90 in interest payments over six months.

If you can't pay off all your debt before the teaser rate runs out, you may be able to keep your rate low by going "credit card surfing"—transferring your balance to a new teaser-rate card whenever your teaser rate runs out. But you have to surf carefully. Credit card companies have started getting wise to surfers, and some of them now charge "transfer fees" of as much as 4% of your balance. Stay away from those cards. And don't let the lower monthly payments that come with low-rate cards seduce you into paying off your debt more slowly; try to pay at least as much every month as you would with a higher-rate card.

Ideally, you'll be able to find a card with a low rate that lasts. The interest rates on such cards tend to be slightly higher than teaser rates, but they are less of a hassle. Though many of these cards are not guaranteed to stay at the same rate forever, they tend to remain stable. Unfortunately, it isn't easy to qualify for these long-lasting low-rate cards. They are targeted to people with stellar credit ratings and not much debt. Here are details on some of the requirements.

- **Bill-paying habits.** If you have recently been 30 days late paying a credit card bill or if you were late more than 60 days in the last four years, you will have a harder time getting a low-rate card.

- **Salary.** In most cases, you need to earn at least $20,000 a year.

- **Stability.** Most issuers want to see that you've been at your job for at least a year. It also helps if you've lived in the same residence for a year.

- **Debt.** Your monthly debt divided by your income, or **debt-to-income ratio,** typically shouldn't be more than 35% to 45%. To figure this out, add up the amount you pay each month on your rent or mortgage, your auto loans, your student loans, and the minimum monthly payments on your credit cards. To get the percentage, divide this total by your monthly income before taxes.

THE TRICKY TEASER

Adam is a dedicated credit card surfer who prides himself on his ability to pay the lowest possible interest rates on the $3,000 balance he tends to carry from month to month. Because he has a good credit history, he gets solicitations in the mail almost daily, offering him extra-low introductory teaser rates. Every few months, he switches cards and gets a new teaser rate, so he never ends up paying a rate of more than 5% on his debt.

Recently Adam transferred his balance to a card with a six-month teaser rate of 3.9%. He used the card to buy hundreds of dollars worth of books and clothing. When he got his credit card statement at the end of the month, he was shocked to see that while the balance he had transferred from his old card was running up interest at 3.9%, the money he had spent on those books and clothes was being hit for 18.9%! What Adam hadn't noticed was that the teaser rate on his card applied only to balance transfers—not to any new purchases Adam made.

Determined not to pay interest rates in the double digits, he

- **Usage.** To measure credit card usage, issuers calculate the ratio of your outstanding debt to your potential debt (that's the sum of the credit limits on all your cards). For example, if you have a $1,000 credit limit and outstanding debt of $900, your **usage ratio** is 90% ($900 divided by $1,000). This ratio should not exceed 80% if you have two cards and should not exceed 65% if you have three or more cards.

For lists of long-lasting low-rate and teaser deals, visit the Web sites of Bankrate.com (www.bankrate.com), CardWeb (www. cardweb.com), and Consumer Action (www.consumer-action.org). If you don't have access to the Internet, call 800-344-7714 or send

sent in a check large enough to cover all the new purchases he had made that month. But when his next statement came, he noticed that none of the 18.9% debt had been paid off; instead, his check had gone toward paying off the older—and cheaper— balance he had transferred from his old card. He would have to pay off the entire $3,000 balance transfer (at 3.9%) before he could even make a dent in his more expensive new balance (at 18.9%). Ironically, his teaser rate was preventing him from paying off his highest-rate debt.

In the end, Adam was forced to engineer a complicated transaction to get at his 18.9% debt. He transferred all the debt on his card to *another* card, then immediately switched it all back. (That way, it counted as a balance transfer again.) From then on, he made all of his new purchases on a second card and paid them off in full every month, avoiding interest payments altogether—and used his 3.9% card exclusively for his old balance.

The moral of the story: Not all teaser deals work the same way. Make sure to read all the fine print before you rush to switch cards, and adjust your habits to fit the deal.

a request and check or money order for $5 to CardTrak, P.O. Box 1700, Frederick, MD 21702. If you belong to a credit union, national association, or labor union, you might be able to get a card with a relatively low rate. Also investigate local banks, which sometimes offer lower rates than large national institutions.

Pointers for Those Who Carry a Balance

About six out of every ten credit card users carry a balance from month to month. While your goal is to pay off your credit card debt entirely, until you can, take note of the following suggestions:

- **Pay your bill the day you get it.** Most credit cards have a grace period, which begins the day your purchases are made or posted (officially recorded) and lasts until the due date specified on the bill. As long as you pay your bill in full by the due date, you won't be charged interest. Unfortunately, with most cards, the grace period exists only for those credit card users who pay their full balance each month. If you don't regularly pay off your bill in full, you will be charged interest immediately on any new purchases you make. In other words, if you carry a balance from month to month—even a very small balance—you lose the grace period. To reduce your interest charges, pay your bill as soon as you get it.

- **Never miss a payment.** If for some reason you can't pay your bill the day you get it, at least make sure you pay it on time. Banks used to be pretty lenient about punctuality, but nowadays late fees are often applied to your account the day after your payment is due. And those fees have been skyrocketing: Many banks now charge $29 for a single late payment. Worse, more and more banks punish late payers by jacking up their interest rates to "penalty rates" of up to 30%. As if all that weren't enough, late payments can also make their way onto your credit report and make it harder for you to get loans and low rates in the future. (For more information about credit reports, see the section at the end of this chapter.)

- **Find out how interest is calculated.** Most lenders calculate interest using a system called the **average daily balance method including new purchases.** Here's how it works. The issuer divides up the year into 30-day periods known as billing cycles. On the last day of each billing cycle, the issuer mails your bill. Say you owe $500. If you pay the entire amount by the due date, you won't pay any interest. But if you leave even just $1 unpaid, expect a nasty surprise on your next bill. Interest charges won't be calculated on just the $1 balance; instead, they will be based on the *average daily balance* of the billing cycle. In this case, your balance would be $500 for 25 days of the billing cycle, and $1 for the last five days, resulting in an average daily balance of $417.

  Another method, the **two-cycle average daily balance**

A NASTY CARD SURPRISE

Kathy and Michael went on a honeymoon to Hawaii and charged all their expenses on a credit card. A week after they got home, the $5,000 credit card bill arrived. They had enough money to pay the whole bill, but Michael decided to pay it over the course of two months so he wouldn't fall below the minimum balance he needed to get free checking at his bank. He wrote a check for $4,900 and mailed it out by the due date. When the next credit card bill came, Michael was shocked to discover that although he owed only $100 from the previous balance, he also owed $63 in interest. Because he didn't pay off his balance entirely, he was charged interest for the average daily balance—in this case, about $4,180—of the billing cycle. The lesson: Don't carry a balance if you can help it. (By the way, if Kathy and Michael had a card that used the two-cycle method, they could have owed as much as $138 in interest!)

method including new purchases, can be even more costly. Basically it allows the issuer to calculate interest based on the two most recent billing cycles. If you sometimes carry a balance and sometimes pay in full, avoid cards that use the two-cycle method. Several major credit card issuers use it. To find out if yours does, check the back of your billing statement, where the method is usually printed in tiny type. For an illustration of just how expensive these methods can be, see the box on page 57.

- **Pay more than the monthly minimum, and resist skip-a-payment offers.** Many banks have lowered the monthly minimum payment from 4% of your outstanding balance to 2%. But if you pay only 2% rather than 4% on a $1,000 balance (with an interest rate of 17%), it will take you about ten more years and $1,070 more to finally pay it off. Ideally, you should pay your balance in full each month. If you can't, pay as much as possible. (See Figure 3-1 to help you calculate how long it will take to pay off your debt.) Also, resist the temptation to go for the skip-a-payment deals offered by many issuers. What they often don't make clear is that you will still be charged interest on your outstanding balance for that month.

If You Can't Get a Regular Credit Card, Try a Secured Card

If you've never had any credit or you've defaulted on a loan within the past few years, it may be difficult to find a lender that will give you a standard credit card. One option to consider is a **secured credit card.** With a secured card, the issuer requires you to provide collateral by depositing money into a special savings account. The issuer usually allows you to charge an amount equal to the sum you keep in the savings account, although in some cases the credit limit is lower or slightly higher than the amount on deposit. You can't withdraw the money from the savings account while you have the card.

If you've misused credit in the past but your problem is now

Figure 3-1
HOW MANY MONTHLY PAYMENTS
YOU'LL NEED TO KILL YOUR DEBT

This table can help you get a rough sense of how long it will take you to get rid of your credit card debt entirely, regardless of how much you have. Here's how it works: Look down the far-left column and ask yourself what percentage of your debt you can comfortably commit to pay off each month. If, for example, you have $1,000 in debt, you may decide that you can pay off 3% of $1,000, or $30, every month until the balance is completely wiped out. Now look across the top row and find the annual interest rate charged by your credit card. Say it's 18%. The point at which 3% intersects with 18% is the number of months it will take you to pay off your debt. In this case, the answer is 47 months. But if you're able to refinance that debt with a credit card that charges only a 10% annual rate, the number of monthly payments you'd make would be 39.

| | | ANNUAL INTEREST RATE | | | | | |
		8%	10%	12%	14%	16%	18%
Payment as a % of Initial Debt	2%	61	65	70	75	83	93
	3%	38	39	41	42	44	47
	4%	27	28	29	30	31	32
	5%	21	22	22	23	23	24
	10%	10	10	11	11	11	11
	15%	7	7	7	7	7	7
	20%	5	5	5	5	5	5
	25%	4	4	4	4	4	4

Source: AT&T Universal Card Services.

under control, you can probably qualify for a secured card. Once you've demonstrated that you can handle a secured card, issuers will be more willing to take a chance on giving you a regular credit card.

Secured cards often charge higher interest rates than traditional credit cards, and most have annual fees. And though some issuers

FRAUD AND CARD SAFETY

If your credit card gets lost or stolen, someone out there could be running up bills under your name. But you don't have to worry about paying the tab for their spending sprees. In cases of fraud, federal law limits your liability to $50—and most credit card companies won't ask you to pay anything at all. If you notice strange purchases on your credit card statement, let your card company know right away so that they can investigate the issue and take the charge off your account.

Debit cards can be trickier. Visa and MasterCard have voluntarily limited your liability to $50 on their signature-based debit cards. (The one drawback is that if your bank account is depleted because of unauthorized use, it could take them a few days to replenish your account while they investigate your case.) If you have a PIN-based debit card, you have to be more careful. If you report a lost PIN-based card within two days of noticing its absence, your liability will be limited to $50. Wait longer than that and you could be held liable for up to $500. And if you don't report a fraudulent use of your card within 60 days of when your bank sends you the statement that shows it, your liability is unlimited. To make sure you don't get cleaned out, don't give anyone your PIN number, and check your bank statement every month to see that it squares with your own records.

pay interest on the required savings account, others do not. That's why you should shop around. CardWeb (www.cardweb.com) and Bankrate.com (www.bankrate.com) provide lists of secured card options and let you compare them side by side. You can get a written report listing details about several dozen secured cards by sending $10 (check or money order) to CardWeb's Secured Card Report, P.O. Box 1700, Frederick, MD 21702.

Get a Debit Card as a Way to Discipline Yourself

If you have trouble controlling your spending, consider cutting up your credit cards and using a **debit card** instead. Like a credit card, a debit card is a plastic card that you can use to make purchases. Unlike a credit card, which allows you to *borrow* money, a debit card simply enables you to *use* money you already have. When you pay by debit card, the money is withdrawn from your bank checking account. (That's why debit cards are sometimes called **check cards**.)

With certain types of debit cards, the funds get siphoned out of your account the day you use the card. These debit cards are basically ATM cards: they require personal identification numbers (PINs) and are only accepted at stores—including many supermarkets—that have special machines to process them. In the industry these are known as **PIN-based debit cards**.

A growing number of banks now offer debit cards with Visa and MasterCard logos, known as **signature-based debit cards**. These cards can usually function as ordinary PIN-based cards, but they have a major added advantage: They can also be used *without* a PIN code wherever you would use an ordinary credit card, even overseas. Instead of entering a PIN when you make a purchase with one of these cards, you simply sign your name on your bill, just like with a credit card. And if you are unhappy with a product or service that you have purchased with your signature-based debit card, you can refuse to pay and have your bank duke it out for you—again, just like with a credit card.

If your bank offers debit cards, ask if there are any annual or monthly fees. Also, make sure to document your debit card purchases the same way you would record purchases made by check. It may take a few days for the money you spend with a debit card to be withdrawn from your bank account. If you don't keep records when you use your card, you may lose track of how much money you have in your account and end up bouncing checks.

Some Final Tips on Credit Cards

Whether you carry a balance or not, here are a few more pointers that will save you some money.

- **Ask your current card company for a better deal.** Because the credit card business is very competitive these days, you may be able to talk a credit card representative into lowering your rate or eliminating your annual fee. Call the toll-free number and explain in a friendly but assured manner that you're thinking of canceling your card if your request isn't met. Say that your other cards have lower interest rates and no fees (but be prepared for the phone rep to ask you to name names). If you hold your ground, there's a good chance the rep will check your record and then offer you some break on the rate or fee, especially if you pay your bills on time.

- **Look through the envelopes your credit card company sends you.** You may notice that your monthly credit card statement is sometimes accompanied by little notices and advertisements known as "envelope stuffers." Most of the time these are junk, but sometimes credit card companies use them to announce changes that might be important to you. For example, many companies have been shortening their grace periods from 25 days to 20 days. Others have been raising their late fees or their rates. So when you get your credit card bill, give a quick scan to the rest of what's in the envelope to make sure you're not getting snookered.

- **Don't use your credit card for cash advances.** Most credit cards can be used to obtain cash from an ATM. When you get a cash advance from an ATM, you are borrowing money from the credit card company in a more expensive way since many issuers charge higher interest rates on cash advances than they do on purchases. And most cash advances don't have a grace period; interest begins accruing the moment you get the advance. On top of the interest, you may have to pay a one-time fee of as much as $20 or 5% of the amount you withdraw. You should also stay away from the "convenience checks" some issuers include with your statements (unless you're using them to transfer balances from higher-rate cards). These usually work the same way as cash advances, and you'll be charged accordingly.

MEMBERSHIP HAS ITS PRICE

Traditional American Express cards may look like credit cards or debit cards, but they're actually a different species of plastic: **charge cards.** Charge cards work on a "pay-in-full" system, which means that you have to pay your bill completely at the end of every month, instead of carrying a balance. If you don't pay every cent you owe, you could get hit with late fees, and eventually your card will be suspended. (American Express also offers a line of regular *credit* cards.)

Some people find that charge cards help them stay disciplined and avoid getting too deeply into debt. Problem is, it has high annual fees: Amex's basic green card charges $55 for the privilege of membership, plus an additional $30 if you want frequent-flyer points through its "Rewards" program; the fee on Amex's "Rewards Plus Gold Card" is $150. Now that credit card issuers are offering gold cards with similar perks and no annual fees, think twice before you pay for a charge card. You could be better off just pretending you have one and paying off your bills in full every month.

• **Before you sign up, evaluate reward cards carefully.** With a reward card, whenever you charge, you earn points toward some product or service. Most reward deals make sense only if you pay off your entire balance each month. That's because the interest rates they charge are often higher than the rates you can get if you shop around. These higher rates can offset any benefit you get from the card. Also, most reward deals—especially airline cards that allow you to earn frequent-flyer miles for every dollar you charge—pay off only if you charge a lot. You have to charge thousands of dollars (recently around $25,000) in order to get one free round-trip ticket from an airline card. If you don't carry a balance and you don't spend very much, look for a reward card that does not charge an annual fee—for example, the Sunoco MasterCard, which offers rebates on gas.

STUDENT LOANS

Most students can expect to graduate from college with thousands of dollars in student debt. If you're having trouble paying back your loans or you're simply looking for a way to reduce your interest payments, this section can help.

Most student loan debt consists of **Stafford loans,** which are guaranteed by the federal government. ("Guaranteed" means that the government will ultimately pick up the tab if you default on your payments.) Other kinds of federally guaranteed student loans include **PLUS loans** (which are made to students' parents) and **Perkins loans** (which are offered to lower-income students). Check your paperwork to see exactly what kind of loans you have; Stafford loans probably make up the majority of them.

There are two ways to get Stafford loans: directly from the Department of Education, through the Federal Direct Loan Program (800-848-0979; www.ed.gov/offices/OPE/DirectLoan); or through a private lender, usually a bank. The Federal Direct Loan

Program keeps its loans throughout the period when you're paying them back, and so do some private lenders, including major ones like Citibank and Chase. But many private lenders sell off their loans to other companies, known as the **secondary market,** which take over the bill collection. The biggest player in the secondary market, Sallie Mae (800-643-0040; www.salliemae.com), handles about one-third of all student loans.

Throughout this chapter, I'll be using the term **servicer** to refer to the company that actually deals with you when you're paying off your student loans—whether it be the federal government, your original lender, or the secondary-market company that has bought your loan.

How to Reduce the Cost of Your Student Loans

Here are four strategies to consider:

- **Pay all your bills on time.** Some servicers have programs that reward you for timely payments. For example, Sallie Mae offers a loan repayment program that allows borrowers with Stafford loans who make their first 48 scheduled payments on time to reduce their interest rate by two percentage points for the remaining **term,** or length of time during which the loan lasts. Sallie Mae calls this program "Great Rewards," and most of the other major private servicers have similar programs in place. That 2% discount may not sound like much, but it can make a substantial difference. If you have $10,000 in Stafford loans at an 8.25% interest rate, a 2% reduction after 48 months would save you $578 in interest over the rest of a ten-year term.

  These programs often have restrictions. In Sallie Mae's case, the loans must have been taken out in 1993 or later, for example. Check with your servicer to see if you qualify. If you got your loans from the Federal Direct Loan Program, you're out of luck; as of this writing, Direct Loan does not offer any incentives for timely repayment.

- **Deduct your interest payments.** The government gives students a tax break: You may be able to deduct the first 60 months of *interest* payments on your student loans, up to a maximum of $2,000 in 2000. (This maximum deduction will grow to $2,500 in 2001.) Money that goes toward repaying the principal is not deductible. For more details, see Chapter 9.

- **Sign up for automatic payment.** If you agree to have your loan payments automatically deducted from your checking or savings account each month, there's a good chance your loan servicer will reduce your interest rate by a quarter of a percentage point. The Federal Direct Loan Program does offer this discount. Call your servicer to find out how to sign up.

- **Prepay your student loans.** If you're not loaded down by credit card balances or other high-rate debt, consider paying back your student loans faster than you're required to under your current payment schedule. One simple way to do this is to double the monthly payment you make. This will save you a substantial amount of interest in the long run. Say you have a $10,000 loan with an interest rate of 7.43%. If you assume interest rates remain the same and you pay back your loan over ten years, your monthly payment will be $118. If you double that amount and pay $236 a month, you will pay off your loan in four years and two months and save more than $2,500 in interest. Remember, prepayment makes sense only if the interest rates on your loans are *higher* than the rates you can earn on an investment. (For an explanation of why this is so, see page 51.)

Simplifying Your Repayment

Here are two ideas that may make paying back your loans a bit simpler:

- **Loan consolidation.** To reduce your paperwork, servicers offer loan consolidation, which lets people combine their major federal student loans (like Stafford loans and PLUS loans) into one massive loan—for a price. Your servicer pays off all your old loans and issues you a new one, with a fixed interest rate equal to the average of the rates on your old loans (rounded up to the nearest eighth of a percent). The interest rate on this new consolidated loan is guaranteed to remain under 8.25%.

Loan consolidation makes it easier for you to keep your payments on track, because you'll have only one bill to pay every month. And there's another reason that it may make sense to consolidate your loans: Only by consolidating can you take full advantage of special repayment plans offered by private lenders (which are outlined in the next section). Basically, with a consolidated loan, you may be able to stretch out your repayment over a longer period of time. That could lower your monthly payments substantially, which is good news for people on a tight budget. But it also means that you'll be shelling out a lot more interest over the life of your loan.

Annoyingly, Sallie Mae and the other servicers won't give you the 2% timely-discount break if you consolidate your loans. So if you don't need to stretch out your repayment, don't consolidate.

The federal government has its own consolidation program, called the Federal Direct Loan Consolidation Program (800-557-7392; www.loanconsolidation.ed.gov). The interest rate on federal consolidated loans is the same as for private loans, but the repayment options differ slightly.

If you're thinking of consolidating, check out the consolidation calculators available from the USA Group at www.usagroup.com (for private consolidation) and from the Department of Education at www.ed.gov/offices/OPE /DirectLoan (for federal consolidation). These calculators help you figure out exactly how much you can expect to pay over the course of your loan and let you compare the cost of different repayment options.

• **Loan serialization.** If you don't want to consolidate, there may still be a way to simplify your monthly payments. Some of the larger private servicers offer "loan serialization," which is a fancy way of saying that they'll send you just one bill for all of your loans that they handle. Serialization won't actually change anything about your loans, but it could make it easier for you to get organized and make your payments on time. And you'll still be eligible for the 2% discount for timely Stafford payments.

Special Repayment Options

The standard way to pay back student loans is by making equal monthly payments for ten years. If you have student loans and you're having trouble making your monthly payments, you have several repayment options to choose from. The rules for these options vary depending on whether you have consolidated your student loans and whether your loans are handled by the federal government or by a private servicer like Sallie Mae.

Be forewarned that although these options may make your monthly payments more manageable, they could severely increase the total amount of interest you pay.

- **Extended repayment.** This option allows you to stretch out your loan repayment over a period of ten to thirty years. If your servicer is a private company, you must consolidate your loans to extend them, but the Federal Direct Loan Program offers the extended repayment option whether you consolidate or not.

- **Graduated repayment.** This option allows you to make lower payments in the early years of your loan. Your payments will then increase every two years. This plan may be combined with an extended repayment plan.

- **Income-sensitive repayment.** This plan is available only to people whose loans are being serviced by private lenders, not by the Federal Direct Loan Program. To ease the burden if you're in a low-paying job, income-sensitive repayment enables you to work with your lender and have your monthly payments determined by your salary and debt load. Your payments will rise and fall based on fluctuations in your income, but will always be at least high enough to pay off the interest you are accruing on your loan. If you're married and file a joint tax return, your joint income is used to calculate the required monthly payments. The maximum term for unconsolidated loans is ten years, but the period can be extended to as much as thirty years for consolidated debts.

- **Income-contingent repayment.** This option is similar to income-sensitive repayment in most ways and is available only to people with Federal Direct Loans. Unlike income-sensitive repayment, it is possible under income-contingent repayment to make monthly payments that are so low they do not even cover the interest you owe on your loan. If this occurs, your debt may actually grow even as you make payments on it—a financially disastrous situation. If at the end of 25 years you still have not paid off your debt, the Department of Education will do something that private servicers won't. forgive you the remainder of what you owe. (They forgive but they don't forget. You'll have to pay income tax that year on the amount that has been waived.)

How much will these plans increase the amount of interest you pay? A lot. For example, if you extended the term of a $20,000 loan (with an 8% interest rate) from ten years to twenty years, you would have to shell out a whopping $11,000 in additional interest. The other repayment plans can be even costlier.

Special Breaks If You Can't Make Your Payments

The government has set up rules that spell out exactly why and for how long you can put off repaying your student loans. A government-approved delay is called a **deferment.** Deferment rules change every few years, so figuring out whether you qualify for a deferment can get pretty confusing.

Deferments are granted for many different reasons. For instance, if you're unemployed, a part-time or full-time student, a professional intern or resident, a full-time unpaid volunteer, or a recipient of an approved graduate fellowship, you may qualify for a deferment. Also, if you teach full-time in a public or nonprofit elementary or secondary school in what is considered a teacher-shortage area, you may be able to defer for up to three years. (Each state has its own definition of a teacher-shortage area.) During deferment periods, the government sometimes pays the interest for you. That's the case with some Stafford loans and most Perkins loans. With all other student loans, you will eventually have to pay the interest that accrues during the deferment period. To learn more about deferments, contact the institution that's handling your loans.

If you don't qualify for a deferment, all hope is not lost. Loan servicers can offer you time off from making payments through a process known as **forbearance.** Forbearance can be granted for a variety of reasons, many of which are based on the discretion of the institution that's holding your loans. You will be responsible for the

A SMART MOVE IF YOU HAVE CREDIT CARD AND STUDENT LOAN DEBT

The interest rates on your student loans are probably lower than the interest rates on your credit cards. If this is the case, you should pay off your credit card debt faster than you pay off your student loans. By consolidating your student loans and extending the number of years over which you pay them back, you can reduce monthly student loan payments and free up some cash to pay off your credit cards. Once you've wiped out your credit card debt, increase your student loan payments to at least their original levels.

interest that accrues on any type of loan during a period of forbearance. Again, speak to someone at the institution that is servicing your loan for details.

CAR LOANS

Once you get a car loan with a high interest rate, you may be stuck
with it; it's often hard to find a lender that will refinance a car loan
with a lower-rate loan. (If you own a home, you may have the option
of transferring your auto debt to a home equity loan. See the next section for details.) For this reason, it's smart to shop carefully for a loan
when you buy a car. For instance, getting a 7% rate instead of a 9%
rate on a $15,000 four-year loan would save you about $675. This
section will offer you some shopping advice on loans and leases.

How to Get a Good Deal on an Auto Loan

To get a good rate, you're going to need to do some legwork. Here
are some pointers:

- **Shop around.** Before you set foot in a dealership, check with
  a credit union and at least two banks. Credit unions tend to
  charge lower rates on car loans than banks do—sometimes
  as much as a full percentage point lower. (For information
  on joining a credit union, see Chapter 4.) In some cities, the
  difference among bank rates can be more than three percentage points. See if your own bank is willing to bargain;
  you can sometimes get a half-percentage-point break if you
  have your payments deducted automatically from your bank
  account or if you're considered a "good customer" (meaning you have anywhere from $1,000 to $5,000, depending
  on the bank, in your account).

- **Use the Internet.** Look around the Web to see if any lenders in your area are offering especially appealing rates.

Good sites for that purpose include Bankrate.com
(www.bankrate.com), LendingTree (www.lendingtree.com),
and RateNet (www.rate.net).

• **Ask your bank if you can get preapproved for an auto loan.**
Preapproval is a process by which the lender looks at your
income, debts, and other financial information and deter-
mines how large a loan you can handle. The benefit is that
you'll be better equipped to negotiate with a car dealer once
you have a ballpark figure on how big a loan you can qualify for.

• **Negotiate and settle on an exact price for the car before you**
discuss financing. Sometimes dealers will give you a break
on one aspect of a car purchase—say, by offering you a low-
rate loan—but then jack up the price of the car to compensate. That's why it's critical to settle on the price first and
then negotiate financing. In general, the sticker price is 10%
to 20% higher than the price the dealer paid for the car. For
all but the hottest models, you shouldn't pay the sticker
price. Instead, check out annual reports in magazines such
as *Money* and *Consumer Reports,* which list estimates of
dealers' costs, or look at the comprehensive write-ups of
specific cars on consumer-oriented Web sites like Edmund's (www.edmunds.com) and Kelley Blue Book
(www.kbb.com). (Edmund's and Kelley Blue Book put out
book versions of their reports as well, but their Web sites are
more up-to-date.) If you have a particular car in mind, you
can get useful information and advice about it for $12 from
the *Consumer Reports* New and Used Car Price Service
(800-422-5039; www.consumerreports.org). Once you've
done your research, try to haggle with the dealer and pay
just 5% or so above the price he paid.

• **Don't tell the dealer how much you can afford to spend on**
monthly payments. This is often the first question a car
dealer will ask. Though you should have a rough idea of the
answer (see Figure 3-2), don't share that information with

the dealer. The reason: Once the dealer knows, he can adjust the terms (for example, the price of the car or the interest rate you are charged) to his liking while matching your monthly payment figure.

• **Be wary of financing options that require "no money down" or a very low down payment.** The lower the down payment is, the more interest you will pay over the life of the loan. That's because a low down payment increases the size of the loan you need. Of course, if you can afford it and don't have other high-rate debt, the best move is to pay the entire cost of the car upfront.

• **In general, go with the shortest-term loan you can afford.** The average term on new auto loans is about four and a half

Figure 3-2
HOW MUCH YOU'LL PAY EACH MONTH
WITH AN AUTO LOAN

This table can help you get a sense of what your monthly car payments will be given a specific term and interest rate on a $10,000 auto loan. Although your monthly payments are lower with a longer-term loan, the total amount you will pay is higher. To figure out the total cost of the car loan, multiply the monthly figure by the number of months it will take for you to pay it off.

		INTEREST RATE						
		7%	8%	9%	10%	11%	12%	13%
Term (Months)	24	$448	$452	$457	$461	$466	$471	$475
	36	309	313	318	323	327	332	337
	48	239	244	249	254	258	263	268
	60	198	203	208	212	217	222	228

Source: Chase Automotive Finance

years. If you don't have any other high-rate debt, get a loan with a term of four years or less. Remember, your goal is to pay off your highest-rate debt as fast as possible.

Some Advice on Leasing a Car

If you've been shopping for a car, you probably know that car dealers push leasing in a big way. And if you're like most people, you've probably found the low down payment and low monthly payments extremely attractive. What you may not know is how leasing works.

When you lease, you are essentially renting a car from a leasing company for a fixed number of years. Although it's most common to lease a car through a dealership, a dealer is actually just the middleman working on behalf of a leasing company. As a leasing customer, you pay for the amount the vehicle depreciates during the lease period—typically two to four years—plus interest on this amount. Your monthly payments are based on the price of the car, the interest rate you're charged, the anticipated resale value of the car at the end of the leasing period, and the number of years in the leasing period.

At the end of your contract, you have the option of buying the car you've been leasing. If you don't want it anymore, you can usually return it and lease a new one—without the time, expense, and hassle of trying to sell a used car. But you won't have anything to show for the money you've put into your auto payments.

Look Before You Lease

Leasing typically makes the most sense for people who want to drive a new or almost-new car at all times. If you plan to keep your car for many years, you'll probably save money by buying. That's especially true if you drive a lot or treat your car badly, because you'll have to pay for damages and extra mileage when your leasing contract is up. And if you plan to move soon, make sure your lease will permit it; some lessors require you to give up your lease if you move and pay hefty charges for early termination.

Before you make a decision about buying or leasing a car, take some time to crunch the numbers. Several good calculators are available online, through such sites as CarWizard (www.carwizard.com) and *Smart Money* (www.smartmoney.com/lease). For about $25, CarWizard also offers a computer program that will allow you to do a more comprehensive lease-versus-buy analysis. To order, call 800-838-8778, or download the program online (and pay by credit card) at www.carwizard.com.

Leasing agreements have their own jargon and can get pretty complicated. As a result, it's easy to get taken for a ride. Here are the main factors you should be aware of while negotiating a leasing deal:

- **The "interest rate."** Technically, there is no such thing as an "interest rate" where car leasing is concerned. There is, however, an implicit **lease rate,** which is the equivalent of an interest rate. The dealer should be able to calculate the lease rate for you. If your dealer balks, insist that he or she tell you the **money factor,** which is a figure most leasing companies use to calculate their monthly charges. You can use the money factor to get an estimate of the effective lease rate you'll be paying: Simply multiply the money factor by 24 to come up with the answer. A money factor of .0042, for example, would give you a lease rate of about 10%.

- **The "price" of the car on which the lease is based.** In leasing lingo, the term **adjusted capitalized cost** is basically the purchase price of the car you're leasing, as set by the dealer, *plus* tax and *minus* your down payment and the value of any trade-in. It may also include extras like insurance, extended warranties, and other optional services; make sure these extra charges are itemized so that you can decide which ones you really want before you agree to include them in your contract. The car's purchase price as proposed by the leasing company should be bargained down the same way you would if you were buying. Ideally, the value you accept should be substantially below the **manufacturer's suggested retail price** (MSRP), also known as the "sticker price," of the car you're interested in. You can find out a car's sticker price online at sites like Kelley's Blue Book (www.kbb.com) and Edmund's (www.edmunds.com).

Try to find a **manufacturer-subsidized lease** if you can; these leases get financial support from carmakers and offer much better deals. You can find updated information on the best manufacturer-subsidized leases through the Internet at IntelliChoice (www.intellichoice.com) and Edmund's (www.edmunds.com).

- **The probable value of the car at the end of the lease.** This is known as the **residual value.** To find out if the dealer is quoting you a fair residual value, look up the car's "residual percentage rate" at the Automotive Lease Guide's Web site, www.alg.com. To make a leasing deal more attractive, some car manufacturers are willing to make the residual value artificially high. If all other factors are equal, a high residual value is better for you, because your monthly payments are based on how much the car is expected to depreciate during the time you lease it. A high residual value means that the car will not depreciate much during your lease; as a result, your payments will be lower.

  High residual value can be a drawback if you're planning to buy the car when the lease is over. But if you do decide you want to buy the car, you may be able to bargain with the leasing company and get them to sell it to you for less than the residual value you previously agreed to in your leasing agreement. Try to negotiate right before the lease is up.

Before you lease, you'll want to settle a number of issues. Find out, for instance, the total mileage you're allowed without being charged extra, and compare this mileage limitation with other leasing companies' offers to make sure you're getting a fair deal. Also, learn what the penalties are for getting out of the lease early. This information should be in your leasing agreement. Before you lease, check out magazines (and their Web sites) such as *Consumer Reports, Kiplinger's, Smart Money,* and *Money.* These publications usually have annual guides to buying and leasing cars. The Federal Reserve publishes a useful (and free) little guide called *Keys to Vehicle Leasing* that can be found on its Web site (www .federalreserve.gov/pubs/leasing) or ordered by phone at 202-452-3244. You may also want to look at what's available at online leasing sites like LeaseSource (www.leasesource.com).

HOME EQUITY LOANS

If you own a home, you have one additional loan source: You're usually allowed to borrow 80% to 100% of your home's value, *minus* the balance on your mortgage. So if you have a $100,000 home with a $60,000 mortgage, you could qualify for a home equity loan of $20,000 to $40,000.

The main advantage of a home equity loan (HEL) is that it offers you a tax break that you don't get with credit cards or auto loans. For this reason, in addition to using HELs to pay for home improvements, many people take out home equity loans and use the money to pay off higher-rate debt, like credit cards. The chief drawback of home equity loans is that borrowers can lose their homes if they can't make their payments. (In theory, auto lenders and credit card issuers can go after your home in most states if you owe them money, but in practice they usually don't.)

Home Equity Loans and Home Equity Lines of Credit

Most banks offer both home equity loans and home equity lines of credit. With a home equity loan, you get all the money at once in a lump sum and you repay it over five to fifteen years. The interest rate on a home equity loan is typically a fixed rate, meaning it's the same throughout the life of the loan. Home equity lines of credit are different. They are similar to credit cards in that borrowers get a set credit line on which to draw over time. Each month they can make the minimum payment or pay more if they want to. Home equity lines generally have variable interest rates that can change on a monthly or annual basis.

The interest you pay on a home equity loan or line of up to $100,000 is *deductible,* meaning you can subtract it from your taxable income when you fill out your tax return. The interest on amounts above $100,000 is not deductible, with one exception: If you use the money for home improvements, you can deduct the interest on a loan of up to $1 million.

Here's what that tax break means in dollars. Say you owe $1,000 on your home equity loan and your interest rate is 8%. If you pay it off in one year, you will also pay $80 in interest. If you're in the 30% tax bracket, you will save $24 (30% of $80) at tax time if you itemize your deductions. So after you factor in your tax savings, the interest you actually paid was just $56. Another way to look at it is that the *after-tax* interest rate on an 8% home equity loan is 5.6%. (See Chapter 9 for details on itemizing.)

Before You Refinance Other Debt with Home Equity, Read This

Although home equity lines and loans offer attractive rates, it doesn't always make sense to transfer your high-rate debt to them. Do not consider refinancing with your home's equity unless you do the following:

- **Plan to pay off your home equity line as fast as you would have paid off the loans you're refinancing.** As I mentioned, you may want to transfer your auto loan to a home equity line, but because *you* can decide how much you want to pay back each month with a home equity line, it can be tempting to make small monthly payments. Dragging out repayment gets expensive, so you have to be disciplined—which is why it's a smart idea to pay off your home equity line over the same number of years it would have taken to pay off your auto loan.

Similarly, if you decide to pay off your credit card debt with a home equity line, you'll also need to be diligent about paying the line off quickly. And don't start using your home equity line as a credit card substitute. Remember, if for any reason you can't make your payments—say you lose your job or have a medical emergency—the lender will be allowed to take your home.

- **Factor in up-front fees.** Some lenders charge hundreds or even thousands of dollars in initial fees when they grant home equity loans and lines of credit. But most lenders are now willing to waive these fees entirely. Shop carefully. And make sure that after you factor in the fees, it still makes sense for you to refinance.

- **Determine whether you're comfortable with a variable interest rate.** The variable interest rates on some home equity lines are enticingly low, but make sure you know just how high your monthly payments could go if you stick to your self-imposed short-term pay schedule. Ask the loan officer how much the rate can rise. Also, ask him to talk you through a worst-case scenario. Many home equity lines offer deeply discounted first-year rates that can increase several percentage points in year two.

- **Steer clear of 125% loans.** Many lenders are now allowing home equity loans of up to 125% of the value of your home, minus your mortgage. So if you have a $100,000 home and a $60,000 mortgage, you could theoretically be allowed to borrow up to $65,000. But there are two problems with 125% loans. First, you will not be able to deduct the interest on your entire loan—only the part that, along with your mortgage, adds up to the fair market value of your home. (In the case above, even though you borrowed $65,000, you would only be able to deduct the interest you pay on the first

BORROWING FROM FRIENDS AND RELATIVES

Patti wanted to pay off the $5,000 balance she owed on her credit card, which charged a rate of 18%. Her parents were willing to lend her the money to do it. Here are some steps they followed to make the transaction harmonious:

- **They made sure the deal was good for both parties.** Patti agreed to pay her parents back with interest, and they settled on a rate of 7%. Not only was this a good deal for Patti, but it was also beneficial to her parents, whose money had formerly been sitting in a bank savings account earning just 3%.

- **They put everything in writing.** Patti's parents wrote up an agreement that included the interest rate charged and the dates payments were due. It might sound formal, but this helped avoid confusion.

- **They made sure there weren't any negative tax consequences.** Bizarre as it may seem, the IRS sets a minimum interest rate—the **applicable federal rate (AFR)** —that family members and friends are required to charge on certain types of loans. Even if your parents, for example, want to lend you money without charging you interest, they may owe tax on the interest they *would have* received had they charged you the AFR. If you borrow less than $10,000 to buy an item like a car or to pay off debts (as Patti did), you don't have to worry about these rules. But if you borrow the money to purchase assets like stocks and bonds or if you borrow more than $10,000 for any purchase, your parents, friends, or relatives may be expected to charge you interest. The rules are very complicated, so check one of the current tax guides for details, looking in the index under "loans." For the current AFR, call your bank or your local IRS office, or look it up on the IRS Web site at www.irs.gov/prod/bus-info/tax-pro/tax-law.html.

$40,000.) More important, 125% loans will get you in debt way above what you can afford. In a worst-case scenario, you could lose your home and still be deep in the hole.

CREDIT
REPORTS

Companies that keep your credit report, known as credit agencies or credit bureaus, are information gatherers and distributors. They supply banks and other lenders with all the dirt on your financial behavior. When you apply for a loan or credit card, lenders request the report and evaluate your history. Frequently, the credit bureau will be asked by the lender to summarize the information in your report into one number called a **risk score**. These risk scores are supposed to predict how likely you are to default on a loan, declare bankruptcy, or even make late payments. Unfortunately, at the time of this writing, you cannot find out your risk score, but you do have access to your credit report. Because so much rides on a credit agency's evaluation of your credit history, it is essential to check your credit report before applying for a major loan.

Q: *What kind of information is in my credit report?*
A: Your report lists the basics, such as your age, birth date, Social Security number, current and previous addresses, current and previous jobs, and spouse's name (if you are married). The credit information describes all the credit relationships you have, such as bank credit cards, store credit cards, and student loans. Included is the date you opened each account, how much you owe, the maximum amount you can borrow, and your payment history. The report typically does not include information about your rent or utility payments, but it does indicate whether you've ever had any major financial problems, like defaulting on a loan or declaring bankruptcy.

Q: *How do I get a copy of my credit report?*
A: There are three major credit agencies that maintain credit

reports: Equifax, Experian, and Trans Union. The information may be very different in each report.

If you haven't been denied credit but simply want to see what's in your credit report, order a copy of it from Equifax at 800-685-1111 (www.equifax.com), Experian at 888-397-3742 (www .experian.com), or Trans Union at 800-888-4213 (www.tuc.com). You'll have to pay $8 in most states. As of this writing, you'll pay less than that if you live in Connecticut, Minnesota, or Maine. And you're entitled to at least one free report every year if you live in Colorado, Massachusetts, Maryland, Virginia, Georgia, or Vermont.

Q: *If I'm turned down for a loan, can I find out why?*

A: Yes. The Equal Credit Opportunity Act says that if your application for credit is denied, the lender must either give you an explanation for the rejection or inform you how you can get an explanation. If you ask for a specific reason, the lender must provide you with one. According to the Federal Trade Commission, acceptable explanations should be fairly specific—for example, you earn too little money or you haven't worked long enough. Vague reasons—such as not meeting the creditor's "minimum standards"—aren't acceptable.

If the denial was due to something in your credit report, the lender must tell you the name and address of the credit agency that provided information about you. If you are denied credit, credit agencies are required by law to send you a free report if you request it within 60 days. The same is true if you've been turned down for a job or an apartment because of your credit history.

Q: *How long will my credit report show my misdeeds?*

A: Most negative information will be deleted from your report after seven years. If you ever file for bankruptcy, it could take ten years before your credit report will be clean. This doesn't mean you won't be able to get credit before then. Lenders usually look at your behavior in the past two years or so when evaluating your credit-worthiness.

Q: *I've heard of companies that claim to repair credit ratings. Should I consider one?*

A: Definitely not. There are all kinds of sleazy firms that promise to fix credit reports. Don't waste your money on them. At best, these fly-by-night companies work the legal fine print to trip up the credit bureaus and force them to remove negative information. But most of the time these tricky maneuvers don't work, and you end up paying hundreds of dollars for nothing.

Q: *What should I do if I find a mistake in my credit report?*

A: Credit bureaus have a reputation for making mistakes. Sometimes it's simply misspelling your name or giving a wrong address, but sometimes it's a potentially damaging error, such as mistakenly showing that you've defaulted on a loan.

If you find a mistake on your report, write to the credit agency right away, and be specific about your concerns. The agency gets 30 days to investigate your complaint; if it can't verify the information on the report by then, the agency is legally required to delete it. If that happens, you can ask that copies of the corrected report be sent to any lender that has seen the report within the past six months or any potential employer that has seen it within the past two years. (You'll find a list of these people on the credit report itself.) If you don't agree with the outcome of the investigation, write a short statement (100 words or less) and have the credit agency include it in your credit report. If you ask, the credit agency should send a copy of your version of the dispute free of charge to potential employers who have received the old report within the last two years or potential lenders who have received it within the past six months.

Q: *Will "credit card surfing" hurt my credit report?*

A: Hopping from credit card to credit card whenever your teaser rate runs out can save you money, but it could also slightly drive down your credit rating. Every time you apply for new credit, an inquiry is noted on your report. Credit scoring systems tend to punish people with a lot of inquiries on their credit report, because those inquiries may be a sign that you are applying for more credit than you can handle. Similarly, if you do switch cards, don't forget to cancel your old card. If you keep the card open, potential lenders might think you have too much available credit already. Neither of these two factors will matter much if your credit is in good shape. But if you have a number of red flags on your credit report—like defaulted loans, a history of late payments, or a number of cards that are almost maxxed out—surfing may not be a good idea.

Q: *How can I fix my credit report if I've been the victim of fraud?*

A: Unfortunately, the technological revolution has made it easier than ever before for thieves and con artists to get hold of your personal information, including your Social Security number, driver's license number, and even your PIN codes. Using this information, they can pass themselves off as you, set up accounts in your name, run up huge bills, and leave you to clean up the mess they leave behind. This phenomenon, known as **identity theft**, is becoming more and more common. Under federal law you can't be held financially responsible for the false charges made in your name, but your credit report might well be wrecked. If that happens, it's important to start cleaning up your record right away. The first step is to contact the fraud departments of all three major credit bureaus: Equifax (800-525-6285), Experian (800-301-7195), and Trans Union (800-680-7289).

To minimize the danger of your identity's being stolen, check your credit report on a regular basis, and be careful about sharing your personal information. Tear up personal documents, including credit card offers you get in the mail, before you throw them in the garbage. For more information about identity theft, contact the Privacy Rights Clearinghouse (619-298-3396; www.privacyrights.org), a nonprofit consumer group.

Q: *I'm married. Does that mean my spouse and I have the same credit report?*

A: If you each had your own credit cards before you were married, then you each have a separate credit report. If you have a joint credit card or loan, that will be noted on both of your individual credit reports. Keep in mind that whenever you share a card or cosign a loan, you are liable for each other's debts.

It is important for you to keep at least one loan or credit card in your own name, and for your spouse to do the same, so that each of you establishes a separate credit history. If you don't, you will have trouble getting credit if you get divorced or if your spouse dies.

Q: *Who can look at my credit report?*
A: The law says that credit bureaus can disclose information about you to any person or organization with a "permissible purpose" for seeing the information. That can include a lender or landlord who wants to find out about your past financial habits or even a potential employer who wants to know more about you. (Potential employers, unlike lenders or landlords, must get your written permission before requesting your credit history.) A copy of your report will show you who has made inquiries about you in the past two years.

IF YOU'RE IN
SERIOUS DEBT

If you're having severe trouble making your payments, contact your lenders directly and explain your financial situation. Often you will find that a lender will be willing to work with you to come up with a more flexible repayment schedule.

If your creditor has hired a debt collector to get you to pay up, know your rights. Debt collectors can contact you by phone, mail, fax, or in person. They must contact you during reasonable hours (not before 8 A.M. or after 9 P.M.) unless you agree to a different arrangement. They can't harass you or repeatedly phone you with the intent to annoy you. You can stop a debt collector from continually contacting you by sending a letter to the collection agency he or she represents. Under the Fair Debt Collection Practices Act, the collection agency must stop contacting you at your written request, except to notify you of plans to bring legal action against you.

If you need help negotiating with lenders to lower your monthly payments and possibly reduce the interest rates on your loans, you may want to contact the nonprofit Consumer Credit Counseling Service (CCCS). This service is often free for general budgeting

IS BANKRUPTCY AN OPTION?

Tom, a 25-year-old social worker, earns $22,000 a year and doesn't expect his salary to increase any time soon. Unfortunately, he owes more than $50,000 in student loans and $5,000 in credit card debt. Feeling desperate, he wonders if it makes sense for him to declare bankruptcy.

The fact is, declaring bankruptcy, especially a certain type known as Chapter 7, can seem very appealing. It will cost some money up front: You will have to fill out some paperwork and submit it with a fee (recently $200) at a federal bankruptcy court, and you will also probably want to pay a bankruptcy lawyer to help you make your case. But if your petition for bankruptcy is accepted, your debts will be "discharged," meaning you will be absolved of responsibility for the money you owe to creditors such as your landlord, doctors, and credit card companies. Some of your assets can be seized to pay off these creditors, but depending on what state you live in you may be able to keep your car, home, and household possessions. And it may not be long before you can start borrowing again. One study found that more than a third of those who declared bankruptcy were able to get credit within three years of filing.

Although this sounds like a great deal, it's not an option that Tom—or most of us, for that matter—should consider. For starters, there's a long list of debts that can't be discharged if you file Chapter 7. Student loans, for instance, usually can't be wiped out. What's more, bankruptcy is noted on your credit report for ten years. True, you may be able to get some form of credit soon, but you probably won't be eligible for low-rate credit cards or other attractive loan deals for many years. Finally, because prospective employers will learn from your credit report that you declared bankruptcy, you may have trouble changing jobs— especially if you're trying to get a position that requires you to be financially responsible.

If your debts are pressing down on you but you can afford to make some payments, consider filing for Chapter 13 bankruptcy instead of Chapter 7. With Chapter 13, your debts won't be wiped clean, but the court will set up a repayment plan that will keep your creditors away from you and let you pay off all or part of your debts. It may be possible under Chapter 13 to hold on to major property that you would not been entitled to keep under Chapter 7. Also, some lenders consider Chapter 13 to be the more respectable form of bankruptcy and may treat you more favorably. But beware: Many people who try to live up to their obligations under Chapter 13 find that they can't. Unfortunately, you may not have much of a choice: Bankruptcy declarations sky-rocketed in the 1990s, and Congress is considering legislation to make it harder to qualify for Chapter 7.

For more information about bankruptcy, visit the American Bankruptcy Institute online at www.abiworld.org.

advice and typically charges a small monthly fee for its debt management program, based on your ability to pay and your state's banking laws. If you can't afford to pay, CCCS says it will not turn you away. To locate an office near you, call 800-388-2227. Another helpful source for debt advice is Debt Counselors of America (800-680-3328), which boasts a particularly user-friendly Web site (www.dca.org).

You may also want to look into other nonprofit counseling services available in your area. Some colleges and credit unions offer such services, and you might be able to get a referral from a local bank or consumer protection office.

FINANCIAL CRAMMING

- Take any savings you have and pay off your high-rate credit card debt. Paying off a balance on a credit card that charges 18% is the equivalent of earning more than 18% interest on your money *guaranteed*, after taxes. This is one of the best investments most of us can make.

- If you have a decent credit history and can't pay off your high-rate credit card debt immediately, try to get a low-rate card and transfer your debt to it. You can find listings of low-rate cards on Web sites like www.bankrate.com, www.consumer-action.org, and www.cardweb.com.

- If you are having trouble paying off your student loans, consider consolidating them and extending your repayment period. See page 66 for details.

- Before you visit a car dealership, shop around to get an idea of current auto loan rates and car pricing information. Once you find the car you want, negotiate an exact price for a car with the dealer before you discuss the financing he has to offer. You can find pricing information online at Kelley Blue Book (www.kbb.com) or Edmund's (www.edmunds.com).

- If you own a home, consider taking out a home equity line in order to pay off your high-rate debt. But plan to pay off your home equity line at least as fast as you would have paid off the loans you're refinancing.

- Before you apply for an auto loan or a low-rate credit card, get a copy of your credit report from Equifax (800-685-1111; www.equifax.com), Experian (888-397-3742; www.experian.com), or Trans Union (800-888-4213; www.tuc.com). Because each credit bureau may have different information, your safest bet is to check with all three of them. A credit report costs $8 in most states.

BASIC BANKING

Learn How to Get the Most from Your Bank for the Least Amount of Money

CHANCES ARE, your parents' financial lives have revolved around their local bank. They keep their savings there. They got their mortgage there. They obtained their first credit card there. They probably even got their clock radio there.

But that may not be true for you, because today many of the services that were once the domain of your local bank are better handled elsewhere. You may have obtained an auto loan through a car dealership rather than from your bank because the dealership offered more attractive terms. Perhaps you got an American Express card because it allowed you to rack up airline frequent-flyer points. Or maybe you've switched to an Internet bank because it doesn't charge monthly fees.

Why do you need a bank at all? The main reason is that banks offer two services that are difficult to get anywhere else: an all-purpose checking account and easy access to your cash through bank machines, also known as **automated teller machines (ATMs).** So the key factors to consider when choosing a bank are the costs of its checking and ATM services. If you take the time to investigate these charges before you choose a bank, you could save yourself hundreds of dollars each year. This chapter shows you how to shop for a bank, whether it's down the block or on the Internet. It also highlights your various savings options and offers you tips on reducing all your banking costs.

A BANK BY ANY OTHER NAME

For our purposes, it doesn't matter whether an institution calls itself a bank, a savings bank, or a savings and loan (S&L). These classifications reflect the government agency that oversees the institution and have no impact on you whatsoever. A **credit union** is a special kind of bank formed by people who have something in common, such as a shared workplace or profession. Credit unions tend to offer lower-priced services than ordinary banks. (For details on the advantages of credit unions and how to join, see the box on page 92.)

Nearly all banks, savings banks, and S&Ls in the United States are covered by something called federal deposit insurance. It guarantees that if the institution should fail, the money in your federally insured accounts (up to $100,000) will be protected. Look for signs that tell you that your money is covered by the Federal Deposit Insurance Corporation (FDIC). Federally insured credit unions have signs indicating that they are protected by the National Credit Union Share Insurance Fund (NCUSIF). If you don't see a sign or sticker at your institution, ask. Keep in mind that many banks, savings banks, S&Ls, and credit unions sell *uninsured investments* these days, so it is also important to make sure that the type of account you're opening is covered by federal deposit insurance. (These uninsured investments are explained later in this chapter.)

For simplicity, I'm going to stick with the term *bank* when discussing any of these financial institutions.

FINDING A LOW-COST CHECKING ACCOUNT

The interest rates that banks pay on savings accounts generally do not vary dramatically from bank to bank. It would be unusual to find one bank paying 3% on a savings account, for example, and

SIGN ON WITH A CREDIT UNION IF YOU CAN

Doing your banking at a credit union can often save you money. Credit unions tend to charge lower rates on loans and pay higher rates on savings accounts than ordinary banks. Even better, about two-thirds of credit unions (versus about a fifth of ordinary banks) offer free checking and no minimum balance requirement. And credit unions typically charge less for everything from money orders to bounced checks.

Before you sign up with a credit union, see if it offers all the services you want. For instance, most credit unions do not have their own ATMs, which means their members must use bank ATMs and pay higher fees for the privilege. Also, many credit unions don't return your canceled checks with your statements the way some banks do.

If these drawbacks don't bother you, you should definitely see if you're eligible to join one. If you work for your city, chances are there's a credit union available to you. Your church or synagogue may have one, or your community may have a credit union whose members are people who live in the neighborhood. If you have a relative who belongs to a credit union, you might be eligible to enroll; some credit unions accept immediate family members only, while others allow members of the extended family to sign up. For assistance, contact the Credit Union National Association (800-358-5710; www.cuna.org) and get the phone number of your state's credit union league. The league will help you locate a credit union that you may be able to join.

another bank down the street paying 8%. The important distinction among banks has to do with the fees you pay for services and the minimum balances required to avoid such fees. And the biggest challenge you may face is finding a bank that does not require you to maintain a high minimum balance to get free checking.

Many banks do not charge you monthly checking fees if you keep an average of $1,000 in a checking account. But some banks in major cities have much higher balance requirements—from $1,000 to $10,000. If you can't maintain these minimums, you have to pay a monthly checking charge of between $3 and $10. You may also have to pay 50 cents or more for each check you write above a predetermined limit.

To find the best checking deal, you'll have to do some scouting around. First, make sure you fully understand your current bank's minimum balance requirements. Then ask friends and coworkers if they know of a bank that has a lower balance requirement to qualify for free checking. If they don't have any leads for you, use the Yellow Pages to pinpoint banks nearby and start calling around. In most areas—even big cities—you're likely to find one. In New York City, for example, at least one bank (Amalgamated Bank of New York) currently offers totally free checking to all customers regardless of the size of their balances. In general, credit unions and smaller community banks tend to offer better deals than large, big-name national banks. And many banks that operate only over the Internet currently offer free checking regardless of your balance. Keep this in mind when you hunt for an institution.

Here are some tips on reducing your checking costs:

- **Pay attention to how a bank calculates minimum balance.** Some institutions use what is called the **minimum daily balance method.** This system requires you to maintain the minimum balance every single day—typically $500, though it can be much higher in big cities—in order to get free checking. If your balance drops below the minimum for even one day, you will be charged a fee. Other banks use the **average daily balance method.** With this method, the bank adds up all your daily balances and then divides that total by the number of days in the billing cycle to get an average figure. So if your bank's balance requirement is $1,000 and your account dips below that a couple of times during your billing cycle, you won't be penalized as long as your *average* balance is at least $1,000.

- **See if your bank allows you to "link" accounts to meet balance requirements.** Some institutions insist that you keep a set amount of money in your checking account in order to get free checking. Others offer free checking if you maintain a minimum balance in a *combination* of accounts—including checking accounts, savings accounts, certificates of deposit (CDs), and money market accounts (MMAs). This is known in the banking industry as "relationship banking." You may have to keep about twice as much money in the combination of accounts as you'd have to keep in a checking account alone. But since CDs and MMAs pay interest, relationship banking may be a good way to make sure you stay comfortably above your bank's minimum balance requirements—and earn a little bit of interest while you're at it. (For more details see the section "Different Ways to Save in a Bank" later in this chapter.)

- **Ask your employer to deposit your paycheck directly into your bank account each month.** Some banks waive their minimum balance requirements and checking fees if you sign up for **direct deposit** through your employer. This increasingly available arrangement permits your company to automatically deposit your entire paycheck into your checking or savings account.

- **Use your computer.** Some large banks reduce their minimum balance requirements if you agree to do all your banking with them online, at their Web sites. If you don't mind never seeing a teller again (or paying a fee when you do), this could be a good option.

  It's also a good idea to look into banks that operate *only* through the Internet and have no branches at all, like

CompuBank and Wingspan. These virtual banks, which I'll be referring to as **Internet banks,** are aggressively pursuing customers. As of this writing, they offer attractive interest rates on their checking accounts, often with no minimum balance requirements at all. But Internet banks are not for everyone. For more information about Internet banking, see the box on page 100.

- **If you write only a few checks a month, consider alternatives to a regular checking account.** Many banks offer what are called "basic" or "lifeline" checking accounts. These accounts charge a smaller monthly fee (about $3) and limit you to eight or ten free checks per month. (Some banks waive the checking fee if you keep at least $250 in a combination of your bank accounts.) If you exceed the monthly check limit, you pay a fee for each additional check you write, so if you usually need more than eight or ten checks a month, basic banking is not for you. Also, these programs often limit your free ATM transactions to a few per month, ruling them out for many young people addicted to ATMs. But if you can comfortably comply with the restrictions, a basic banking account is a worthwhile alternative.

  Some banks are willing to loosen the checking limitations on their no-frills accounts if you do your bill paying online, instead of writing paper checks. For more on online bill payment, see the box on page 96.

- **Avoid interest-bearing checking accounts that require you to maintain high minimum balances.** Checking accounts that pay interest, also called **NOW accounts,** can be very appealing. (NOW stands for—get this—negotiable orders of withdrawal.) But some banks require you to keep a minimum of $1,000 in a NOW account at all times, and others require an average daily balance of $2,000. If you fall below the minimum, you're slapped with a fee. The interest rate you're paid on such a NOW account is often so meager that it probably doesn't make sense to tie up your money in one. Odds are you're better off sticking with a regular checking

PAYING YOUR BILLS ONLINE

Most larger banks now let you do a lot of your banking at home by logging on to their Web sites. These sites allow you to transfer funds from one account to another, determine whether checks have cleared, keep track of ATM withdrawals and debit card purchases, and even apply for a loan—all without changing out of your pajamas.

One of the best features of online banking is electronic bill payment. Some banks charge $5 a month for electronic bill payment, but many provide it for free. The way it generally works is that you type in a list of merchants you want to pay and the dates on which the payments should be made. After setting up your system, you can pay your bills electronically with the touch of a button. You can also arrange for your bank to automatically pay recurring bills that are the same amount each month, like your cable bill. Just make sure you remember when you've arranged to have your bills paid, so you don't end up bouncing checks.

If your bank does not offer electronic bill payment, you may

account and a savings account (which is discussed later in this chapter). The exception to the rule: Some Internet banks pay interest on checking accounts regardless of how much money you keep in them.

MANAGING YOUR CHECKING ACCOUNT

Once you find a low-cost checking account, you'll want to make sure you manage it wisely. If you don't, you could find yourself

still have a few options. Many utility companies allow you to have your monthly payments electronically siphoned out of your checking account. There are also a handful of national billpaying services, like CheckFree (800-297-3180; www.checkfree.com), that allow you to pay all your bills electronically by computer or by using a Touch-Tone telephone. But these electronic bill-paying services can be expensive—they generally cost about $10 a month.

A few warnings. First, don't wait until the day a bill is due to pay it electronically. There is a lag, typically between two and five days, between the time you initiate a payment and the time a merchant actually receives it. To avoid any slip-ups, make electronic payments at least six business days before your bills are due. Second, don't assume that your account balance will be adjusted automatically when you make an electronic payment. Your electronic check will be subtracted from your account when it is cashed by the recipient, not when you send it. Finally, be prepared for technological glitches. In 1999, for example, CheckFree went down for a week, causing hassles for customers, although the company did cover late fees caused by the glitch.

zapped with $20 bounced-check fees. Here are some tips that will help you avoid such outrageous charges, and in general gain control of your checking account:

- **Balance your checkbook.** For some reason many people dread this chore even though it isn't difficult. Unless you're wealthy enough to keep so much cash in your checking account that you never have to worry about covering all the checks you write, you've got to balance your book. It helps to carry your check register with you, so that you can record checks the minute you write them and ATM withdrawals (and deposits) as soon as you make them. If your employer deposits your paycheck into your checking account, make sure to enter that deposit into your check register every payday as well. If you need help balancing your checkbook, look at the back of your bank statement; many banks provide a useful worksheet that can help you keep your checkbook in order. You might also consider using a personal finance computer program like Quicken or Microsoft Money to do the math for you.

- **Adopt a system that suits your financial situation.** If you tend to live from paycheck to paycheck, one way to help ensure that you always have enough in your account to cover your checks is to sign up for direct deposit and have your paycheck deposited into your checking account. With direct deposit, the money will typically show up in your checking account within two days of payday. The drawback to this method is that it could result in your having all your money sitting in a checking account that doesn't pay interest. That's why, if you opt for this system, you should sign up for an automatic savings plan at your bank. You might, for example, ask your bank to withdraw $50 a month from your checking account and transfer it into a savings account or another interest-bearing account. (For details on how these automatic savings plans work, see the box on page 108.)

  If your financial situation is less hand-to-mouth, another alternative is to deposit your paycheck directly into an interest-bearing account and then transfer money into your checking account to cover checks as you write them. You'll earn more interest using this method, but if you're not extremely conscientious about transferring money into your checking account, you'll end up bouncing checks. For many people, this system isn't very practical.

- **Sign up for bounced-check protection.** Many banks offer what is called **overdraft protection.** This is basically an automatic loan that kicks in if you write a check for an amount greater than the amount you have in your checking account. The interest rate you pay on the overdrawn amount is often high (19% or so), but if you don't abuse it, the service will cost you much less than a bounced-check penalty. That said, it's important to keep in mind that you'll probably have to write a check to pay off the overdraft account; it will not automatically be paid off as you deposit money in your checking account. Also, understand that some banks allow you to access your overdraft protection via your ATM. I have a friend who ran out of money and simply withdrew the $1,000 in overdraft protection via the ATM to cover the cost of a trip to France. It took her three years and more than $300 in interest to pay off the loan.

- **Don't rely on the ATM to keep track of your checking account.** One common reason people get nailed with annoying bounced-check fees is that they don't realize how the check-clearing process works. If you don't keep track of the checks you write, you could find yourself in trouble. Say you have $200 in your checking account, and you mail an $80 check to the phone company. Assume it takes a week for the phone company to deposit your check. If five days go by and you suddenly remember that you need $150 to renew your health club membership, you would see at the ATM that you have $200 in your account. If you forgot about the check you wrote to the phone company, you might withdraw $150, in which case your phone company check would bounce. The point: Keep track of your checking account.

USING THE ATM WISELY

You've heard of the MTV Generation? Well, most of us are part of the ATM Generation, a group that relies on bank machines for survival. Just a few years ago, banks didn't charge for ATM use because they wanted to encourage customers to become comfortable banking by machine. It worked. Now that so many people are hooked on them, ATMs can cost up to $2 or more per transaction. Here are some tips on keeping your ATM habits—and your spending—in check:

INTERNET BANKING

This is not a great time to plan a career as a bank teller. Large banks across the country increasingly encourage their customers to do their banking online or by phone. And now there are banks that operate almost completely online and may not have any branches at all. If you're comfortable with the idea of handling your financial transactions online, you should consider banking with Internet-only banks like CompuBank (888-479-9292; www.compubank.com), Telebank (800-TELEBANK; www.telebank.com), Net.B@nk (888-256-6932; www.netbank.com), and Wingspan (888-736-8611; www.wingspan.com). Most Internet banks issue paper checks for payments you don't want to make electronically (see the box on page 96) and an ATM card for cash withdrawals and debit card purchases.

Internet banks have a number of advantages. Their minimum balance requirements are generally very low or nonexistent, which could save you a lot of money in checking fees. They also let you earn interest on your regular checking account, regardless of your balance. The money you keep at an Internet bank should be federally insured for up to $100,000, just as it would be at a traditional bank, so if the bank goes out of business, you won't lose your savings. (Before you make any deposits, make sure the bank is federally insured by calling the Federal Deposit

• **Limit yourself to four ATM withdrawals per month if possible.** Not only is it often expensive to withdraw $20 a day from an ATM, but it's also a bad way to keep track of where your money goes. Use the worksheet you filled out in Chapter 2 to estimate how much cash you need each week. Then pick one day a week to withdraw cash from the machine—say, every Monday. Make a pact with yourself to

Insurance Corporation at 800-934-FDIC or searching its Web site at www.fdic.gov.)

Before you rush to sign up at an Internet bank, though, consider the downside. If you're accustomed to banking in person, you may miss some of the teller services that banks with branches can provide. Customer service at Internet banks can be pretty limited, and you may have a hard time getting through to a human being. And every time you want to deposit a check, you'll have to mail it in to the bank, which could be a problem if you need the money in your account right away. You can sign up to have your paycheck deposited directly into your account, but that won't work for birthday checks from your grandmother.

Also, since Internet banks have no physical branches, you will always get hit with surcharges when you use an ATM. To lessen the load, Internet banks provide lists of ATMs that do not impose surcharges, but there aren't too many of those around anymore. When I asked for a free ATM near my home in New York City, the closest one they could come up with was in New Jersey. Some Internet banks will go further and reimburse you for four ATM charges a month, with a limit of $1.50 for each withdrawal.

As Internet banking catches on, expect it to become more customer-friendly and less economically advantageous. But for now, Internet banks can be appealing. You can open an account by applying online or by printing the application and mailing it in to the bank.

make that cash last for the entire week. Promise yourself that once it runs out, you won't get more. This strategy will also help you rein in your spending habits.

• **Find out what it costs to use another bank's ATM.** Some banks charge their own customers for using their ATMs. Others don't, but do charge you for using bank machines

MANAGING A JOINT CHECKING ACCOUNT

If you and your mate decide to have a joint checking account, you'll need a system for keeping track of the checks each of you writes, so that you can avoid bouncing checks. The best way to handle it is to put one person in charge of balancing the checkbook. Marty and Andrea use checkbooks that have carbon copies. Each time they write a check, they toss the carbon copy into a box located in the kitchen. They also put ATM and bank withdrawal and deposit slips into the box, as well as incoming household bills. Twice a month Andrea goes through the box, writes checks to pay all the current household bills, and balances the checkbook.

that are affiliated with other banks. The fee your bank charges you for using a "foreign" ATM, as it is called, could be as high as $2 per transaction.

- **Ask about the minimums for avoiding ATM fees.** Some banks require you to maintain a minimum balance in your account in order to avoid ATM fees. If you don't meet the minimum, you could be charged 25 cents per withdrawal to use your bank's ATM and $1 to use another bank's machine. That may not sound so bad, but if you use cash machines a lot, you could easily end up throwing away $50 or $100 a year. Look for a bank that will waive its ATM fees if you maintain a low minimum balance.

- **Beware of surcharges.** In addition to the fees your own bank may charge, you could end up having to pay so-called **surcharges** of $1 or more when you use another bank's ATM. These fees are collected by the company that owns the ATM you're using, and they can be especially high in places where people need money fast, like malls and casinos. One cruise ship line has reportedly charged $9.50 to use its ATM. Surcharges are another good reason to use your own bank's machine whenever possible. At the very least, remember which ATMs carry high surcharges and avoid them when you can.

- **Use your debit card.** If you have the kind of debit card that requires a PIN code (as described in Chapter 3), you may be able to make ATM-style cash withdrawals when you make a purchase at your local supermarket. If your grocery bill comes to $20, for example, you could enter it as $60 and get the $40 difference from the cashier. This is a good way of getting money from your account without paying ATM fees. Just make sure to keep your receipt and enter the transaction into your checkbook.

- **Know the different ATM fees your bank charges.** Some banks also charge for transactions other than withdrawals. Finding out your balance or transferring money between accounts might cost from 25 cents to $1. If you use the ATM a lot, find a bank with low transaction fees, or look for one that waives ATM charges when you maintain a low minimum balance.

JOINT VERSUS SEPARATE ACCOUNTS

If you're involved with someone but not married, don't open a joint account with that person without giving it serious thought. With a joint account, either person has complete access to all the money in the account. What's more, if you break up, dividing up the money in a joint account could get ugly.

Still, if your relationship is very serious, you may decide that you do want to open a joint account with your partner. Many people do this for convenience and also because they think a joint account ensures that their partner will get all the money in the account in case they die. But this can be very tricky. Having one type of joint account with your partner, called a **joint convenience account,** does not entitle one person to inherit all the money in the account if the other dies. With another type of joint account called a **joint account with the right of survivorship,** the person with whom you share the account usually gets to inherit all the money in the account. An account with the right of survivorship doesn't offer your partner total protection; parents and other family members can challenge the arrangement in court. To protect your partner better, you should also write a will.

If you're married, you and your spouse should still discuss the joint account question. If you favor separate accounts but your spouse wants joint, there is a way to compromise: Consider keeping a portion of your savings in a joint account and putting a percentage—say, 5% of each paycheck—into separate accounts. That way you have the freedom to spend some of your money without having to confer with your partner. (Of course, you'll want to be sure to meet the minimum balances for free checking in all of your accounts.) You should also discuss what will happen in case of death. In some states, your parents would split your assets with your spouse if you die. Again, write a will to prevent such a situation.

DIFFERENT WAYS TO SAVE IN A BANK

Bank savings options don't offer the potential for phenomenal gains, but that's not what you're after here. You're just looking to meet the requirements for free checking and low-cost ATM usage. You'll make your fortune elsewhere.

Some banks, including most Internet banks, offer free checking with no strings attached. But many banks waive their checking fees only if you keep an average of $1,000 in a checking account, and in large cities the minimum can be much higher. As I mentioned earlier, you may be able to find a bank that offers you free checking for keeping, say, $2,500 in a *combination* of accounts—including CDs, money market accounts, savings accounts, and checking accounts. The advantage of this arrangement is that these linked accounts pay some interest, unlike regular checking accounts. Whether you should opt for linked accounts depends on your situation.

If you're not sure you can maintain the required $2,500 in combined balances, you're better off keeping all your money in a non-interest-bearing checking account. The reason: The interest you would earn from your linked accounts is too low to offset the monthly checking fees you would pay if you unintentionally fell below the minimum. It's better to meet the lower balance requirements on a checking account, even though you won't be earning interest, than to fall short of the balance requirements of a combination of accounts.

But if you *can* comfortably maintain the $2,500 combined minimum, keeping it stashed in linked interest-bearing accounts may make sense—especially if you were planning to invest that $2,500 in relatively safe, low-paying investments anyway. The interest you'll earn in your linked accounts won't be very impressive, but they will let you avoid having to keep money in a checking account that pays *no* interest at all. When all is said and done, it could work out in your favor. Bank savings options like the following can help you avoid checking fees and are not a bad place to accumulate part of the "three-month emergency cushion" discussed in Chapter 2.

Here are some details on the interest-paying accounts most banks offer:

- **Savings accounts.** This plain-vanilla type of account is the simplest way to keep money in the bank and earn interest on it. Generally there is no initial minimum deposit (but some banks do charge a monthly fee of $3 if the amount in your savings account drops below $200). Money in a savings account is **liquid,** meaning you can withdraw it whenever you want without paying a penalty. The bummer about savings accounts is that they tend to pay very low interest rates. Although banks occasionally raise the rates on savings accounts when interest rates in the economy rise, they are very slow to do this.

- **Money market accounts.** A money market account (MMA) is
  little more than a savings account with a relatively high minimum balance requirement and a complicated name. You will
  likely need $1,000 to $2,500 to open a money market
  account, and you may have to keep at least $1,000 in your
  account at all times to avoid paying a monthly account maintenance fee. Like savings accounts, MMAs are liquid (except
  for the minimum balance requirement) and usually pay a low,
  variable interest rate.

WHY IT PAYS TO KNOW YOUR BANK MANAGER

You don't have to present your bank manager with a shiny
apple each time you visit, but it's a good idea to get acquainted.
You can simply say that you've signed on as a customer and
wanted to introduce yourself. If you think this sounds a little
weird, invent a reason—ask about loan options or something.
The point is to make sure the manager recognizes your face.
It may even make sense to add your bank manager to your
holiday card list. If you ever have a problem, it can really help
to have someone at the bank who knows you as more than
just another multidigit account number.

And if you ever encounter an outrageous fee, don't hesitate
to speak up. When a friend of mine was charged $30 for two
bank checks—an amount he felt was too high—he protested
to the bank manager, who waived the fee. The fact is, bank managers often forgive fees for customers who complain, especially
customers who have clean banking records. And if you're penalized for something you had no control over—like unknowingly
depositing a bad check—you should definitely talk to the bank
manager; he or she may be willing to erase the charge.

When MMAs were introduced in the 1980s, they paid higher interest rates than savings accounts. Banks offered these higher-rate accounts to keep customers from fleeing banks for higher-paying investments offered elsewhere. But customers *did* move away from banks to invest their money elsewhere, so many banks gave up trying to compete; they stopped offering MMAs with significantly better rates than savings accounts. Today most money market accounts pay only slightly higher rates than savings accounts.

- **Certificates of deposit (CDs).** A certificate of deposit is a "savings product" that usually pays a fixed interest rate if you keep your money invested in it for a specified period of time (known as the CD's **term**). CDs almost always pay better rates than savings or money market accounts. With a CD you make a one-time investment and earn interest until the CD's term is complete. You do not continually add money to a CD; if you want to invest more money, you can open a new CD. You can find a CD with as short a term as three months or as long a term as ten years. A common type is a one-year CD.

At many banks you need at least $500 to open a CD. Usually, the longer the CD's term, the higher the interest rate. With a CD, you give up the liquidity you have with a savings or money market account and are rewarded with a higher rate.

The big drawback of a CD is that if you take out the money you've deposited before the CD's term is complete, you will be hit with an early withdrawal fee. These penalties can be steep; if you withdraw money very early in the CD's term, you could lose interest plus part of your initial investment.

There's another issue to consider before choosing a CD over a savings account: When you lock yourself into a CD, you are in effect placing a bet on the direction of interest rates. Here's why. Say you deposit money in a two-year CD that promises to pay you 5%. Now suppose six months later, interest rates increase dramatically, and banks are now paying 7% on two-year CDs. You have a problem.

AUTOMATIC SAVINGS PLANS

Although you're probably not going to keep your life's savings in a bank forever, a bank savings account is the first place most of us start to save. If you haven't been able to accumulate much savings on your own, have someone save *for* you. There are a couple of ways to do this. One way is to ask your company payroll office if you can have a fixed sum taken from each paycheck—say, $50 a month—and funneled directly into your bank savings account. Some employers offer such arrangements. If your employer doesn't, ask your bank to siphon off a set amount from your checking account at the same time each month and deposit that money in your savings account. (Remember to record the amount of money you withdraw in your checkbook to avoid bouncing checks.) These "forced savings" methods offer you an effortless way to build up a nest egg. Because you don't even see the money that's being set aside, before long you also won't even miss it. (For more information on automatic savings options offered by mutual funds and retirement savings plans, see Chapters 5 and 6.)

You're stuck with the 5% CD for another year and six months. Though you would like to get out of the 5% CD and into a 7% CD, the early withdrawal penalty you'd have to pay might be so large that it wouldn't be worth it. You won't face this risk with a savings account because the rate you receive will rise (slowly but surely) as interest rates in the economy rise. Of course, this works in reverse, too. If interest rates fall and new CDs are paying 3%, you'd be a winner with your 5% CD.

A WARNING ABOUT BANK-SOLD INVESTMENTS

Just a few years ago, banks offered only three savings options—savings accounts, MMAs, and CDs—all of which are federally insured. That's no longer the case. Today many banks offer a wider array of investment choices, including mutual funds. Although you will learn everything you ever wanted to know about mutual funds in Chapter 5, I want to mention something right away: Mutual funds, even those sold in banks, are *not* protected by federal deposit insurance. That means you *can* lose money with a mutual fund. Bank salespeople, who like to call themselves "financial counselors," are supposed to explain this; they sometimes forget.

As a rule, you are probably better off buying stock and bond mutual funds directly from low-cost mutual fund companies rather than from banks, because most banks offer limited investment choices and charge commissions on the mutual funds they sell.

FINANCIAL CRAMMING

- Shop around for a bank that offers free checking and waives ATM fees if you maintain a low minimum monthly balance in your checking account or in a combination of accounts. This can save you hundreds of dollars a year.

- Sign up with a credit union to minimize your banking costs. To find out if you're eligible to join one, call 800-358-5710 (www.cuna.org), and ask for the phone number of your state's Credit Union League.

- Avoid bounced-check charges by balancing your checkbook regularly. If your bank offers overdraft protection, sign up for it.

- Look into the checking accounts at Internet banks like the ones mentioned in the box on page 100. They currently pay higher interest rates and charge lower fees than traditional banks.

- If you've been charged an excessive fee for a bank service, complain. Being firm but polite will often help you persuade the bank's manager or customer service rep to waive the charge.

- Resist buying mutual funds that charge commissions from your bank. Instead, look into some of the low-cost mutual fund companies discussed in Chapter 5.

5

ALL YOU REALLY NEED TO KNOW ABOUT INVESTING

For New Investors, the Feeling Is Mutual (Funds)

YOU DON'T HAVE to have a business degree—or even know how to do long division—to know that the stock market has had an amazing run in recent years. Yet if you're like a lot of people, you still have all your money sitting in a low-interest checking or savings account in the bank. Maybe you have no idea where to invest. Maybe you have just enough money to get by, and investing doesn't seem possible. Or maybe you're terrified of making a mistake and losing what little savings you *do* have. But whatever your own maybes may be, the fact is that once you have enough money in your bank account to qualify for free checking, you're ready to learn about investing. Fortunately, this is a lot easier than it sounds.

Instead of betting your life's savings on some half-baked stock tip that promises to make you rich (but probably won't), you should be thinking about a fully baked investment known as a mutual fund. In fact, you can consider mutual funds your entire investment universe, at least for now. This chapter first explains what mutual funds are and how you can use them to meet the goals you formulated in Chapter 2. Later in the chapter, you'll learn how to go about investing in them.

Whether you're interested in super-safe investments that will pay a little more than a bank savings account or willing to jump into riskier investments that give you a greater chance of earning more money, this chapter will show you how to take the plunge.

But first, a brief reality check. The stock market skyrocketed in the 1990s, but there will surely be down periods—possibly major down periods—in the future. In fact, by the time you read this, the stock market may already have taken a tumble. But whether the market is climbing or falling, one thing is sure: No one really knows where it will go next. Your best bet is to decide how much risk you are willing to take and then start investing.

MUTUAL FUND FUNDAMENTALS

Mutual funds should be the foundation of your investment life. But before I get into the details, you'll need to know what a mutual fund is. Mutual means shared, or in common. A fund is a sum of money set aside for a particular purpose. A **mutual fund** is a type of investment that pools together the money of thousands of people. At the helm is a fund manager—the person (or company) in charge of investing the money. Depending on the type of fund, the fund manager generally invests the fund's money in a mixture of stocks, bonds, and money market instruments; these are all known as **securities.** (I'll explain what stocks, bonds, and money market instruments are in a moment.)

What's So Great About Mutual Funds?

Pooling your money with the money of other people works to your advantage because it allows you to reduce the risk you take as an investor. At any given time, a mutual fund is typically invested in dozens (and sometimes hundreds) of different stocks, bonds, or money market instruments. If you bought just one of these securities on your own, your success or failure would depend solely on the performance of that one security. When you invest in a mutual fund, though, you avoid putting all your eggs in one basket. So even if half the securities in the mutual fund lose value, you won't necessarily lose money; the other half may be profitable and may offset the losses with gains. The term for this investing principle is **diversification.**

Is there a downside to buying mutual funds? Some people would argue that you're not really an investor unless you put money in individual stocks. And there's no doubt that it's much more exciting to follow one stock closely and watch it rise or fall. But I don't recommend individual stocks for people who are just starting out—or even for people who have been investing for a while. Buying individual stocks does not offer the diversification you get with mutual funds, which makes them riskier investments. And I don't know many people willing to risk their life's savings on a single bet. (If you still want to buy individual stocks despite my warnings, see page 146 for the best way to go about it.)

Mutual Fund Shares and Where They Are Sold

When you invest in any type of mutual fund, you are technically purchasing units known as **shares.** As shareholders, you and thousands of others are in fact the owners of the fund. The fund's share price—meaning the price at which you can buy or sell a share in the fund—is called the **net asset value (NAV).**

There are several ways to buy shares in a mutual fund. The simplest is to buy them directly from a **mutual fund company** (a company that—you guessed it—sells mutual funds). **Brokerage firms,** which tend to specialize in trading individual stocks and bonds, offer mutual funds as well. So do the investment arms of many banks. As you will see in this chapter, I think your best bet is to go with a low-cost mutual fund company. I'll offer recommendations about specific mutual fund companies a little later on.

Two Pointers for New Investors

Before I get into the details of the various types of mutual funds, I'd like to acknowledge two sad truths of investment life. Though these points may seem obvious, they are often lost on many investors who should know better. And they are especially important to keep in mind during boom times, when everyone and her grandmother seem to be hitting the jackpot in the stock market.

- **There's no easy way to pick a winner.** The fact that a given stock did well last year, for example, provides little or no information about how well it will do in future years. More generally, there's no proven investment strategy that will always beat the others. If people tell you otherwise, don't believe them—including the analyst from a major brokerage firm who appears on CNBC, the distinguished economist who is quoted regularly in the newspaper, or your favorite uncle on your mother's side who had the foresight or luck to buy stock in Microsoft when it was trading for a tenth of its current price.

- **In general, you don't get something for nothing.** With rare exceptions, the only way to get an unusually high rate of return on your investments is to accept an unusually high level of risk. So if anyone promises you a very high return with "no risk," be skeptical.

MONEY MARKET FUNDS

As soon as you have enough money in the bank to get free checking, you're ready to learn about a particular type of mutual fund called a **money market fund.** Also known simply as money funds, these offer a good way for first-time investors to get their feet wet. They're the safest, most stable type of mutual fund, and they tend to pay returns that are typically one to two percentage points higher than the rates paid on bank savings accounts.

Why Invest in a Money Market Fund?

Don't let the name confuse you. Money market funds are very different from bank money market deposit accounts (MMAs), which you learned about in Chapter 4. For one thing, money funds are not federally insured like money market deposit accounts. But they are considered nearly as safe. Since money funds generally pay a higher rate than bank money market accounts, you can view them as a smarter type of bank account.

Aim to save at least three months' worth of living expenses in a money fund before you even think about branching out into stock funds and bond funds. This money fund savings stash will serve as an excellent emergency financial cushion in case of a temporary job loss or illness.

What Are Money Market Instruments?

To understand better what money funds are, you'll need a crash course in money market instruments—the securities that money funds invest in. When large companies or governments need money for very short periods of time, they issue money market instruments in exchange for the cash they need. These **money market instruments** are basically IOUs. Money market fund managers invest mainly in money market instruments issued by reliable institutions like the federal government, various state governments, and big-name corporations.

Since money market funds invest primarily in large, financially stable institutions that promise to repay their money market debts very quickly, they are considered quite safe. On those relatively rare occasions when an institution hasn't made good on its obligations, the money fund manager has generally been willing to reimburse the fund, thus protecting the fund's investors from any loss. Over the past 15 years, just one money fund has lost money for its investors, and even then it lost only 4% of their investment. Practically speaking, this probably isn't worth losing sleep over.

How Your Money Grows in a Money Market Fund

As with any mutual fund, when you invest in a money fund you're actually purchasing shares of that fund. Money fund managers try to keep the price (or NAV) of each share equal to a dollar at all times by investing in short-term debt securities they believe to be very safe. So when you invest $250 in a money fund, what you're really doing is buying 250 shares of the fund. The fund manager then loans your $250 (together with money from other investors) to various governments and/or corporations, receiving IOUs (money market instruments) in return.

In addition to repaying their debts, these governments and corporations must pay the money fund interest on the money they're borrowing from it. Now here's the good part. The fund then passes these interest payments on to you in the form of **dividends**, which are typically credited to your account every business day. If you like, most money market funds will wire these dividends into your bank account or mail them to you (usually once a month). Many investors, however, choose to have their dividends automatically **reinvested** in the money fund. In this case, their dividends are used to buy them more shares in the fund. This is a smart thing to do; in addition to saving you the hassle of depositing an additional 12 checks each year, it's a relatively painless way to increase the size of your account and keep yourself from simply spending your monthly dividend checks.

The **yield** of a money fund is analogous to the interest rate paid on a savings account. You can calculate the yield by dividing the fund's **dividends per share** by its share price (which is generally a dollar). The yield of each money fund fluctuates from day to day. Since all money funds calculate their yields in the same way, you can compare the yields of several money funds before selecting one. Call the fund company's toll-free number and ask for the money fund's **SEC seven-day yield,** which is the average yield for the past seven days.

Some money funds send out statements monthly; others mail them out quarterly. Your statement will indicate the number and value of the shares you own. The two figures are usually the same because the price per share is almost always a dollar.

Different Types of Money Market Funds

There's not just one kind of money fund but a variety of types to choose from. Your choice of fund type may be influenced by your tax bracket and the state you live in. In addition, some types of money funds are, at least in theory, slightly riskier than others. Because money market funds hardly ever lose money, though, many sophisticated investors treat them all as essentially risk-free. They go for the highest-yielding fund they can find (subject only to tax considerations), regardless of the variety.

The choices are listed below. They can be divided into two basic categories: taxable money funds and tax-exempt money funds. Although you don't need to memorize all the details, you'll want to refer to this information when you're choosing a money fund. Here's a brief rundown:

- **Taxable money market funds.** With a taxable money market fund, you are required to pay federal taxes on the dividends you earn (although in some cases, you may be exempt from certain state or local taxes on those dividends). Here are the major subcategories of taxable money funds.

  — *U.S. Treasury money funds* invest in short-term federal government IOUs called Treasury bills. These money funds are closest in terms of safety to bank accounts, because Treasury bills are issued by Uncle Sam and are said to be backed by the "full faith and credit" of the U.S. government. (This basically means that the government crosses its heart and promises to pay you everything you're entitled to, even if it has to raise taxes or print more money to do so.) Although the dividends you receive will be taxed by the federal government, they will most likely be free from state and local taxes.

  — *U.S. government money funds* invest in various types of money market instruments issued by the U.S. government itself and/or by federal agencies like the Small Business Administration or "quasi-federal" agencies like Fannie Mae (formerly known as the Federal National Mortgage Association). Because U.S. government agency securities are backed only by the "moral obligation" of the federal government, not by its "full faith and credit," they are considered just a little bit riskier than U.S. Treasury bills. To compensate investors for this slight degree of additional risk, the yield on government money funds is generally slightly higher than that of money funds that invest exclusively in Treasuries. Some of the dividends may be free from state and local taxes in certain states.

—*Corporate money funds,* also known as **prime money funds,** invest in money market securities issued by private companies in the United States and abroad. Because the risk that a corporation will fail to repay its debts is considered higher than the risk of default by the federal government or a federal agency, and because the dividends paid by a corporate money fund are not exempt from state tax, corporate money funds tend to offer somewhat higher yields than money funds that invest in government instruments. Neither the additional risk nor the additional yield is very large, however.

• **Tax-exempt money market funds.** When people refer to a money market fund as tax-exempt, they generally mean only that its dividends are exempt from *federal* tax. The dividends of tax-exempt funds are sometimes exempt from state (and in certain cases, local) tax, but this is not the case for all such funds. In either case, the yield on tax-exempt money funds is lower than the yield of taxable funds, but since the dividends aren't subject to federal income tax, you may end up earning more money in the end with a tax-exempt fund. Here are your choices:

—*Federal tax-exempt money funds* (sometimes referred to simply as tax-exempt money funds) invest in money market instruments issued by various states, counties, cities, and towns, along with tax-exempt entities like turnpike authorities and utilities. The dividends paid by these funds are not subject to federal tax, but if you live where there's a state or local income tax, you'll have to pay these taxes on all or most of your dividend income. In most cases, federal tax-exempt funds invest in the securities of a number of issuers in a number of different regions, in an effort to reduce risk through diversification.

—*Double tax-exempt money funds* invest in money market instruments issued by a single state (or by counties, cities, towns, or tax-exempt authorities located within that state) and pay dividends that are exempt from both federal *and* state income taxes, as long as you're a resident of that state. Because such funds are not able to invest in the securities of as many issuers in as many regions, they may be somewhat riskier than multi-state federal tax-exempt money funds.

—*Triple tax-exempt money funds* may be of interest to you if you live in a city like New York, where residents pay income tax not only to the IRS and to the state but to the city as well. These funds are similar to double tax-exempt money funds but restrict their investments to a single city. Although they offer a triple tax break (federal, state, and local) for residents of that city, such funds are even less diversified (and thus a bit riskier) than double tax-exempt money funds.

Tax Considerations When Choosing a Money Fund

With the possible exception of the double and triple tax-exempt funds, risk should probably not be a big factor in your choice of a money fund, since all money funds are comparatively safe. The main thing you'll want to focus on is the yield—or to be more precise, what's left of the yield after you pay your income taxes. For this reason, your choice of a money fund may be influenced by your federal income tax bracket and, if you live in an area where you're required to pay state and city income taxes, by your state and city tax brackets as well. (To figure out your tax bracket, see Chapter 9.)

Say you're considering investing in a corporate money fund that pays 5%. Assuming that there's no state or city income tax where you live and that you're in the 28% federal tax bracket, 28% of that 5%, or 1.4%, will go to Uncle Sam, leaving you with an after-tax yield of only 3.6%. That means you'd need to earn more than 3.6% from a tax-exempt money fund in order to beat the return you'd get on the taxable fund. In this case, a tax-exempt fund paying 4%, for example, would be better than a taxable fund paying 5%. Since the yields on money market funds fluctuate, you should repeat this comparison every few months. If you discover at some point that you'd be better off investing in, say, a taxable fund instead of a tax-exempt fund, it's easy to transfer your money from one to the other.

If you're subject to state and/or city income tax, do the above calculation using your combined federal, state, and local tax rate. You can then decide whether a double or triple tax-exempt money fund would give you enough additional after-tax yield to make it worth taking a bit more risk.

Where to Find a Money Market Fund

You can invest in money market funds at brokerage firms, mutual fund companies, and many banks. To find lists of the highest yields currently being paid by money market funds, check out Web sites like Bankrate.com (www.bankrate.com) and IBC Financial Data (www.ibcdata.com). If you don't have access to the Internet, consult recent issues of personal finance magazines like *Money* or *Kiplinger's*.

The easiest strategy may be simply to open a money fund at the low-cost mutual fund company where you do the rest of your investing, or plan to do so in the future. You might not get the best deal available on your money fund, but it will make your life simpler to have all your investments in one place. (For recommendations on specific mutual fund companies that might satisfy all your fund needs, see the section "Deciding Where to Buy Your Mutual Funds" later in this chapter.)

CHECK WRITING AND MONEY FUNDS

Whether you get your money fund at a mutual fund company (my recommendation), a brokerage firm, or a bank, chances are you'll be offered some sort of check-writing privileges. But before you dump your ordinary checking account, understand the limitations of writing checks against your money fund accounts at these institutions:

- **Mutual fund companies.** Many fund companies won't permit you to write checks from your money fund for amounts less than $250. Also, they usually don't provide you with an ATM card to access your money fund.

- **Brokerage firms.** Nearly all brokerage firms allow their customers to buy money funds and write checks against them. Some have minimum investment requirements as low as $1,000. But although many brokerage firms do offer ATM cards, none of them have their own ATM networks— which means you can expect to get hit with ATM surcharges whenever you make a withdrawal.

- **Banks.** Many banks now sell money funds to their customers. But most banks don't let you write checks against your money fund, or they limit you to checks of $250 or more.

All things considered, you're probably best off investing in a money fund offered by a low-cost mutual fund company and using a bank to meet your checking needs.

A WORD ABOUT
INFLATION

You may wonder why people don't keep all their money in nice, secure money market funds. After all, even if your money won't grow quite as fast in a money fund as it might in some riskier investment, at least it will be growing, right?

Well, maybe not—at least not in the way that matters most. After paying any taxes due on your earnings from a money fund, you'll probably have a hard time even keeping up with **inflation**— the tendency of prices to increase steadily over the years. If you earn, say, a 5% yield on a taxable money fund one year but are in the 30% (combined federal, state, and local) tax bracket, you'll be left with only 3.5% at the end of the year. While this doesn't *sound* so bad, if everything you want to buy costs 3.5% more on average at the end of the year than it did at the beginning, you may *look* richer on paper, but you're actually right back where you started.

It's easy to forget about the effects of inflation when you think about how your money will grow over the years. To help put things into perspective, it's worth taking a look at the way inflation has weakened the "purchasing power" of the dollar over the past few decades. Say your parents bought a new car for $3,500 in 1969. If you bought a comparable auto today, you'd pay about $21,000. Put another way: $3,500 today buys only about one-sixth of what it could buy back in the late 1960s. Amazing.

Inflation has bounced around a lot over the years—it was about 12% in 1980, for example, and only about 1% in 1986—and it's hard to predict how high it will be in the future. One thing that seems pretty likely, though, is that inflation will continue to erode the value of the dollar over the next few decades, just as it has in the last few. If you put $20,000 under your mattress and inflation increases at, say, an average of 3% a year, after thirty years, your $20,000 will have reduced in value to the point where it buys only what you can now buy for $8,240.

The rate of return you receive on an investment (known as the **nominal rate of return**) minus the rate of inflation is called the **real rate of return.** So if an investment is paying 5% and the inflation rate is 3%, your real rate of return is 2%. Take a look at Figure 5-1. It

Figure 5-1

HOW VARIOUS INVESTMENTS
HAVE FARED OVER TIME

Type of Investment	Average Return[1] (Nominal)	Average Return[1] (Real)	Highest Return[2] (Nominal)	Lowest Return[2] (Nominal)
U.S. Treasury Bills	3.8%	0.7%	14.7%	2.9%
Government Bonds (Long Term)	5.3%	2.2%	40.4%	−7.8%
Government Bonds (Intermediate Term)	5.3%	2.2%	29.1%	−5.1%
Corporate Bonds (Long Term)	5.8%	2.6%	42.6%	−5.8%
Large Company Stocks	11.2%	7.9%	37.4%	−4.9%
Small Company Stocks	12.4%	9.1%	44.6%	−21.6%

[1] Compound annual total return, 1926–1998
[2] Best and worst years, 1979–1998
Source: Ibbotson Associates

shows the nominal and real rates of return (without considering the effect of taxes) associated with various categories of securities between 1926 and 1998. Don't worry for now about the exact definitions of these different securities; I'll explain that later. For now, the thing to notice is that stocks and bonds (and although it's not shown in this table, the mutual funds that invest in them) have done a much better job of overcoming the effects of inflation over this period than Treasury bills (which are often found in money funds).

It's clear from the table that if you'd kept your money in a money market fund that invests in Treasury bills, you would barely have kept pace with inflation. Although Treasury bills had a *nominal* return of 3.8%, the real rate of return, after accounting for inflation, was a pitiful 0.7% per year. And things look even worse when you take taxes into consideration. Although after-tax returns vary depending on an investor's tax bracket, most investors would actually have *lost* money by investing in Treasury bills over this period, after accounting for taxes and inflation. By investing in stocks and bonds, they would have done considerably better.

As mentioned at the beginning of this chapter, the fact that a particular stock has done better historically than most other stocks tells us little or nothing about how well it's likely to do from now on. Still, it's the best guess of many financial analysts that over the long term, stocks and bonds *as a whole* will continue to offer rates of return that are significantly higher than the rate of inflation. Although there's no guarantee that this will actually happen (or even that you won't *lose* money by investing in the stock and bond markets over the years), my guess is that these analysts are guessing right.

So although the safety of money funds makes them a good place to keep your three-month emergency savings cushion, if you want a fighting chance at keeping up with inflation and can tolerate a bit more risk, your next step should be to consider two more aggressive types of investments: stock mutual funds and bond mutual funds.

STOCK FUNDS

Just as money market mutual funds invest in money market instruments, **stock mutual funds** invest in—you guessed it—stocks. The appeal of a stock fund is that your return over the long term may be significantly higher than the return you'd get with a money market fund. The downside is that with a stock fund, you risk losing money. (See Figure 5-1 for a look at how stocks performed in their best and worst years over the past two decades.)

What Is Stock?

To understand stock mutual funds, you must first understand stock. Stock is sold in units known as shares. A **share of stock** represents a small piece of a company; if you buy stock in a company, you become the owner of a fraction of that company. The more shares you buy, the more of the company you own. The amount of money paid for one share is called the **stock price** or the **price per share.**

A stock's price rises and falls depending on supply and demand. When a lot of people want to buy a stock, they'll tend to "bid up" its price, the same way that rival bidders at an art auction might bid up the price of a painting. If, on the other hand, there are more sellers than buyers, the price tends to fall. Anything that might influence investors to buy or sell a company's stock may affect the share price. New information that might lead investors to believe that a company will make more money than previously expected, for example, will generally cause its share price to rise. Unanticipated bad news typically leads to a decrease in price.

In some cases a company's stock price may move up or down for reasons that have nothing to do with changes in the firm's expected profitability. A stock may fall, for example, because a large investor decided to sell lots of shares to raise money for some other purpose and had to settle for a lower price in order to cash in quickly. And in many cases, stock prices may go up or down for what appears to be no particular reason at all.

Stocks do not pay interest like a savings account. The most common way to make money from stocks is to sell your shares for more than you paid for them. That difference between the price you sell them for and the price you paid for them is called a **capital gain.** Certain types of stocks pay **dividends,** which are regular cash payouts companies make to keep shareholders happy. Typically, older, well-established firms pay dividends on their stocks, while newer firms do not. Some stock fund managers invest in stocks they believe will reap hefty capital gains; others focus on companies that have historically paid substantial dividends on a regular basis, even if they're unlikely to increase much in price.

What Is the Stock Market?

You've probably heard reports on television that the stock market was up or down. Loosely speaking, the stock market is said to have gone up if the prices of most stocks have risen. The barometers most people use to keep track of "the market," though, are not based on *all* of the thousands of stocks that people trade but on some sort of more-or-less representative sample. The prices of all stocks in the sample are generally averaged in some way (the details of which may vary) to calculate what is known as an **index.**

The most widely known index is probably the **Dow Jones Industrial Average,** which, despite its fame, is actually based on the stock prices of only 30 large companies, and for that reason doesn't provide an especially accurate reading of the direction of the market as a whole. Another closely followed indicator is the Standard & Poor's **S&P 500 Index,** which tracks changes in the stock prices of 500 large companies. Someone who tells you that "the market" has gone up is usually referring to one of these two indexes.

Different Types of Stock Funds

Stock mutual funds can be divided into two basic categories. The vast majority are **actively managed funds,** which means a fund manager uses his or her own judgment to pick and choose among the thousands of stocks available. The other major type of stock fund is an **index fund.** An index fund invests in nearly all the stocks that make up a particular index, such as the S&P 500. Some people refer to index funds as **unmanaged** or **passively managed** since the fund manager exercises little discretion over which stocks go into the fund. With an index fund, the manager's job is simply to come as close as possible to replicating the performance of the index it tracks.

I recommend that you go with an index fund. Although it might seem surprising, a number of studies suggest that over long periods of time, stock portfolios managed actively by "expert" fund managers actually do no better on average than the passively managed portfolio of an index fund. (In his extensive research on this topic, for example, Princeton economics professor Burton Malkiel found that most active managers have underperformed the S&P 500 in the long run.) What is different about an actively managed fund, though, is that the fund manager usually charges a lot more for his or her services than the manager of an index fund. Most index funds provide the same or better diversification and allow you to participate in the (historically attractive) returns associated with the stock market without paying too much for the privilege.

This is not to say that index funds are in any way a sure thing. Whether you invest in index funds or in actively managed funds, you are always taking a risk when you put money in the stock market. Still, the lower expenses associated with index funds have given them an edge over time.

Let's put some numbers on this. In 1996, in the first edition of *Get a Financial Life,* I strongly recommended index funds. Over the next three years, the average S&P 500 index fund had an annual return of 28.5%. Meanwhile, the average actively managed large-company stock fund returned 24.7%. In fact, according to fund experts at Lipper Inc. in New York, index funds have beaten their actively managed counterparts not just over the last three years, but over the last five years, ten years, and twenty years. So, for example, if two people had put $10,000 into the stock market twenty years ago—one in a managed fund and one in an index fund—the average index fund investor would have an extra $29,031 today.

But don't expect to hear this from a salesperson at a brokerage firm or mutual fund company. Higher expenses may be bad for you, but they're great for the companies that offer actively managed funds. (I'll say more about fund expenses later in this chapter.)

Questions and Answers on Stock Funds

Q: *Wouldn't I be better off choosing a top-performing managed stock fund?*

A: That would be true if you knew which funds were going to perform well in the future. After all, it would be well worth paying a bit more in expenses if the fund manager could deliver high enough returns to more than pay for them. Researchers have found, though, that funds whose returns have been unusually high in the past don't perform substantially better on average than funds that have performed poorly. If there's any advantage at all to betting on past winners, it's not large enough to justify paying the higher fees that active managers charge.

Q: *But what about those few fund managers who've done well year after year?*

A: Maybe they're brilliant, and maybe they're not. But before jumping to conclusions, it's worth remembering that given the number of stock funds that have been formed over the years, it would be surprising if some of them didn't do better than average for a number of years by sheer chance.

Let's talk odds for a minute. Suppose all fund managers pick their stocks completely at random. The chance that a particular fund will perform better than average (that is, better than half of all the funds that are out there) during any given year is 50%, or one chance in two. There's one chance in four (two times two) that this fund will do better than average for two successive years, and one chance in eight (two times two times two) that it will be in the top half of its class for three years in a row. Do this ten times, and you'll discover that there's one chance in 1,024 that a given fund will beat the average for ten years running through sheer luck. These may sound like pretty slim odds, but with more than 5,000 fund managers out there picking stocks, we should expect something like five of them to do better than average ten years in a row—enough to convince most anyone that they're financial geniuses even if they're in fact choosing their stocks at random.

To be fair, this doesn't prove that there aren't any mutual funds

A FINANCIAL JOURNALIST COMES CLEAN

Many readers think I'm holding back on them. "Sure, you recommend index funds in your book," they tell me, "but what investments do you *really* like?" Many people believe there's an insider trick to investing, and that if only they knew the truth they'd strike it rich. For years, publications like *Money* (where I worked for eight years until 1995), *Smart Money,* and *Kiplinger's* have offered the hope of big returns in just about every issue—if you follow their advice. These magazines provide a lot of valuable personal finance advice, but how have their stock picks panned out?

Back in 1994, before I found index fund religion, I was asked to write a cover story for *Money* called "Eight Investments That Never Lose Money." Being a diligent reporter, I did a thorough search of investments and interviewed dozens of Wall Street gurus to determine which stocks were expected to continue to do well.

In 1999, a magazine called *Brill's Content* looked at my article, among others, and asked the big question: How did the advice pan out? According to their calculations, if you had put $10,000 into the eight investments that I recommended, your money would have grown to $22,425. Not too shabby, and it's true that my recommendations didn't lose money. *But:* If you had simply put that cash in an S&P 500 index fund, you would have had $32,814—over $10,000 more.

My bottom line: Go with index funds.

whose managers are genuine stock-picking geniuses. But even if there are, how are you going to tell them apart from the ones who've just been lucky? My advice: Don't try.

Q: *What kind of stock index fund should I invest in?*

A: Later in this chapter I list some of the different mutual fund companies that offer funds based on various stock market indexes. First, however, you'll need to know a little about the indexes themselves. Here are a few of the better-known ones:

- **The S&P 500.** The most popular index is the S&P 500, which is based on 500 of the largest U.S. companies, including such major firms as General Electric, Microsoft, and Coca-Cola. There are a lot of S&P 500 index funds out there, some of which have very modest fees and are willing to accept a relatively small initial investment. While this is a fine place to get started, especially if you don't have much money to invest, the S&P 500 has some drawbacks as well. Large-company stocks did incredibly well throughout the 1990s, but they probably can't continue this upward trend forever. For better diversification you might want to invest in an index that includes the stocks of small- and medium-sized companies as well—or invest in a number of different index funds, including ones that focus on smaller stocks.

- **The Wilshire 5000 Equity Index.** This index comes closest to reflecting the performance of the U.S. stock market as a whole. Despite its name, the Wilshire 5000 is actually made up of approximately 7,000 stocks, including those of a wide range of small, medium, and large companies. I like funds that track the Wilshire 5000 because it offers somewhat more diversification than the S&P 500.

- **The Morgan Stanley EAFE Index.** If you're the adventurous type, you may want to consider investing a small portion of your money in the stock markets of other countries. The Morgan Stanley EAFE Index tracks the performance of about 1,000 companies based in Europe, Australasia (a spiffy name for Australia and New Zealand), and the Far East (hence the acronym EAFE). Investing in a mutual fund that mirrors this index provides a convenient way of achieving some degree of international diversification. Foreign stock markets are sometimes quite volatile, though, and the fees charged by international fund managers tend to be higher on average than those of U.S. funds.

BOND FUNDS

Bond mutual funds invest in bonds, which will be discussed in a minute. First, though, you should know where bond funds fall on the risk/return spectrum. While the exact answer depends on the type of fund, bond funds are generally riskier than money market funds but less risky than stock funds. Not surprisingly, the returns of bond funds have historically been somewhere in between those of stock funds and money market funds.

What Is a Bond?

Like a money market instrument, a bond is an IOU issued by a company, a government, or some other institution. The main difference is that in the case of a bond, the issuer has more time to repay its debt.

When you buy a bond, you're basically lending a sum of money (the **principal**) to the issuer for a fixed period of time (the **term**). In return for the loan, the issuer pays you interest, computed at a fixed rate called the **coupon rate**. Interest is generally paid monthly or quarterly, but in the case of a **zero coupon bond** you won't receive any interest at all until the end of the bond's term. (The bonds you received as graduation or bar mitzvah gifts may have been zero coupon bonds.) When a bond reaches **maturity** at the end of its term, you're entitled (at least in theory) to get back your full initial investment.

So What's Risky About a Bond?

The risks associated with buying a bond can be divided into two categories. The first, which is often referred to as **default risk** or **credit**

risk, is the possibility that the issuer may fall on hard times and be unable to pay you interest or repay your principal the way it's supposed to.

The second, which is somewhat more complicated, is known as **interest rate risk.** Here's one way to think about this kind of risk: If interest rates rise unexpectedly fast during the period in which you own the bond, you won't be able to take advantage of them. You'll be stuck with the same fixed coupon rate, which will start to look worse and worse by comparison with prevailing market rates. And since inflation tends to rise along with interest rates, the dollars you receive when the issuer finally pays you back probably won't buy as much as you'd originally thought they would.

So why not simply sell your bond if interest rates rise unexpectedly and buy another one with a higher coupon rate? Unfortunately, you're not the only one who's thought of this. Nobody is going to buy your low-coupon bond if a new, high-coupon bond can be had for the same price. Since the bond market, like the stock market, obeys the laws of supply and demand, the price you'll be able to get for your bond will drop as soon as interest rates rise. The higher that interest rates climb, the less your bond will be worth.

A bond that doesn't have much time left until its final payback date, though, won't drop in value all that much when interest rates rise. This is because its holder won't have to put up with a lower-than-market coupon rate for very long and because inflation won't have much time to erode the value of the principal. A bond with many years left until its final payback, on the other hand, will fall much further when interest rates go up by the same amount.

So far, I've talked only about how interest rate risk can hurt you when interest rates increase. The other side of the coin is that when interest rates *fall* more than the market expects, bonds tend to *rise* in value. Before you quit your job to become a bond trader, though, you should review the exact wording of the previous sentence. It's not enough to know that interest rates are likely to fall if everyone else knows that too, since those expectations will almost certainly already be reflected in the price you'll have to pay to buy bonds. To "beat the market" you'd have to outguess thousands of experts who spend their time thinking of little else.

My recommendation: Don't even try. The point of this discussion is not to teach you how to make extraordinary profits by predicting the future direction of interest rates but simply to help you understand the two major factors—default risk and interest rate risk—that contribute to the uncertainty surrounding a bond's future performance.

Different Types of Bond Funds

Bond funds differ according to the type of bonds they invest in. There are two key variables to look at. The first is who is issuing the bond. This affects the degree of default risk you're exposed to as well as whether the income you receive from the bond is taxable or tax-exempt. As in the case of money market funds, there are bond funds that invest in bonds issued by the U.S. Treasury, by various federal agencies, by cities, states, and counties, and by corporations of varying degrees of creditworthiness.

From a tax perspective, these different types of bond funds work in pretty much the same way as the corresponding types of money market funds. This is true of default risk as well, except that the stakes are higher. Even a somewhat shaky corporation may be able to stay afloat for long enough to repay a three-month money market instrument, but whether it will last long enough to make good on a twenty-year bond may be another story.

That doesn't mean that shaky corporations don't issue bonds. In fact, there's a whole class of bonds (most commonly known as "junk bonds," though brokers prefer the term "high-yield") that are issued by financially troubled firms. Because such bonds are issued by relatively unstable companies, they have to pay higher coupon rates to attract investors. Since a junk bond fund typically invests in the bonds of a *number* of "junky" companies, the failure of any one of them may not be a disaster for the fund's investors. However, if many of these companies were to fail and therefore default on their bonds, investors could earn a much lower return and might even lose a substantial part of the money they originally invested.

The second variable is the average number of years before the bonds in the fund come due, or "mature." **Short-term bond funds** typically invest in bonds that will mature in fewer than four years,

intermediate-term bond funds in instruments with maturities of between four and ten years, and **long-term bond funds** in bonds that won't mature for at least ten years.

Because changes in market interest rates and the financial stability of the issuing companies exert a larger effect on bonds with a long time left until maturity than on those with less time remaining, long-term bond funds are generally riskier than short-term funds. As might be expected, the relative safety of short-term bond funds comes at a price: Historically, they haven't performed as well as intermediate- and long-term bond funds.

The type of bond fund you select will in part depend on how much risk you're willing to take. As we've just seen, funds that invest in the bonds of less creditworthy companies are generally riskier than those that invest in otherwise comparable high-quality bonds; funds that invest in long-term bonds are riskier than funds that

Figure 5-2
BOND RATINGS

	S&P	Moody's	Description
Investment Grade	AAA	Aaa	Highest quality
	AA	Aa	High quality
	A	A	Good quality
	BBB	Baa	Medium quality
High-Yield (Junk Bonds)	BB	Ba	Risky elements
	B	B	Risky
	CCC	Caa	Riskier
	CC	Ca	Highly risky
	C	C	Extremely poor prospects
	D	—	In default

Sources: Standard & Poor's, Moody's, and Investment Company Institute

invest in the short-term bonds of similar companies. Only you can decide how much risk you're willing to accept for the possibility of a higher return.

That said, I'm willing to stick my neck out and recommend a middle-of-the-road approach that may represent a reasonable compromise if you want to choose a single bond fund and have a more-or-less average tolerance for risk: a fund that invests entirely or primarily in intermediate-term bonds issued by "highly rated" corporations. Although there's no guarantee that this will in fact prove to be your best move, there's a good chance that such a fund will provide you with more income than, say, a short-term U.S. Treasury or government bond fund, without subjecting you to a huge amount of default or interest rate risk.

If you have the patience to evaluate and keep track of more than one bond fund, another alternative you might want to consider is spreading your money among several types of funds that fall at different points on the risk/return spectrum. If not, though, don't worry; the guidelines I'll give you in the next section will allow you to hedge your bets reasonably well even if you choose to follow the simpler, single-bond-fund approach.

Questions and Answers on Bond Funds

Q: *Where can I get information about the types of bonds in a bond fund?*

A: Details about the types of bonds a fund invests in are contained in the fund's **prospectus,** a document you can get by calling the fund company. It's not always easy to decipher a prospectus, but you should be able to find enough comprehensible information about the issuers and maturities of the bonds the fund invests in to help you make an informed decision. You may also want to ask for a copy of the fund's most recent **shareholder report,** which gives a breakdown of the **credit ratings** of the bonds that the fund recently held. These ratings are assigned by one of several rating agencies, the best known of which are Standard & Poor's and Moody's. (See Figure 5-2 for the meaning of various ratings.)

INFLATION-PROTECTED BONDS

If the safety of bonds appeals to you but you can't meet the minimum requirements for any of the funds I've mentioned, there is still an alternative: **Series I** savings bonds, or **I Bonds,** a relatively new kind of savings bond issued by the U.S. Treasury. They're different from the savings bonds you might have gotten as a kid because they have a built-in protection against the negative effects of inflation. As of this writing, I Bonds offer a guaranteed real rate of 3.4%—that's the rate you get *after* inflation. If you look at Figure 5-1 on page 123, you'll see that a 3.4% real return is better than the average real returns for any of the bond investments listed.

You don't need a lot of money to get started. I Bonds can be purchased for as little as $50. They can be cashed in anytime after six months, up to thirty years (but there is a three-month interest penalty if you cash them in before five years). Because these bonds are issued by the Treasury, there is no state or local tax on the interest you earn. You do have to pay federal tax, but not until the bonds are cashed in. This means your money will grow tax-

Q: *Within a given category of bond fund, how should I pick a particular fund?*

A: Although it might seem like a good idea to compare the historical returns of various bond funds or do research on various fund managers, my advice is to concentrate primarily on one thing: fees. Studies have shown that bond fund managers have little effect on the performance of bond funds, so there's no point in paying extra for someone who claims to be better than average.

Q: *Are there bond index funds?*

A: Yes, although not many mutual fund companies offer them. The most common bond indexes are those developed by Lehman

free for as long as you hold the bonds. (See the discussion of tax-free compounding on page 152.) And depending on your income, you may be eligible to avoid paying any tax on the interest I Bonds earn, as long as you use the money for educational expenses.

Visit the Treasury Department's Web site at www .savingsbonds.gov for more information. (Make sure that you type in "gov" and not "com.") I Bonds are available at some banks (check the Web site for locations), or you can purchase them online with Visa or MasterCard.

For investors who have more money, there is another type of inflation-protected bond offered by the government: **Treasury Inflation-Protection Securities,** or **TIPS.** These come in minimum denominations of $1,000. You can only get these directly from the Treasury or through a broker (where you'll pay a commission). For details, visit the Treasury's Web site at www .publicdebt.treas.gov. (Go to the section labeled "Treasury Securities at a Glance" and then the area marked "Inflation-indexed.")

Brothers, the New York investment bank. There are a number of different Lehman Brothers indexes, focusing variously on short-term, intermediate-term, and long-term bonds. One of the most popular is the **Lehman Brothers Government/Corporate Bond Market Index,** which tracks the performance of government bonds as well as bonds issued by top-quality companies. Another prominent New York bank, Salomon Smith Barney, has created a variety of bond indexes as well. I'll offer advice on finding a bond mutual fund a little later in this chapter.

THE RIGHT MIX OF INVESTMENTS

As I've said, your first investing move should be to save three months' worth of expenses in a money fund or a high-paying money market account. But what happens after that? If you're ready to start investing more aggressively, how much money should go into stock funds and bond funds, and how much should stay in your money market fund?

Unfortunately, there's little agreement even among "experts" about the right answer to this question. Once again, you'll have to decide for yourself how much risk you're willing to take in pursuit of higher returns. A fairly typical decision, though, might be to allocate roughly 50% of your assets to stock funds and 30% to bond funds, while keeping 20% in "cash" (meaning super-safe places like money market funds and bank accounts). This type of breakdown would put a lot of your money into those investments that have historically had the highest returns, while keeping some of it in safer places, just in case. Most important, you avoid putting all your eggs in one basket, taking advantage once again of the benefits of diversification.

Some financial advisors insist that this allocation is too conservative. They say that young people should put even more of their assets—say, 80% to 90%—in stock funds, since they have much more time to ride out the downturns of the stock market. But others (including Paul Samuelson, winner of the Nobel Prize in economics) have questioned whether it really makes sense to allocate your assets based on your age.

There is no simple answer that will apply to everyone. To help determine the right mix for you, consider these questions:

- **What's your risk tolerance?** Are you a risk taker by nature? Do you like to gamble? Are you willing to lose $10 for the chance of earning $30? If so, you might be willing to put a lot of your money in stocks. But if you're afraid of risk and sickened by the thought of losing any money, a large percentage of your investment portfolio should probably be in a money market fund.

- **Are you diversified?** To reduce the overall risk in your portfolio, you will want to have a mix of different types of investments. Before you make any decisions, examine the types of investments in your company retirement plan. If you invested your company 401(k) plan mainly in stocks, for example, you will probably want your other savings to include some bond and money market funds. (For details on 401(k)s, see Chapter 6.)

- **What are your goals?** If you have $10,000 that you'll need to use in the next year or two for a down payment on a home, you may not want to invest it in a stock fund or a long-term bond fund, where you could lose a lot of it if the market were to crash or interest rates were to soar. But if you're just trying to build up your savings over the next ten or twenty years without a fixed goal in sight, you might want to take some risk in the hope of getting bigger returns.

One final note: Don't be discouraged if you can't create the perfect investment mix immediately. If you don't yet have enough money to meet the minimums required for separate investments in both a stock fund and a bond fund, it's important not to use that as an excuse to postpone investing. Start with a stock index fund, then begin investing in a bond fund after you've accumulated more savings.

MUTUAL FUND EXPENSES

Because there's little evidence that one mutual fund manager is any more likely to beat the market than another, it makes sense to focus on the one thing that will *definitely* affect your investment results: the fund's **expense ratio.** This ratio is computed by dividing the fund's **total annual operating expenses** (which will be discussed in a minute) by the value of all securities held by the fund. The fund's

INTERNET STOCKS

If you had put $1,000 in AOL when it was first offered in 1992, your investment would have been worth over $800,000 by the end of 1999. Another $1,000 in Yahoo in 1996 would have grown to nearly $200,000, and a $1,000 investment in Amazon.com by the end of 1997 would be almost $50,000. Boy, don't we feel dumb.

It's no big secret that there has been an incredible run-up in Internet stocks, and no one knows when it will end. Perhaps it has by the time you're reading this book. Or maybe it will go on for years. But one thing is known: When you invest in a hot area of the stock market, you run the risk of getting burned. In fact, if you had put that same $1,000 into any number of other Internet stocks, you might still be wiping the egg off your face. By the end of 1999, for example, initial investors in Fashionmall.com would

operating expenses are passed on to its investors, so the higher the expense ratio, the less you'll earn on your investment. If, for example, you invest in a fund that earns a 10% annual return on the securities it holds but has a 2% expense ratio, your investment will grow at a rate of only 8% per year.

One component of a fund's total annual operating expenses is the **management fee** paid to the fund manager (or fund company) for investing and managing the fund's money. Management fees typically range between 0.5% and 1.0% of the fund's assets per year. Other expenses include legal fees and administrative charges. Some fund companies also charge investors what's known as a **12b-1 fee,** which is used to cover the fund's marketing costs. Why should you pay for these? You shouldn't. Find a fund without 12b-1 fees.

As of this writing, expense ratios average about 1.6% a year for stock funds, just under 1.1% for bond funds, and around 0.6% for money market funds. As you'll see in the next section, though, the expense ratios of some funds are much lower, and there's no reason to believe that low-expense funds will perform any worse than high-

have lost two-thirds of their money just seven months after the stock was introduced, and those who tried to get in on the ground floor with Musicmaker.com would have seen their investment drop by more than 50% in less than six months. Even brand names are no guarantee: FTD.com sank 35% just three months after it came on the scene. Don't we feel smart?

No matter who seems to be making money these days, individual stocks, especially those in trendy sectors like the Internet, are anything but a sure thing. And though mutual funds that invest in Internet stocks offer some diversification, investing in them means that you're still betting on one narrow, volatile sector of the stock market. If the Internet sector takes a tumble, your fund will fall with it. The bottom line: If you're investing money that you really need— whether to buy a home, car, or your next meal—don't risk that money on volatile investments.

expense ones. The moral of this story is simple: Invest in funds with the lowest expense ratios you can find, and ignore anything a broker, financial advisor, or bank employee might try to tell you about the great track record or bright prospects of the high-expense fund he or she is trying to push.

One other trap you should look out for: **loads.** Loads are typically one-time fees paid at the time you buy and/or sell shares in certain mutual funds (which are often referred to as **load funds**). They aren't included in the fund's expense ratio, so you'll have to look out for them separately. Loads typically range between 3% and 4% but can be as high as 8.5%. Studies show that load funds perform no better on average than **no-load funds.** So why does anyone pay a load? Because they've been talked into a load fund by an aggressive salesperson. Loads are commonly used to provide generous compensation to the people who sell them, so they're highly motivated to convince you that the fund's performance will justify the load. Just say no. What you want is a no-load fund with a low expense ratio. The salesperson will get over it.

To get the scoop on a fund's fees, loads, and expense ratio, read the prospectus that your mutual fund company will send you in the mail. It will spell them all out in detail.

START WITH JUST $50 A MONTH IN AN AUTOMATIC INVESTMENT PLAN

Many no-load mutual fund companies will waive or lower their minimum initial investment requirement if you sign up for their automatic investment plan. With these plans you can have a fixed amount—the minimum is usually $50 or $100—siphoned off once or twice a month from either your paycheck or your bank checking account and funneled into the mutual fund of your choice. When you choose a fund, simply indicate on the application that you want your money to be automatically invested, and specify where you want the money to come from. After that, you won't have to do much except sit back and watch the money accumulate in your mutual fund account (though you may also want to check your investment mix occasionally to make sure it's still in the proportion you want).

DECIDING WHERE TO BUY YOUR MUTUAL FUNDS

Today there are more than 600 mutual fund companies in the United States alone, many of which offer dozens of funds. There are three principal places to purchase a mutual fund: brokerage firms, banks, and mutual fund companies. I recommend focusing on funds offered directly by mutual fund companies. Why not the others? Well, brokerage firms have several drawbacks. They tend to sell funds with

loads and substantial fees, and their minimum investment requirements are usually quite high. If you go with a "discount broker,"
you can avoid most of the fees but you'll have to put up with customer service that can be frustrating and unresponsive. Banks,
meanwhile, generally offer a very limited selection of index funds
and tend to charge loads. So mutual fund companies are the way
to go.

Fortunately, you should be able to meet all your fund needs at a
single mutual fund company. The main advantage of getting all your
funds from the same company (sometimes called a "fund family")
is convenience. You'll get a single statement every month covering
all your holdings, and you'll generally be able to move your money
from one fund to another without much hassle. Depending on your
situation, though, you may want to split your money between two
or more fund families.

Choosing a mutual fund company is surprisingly easy. Look for
a company that offers no-load funds with low expense ratios and
initial minimum investment requirements that you're able to meet.
In this section, I'll direct you to four mutual fund companies that
currently fit the bill. (If things have changed radically by the time
you read this, you may have to look through one of the lists that
appear from time to time in personal finance magazines—*Money,*
Smart Money, or *Kiplinger's,* for example. The Web site
IndexFunds.com is a good online resource.) Although others might
tell you differently, I don't believe it's necessary for you to consult a
stockbroker, subscribe to *Institutional Investor,* or spend your
evenings doing research in the local business school library. Just pick
a fund family that fits the criteria I mentioned at the beginning of
this paragraph, then call them up and ask them to send you the
forms you'll need to open an account.

One company that's definitely worth considering is the
Vanguard Group (800-662-7447; www.vanguard.com). (Just for
the record, I don't get any kickbacks, discounts, or free slide rules
from Vanguard or any of the other firms I mention in this book.)
Vanguard is a no-load firm that prides itself on having some of the
lowest expenses in the business. For example, Vanguard's S&P 500
index fund has an expense ratio of 0.18%—nearly one-tenth of the
industry average for actively managed stock funds. Vanguard also

has the largest range of index funds to choose from, including international index funds, bond index funds, and broad-based U.S. stock
index funds like the "Total Stock Market Portfolio," which tracks
the entire Wilshire 5000 Index. The only problem with Vanguard is
that it has a minimum initial investment requirement of $3,000 per
fund—except in the case of Individual Retirement Accounts (IRAs),
for which the minimum is $1,000. (You'll learn all about IRAs in
Chapter 6.) To squeeze maximum diversification out of your
$3,000, look into Vanguard's "Balanced Index Fund," a hybrid that
is about 60% Wilshire 5000 stock index fund and about 40% bond
index fund.

If you can afford it, Vanguard is your best choice. If not, you'll
have to invest elsewhere, at least until you can build the $3,000 min-
imum. T. Rowe Price (800-638-5660; www.troweprice.com) and
Galaxy Funds (877-289-4252; www.galaxyfunds.com) each offer
several index funds with minimum investment requirements of
$2,500. But both companies will let you start investing with just $50,
as long as you commit to setting aside at least $50 a month through
an automatic investment plan. (For details on automatic investment
plans, see the box on page 142.) Although their expense ratios are
higher than Vanguard's, they are still low compared to those of most
other companies. T. Rowe Price offers a fund that tracks the Wilshire
5000 but does not offer any bond index funds; Galaxy has a bond
index fund but no Wilshire 5000 fund. Another company to consider
if you're interested in bond funds, but don't have the $3,000 required
by Vanguard, is USAA (800-531-8181; www.usaa.com). USAA
doesn't offer any bond index funds, but the expenses on its actively
managed bond funds are quite low. And as long as you sign up for its
$50-a-month automatic investment plan, USAA will waive its usual
minimum investment requirement of $3,000.

SOCIALLY RESPONSIBLE
INVESTING

People often ask me to recommend "socially responsible" investments. There are more than two dozen mutual funds that fall into this

category, and each has a different idea of what it means to be socially responsible. Some funds that consider themselves socially responsible don't invest in tobacco or liquor companies. Others invest in companies that have good records on energy conservation and pollution control, and shun those that don't. Still others zero in on firms that treat employees well by providing child-care services, promoting women and minorities, and offering generous benefit packages.

Are do-good firms also good investments? Nobody knows for sure. There are those who believe that the securities of a socially minded company should perform about the same as the market as a whole, and some even argue that they should do better, since such firms may be the targets of fewer lawsuits (for everything from pollution to discrimination). Others say that by restricting the universe of qualified companies, ethically aware fund managers are limiting

THE DANGERS OF DAY TRADING

We've all seen stories on *Dateline* about garage mechanics who play the stock market during their lunch hour or great-grandmothers who have switched from daytime soaps to CNBC. Some high rollers actually quit their regular jobs to trade stocks full-time.

Amateur "investors" who buy and sell stocks online all day, frantically trying to make a profit from the ups and downs of volatile stocks, are known as **day traders.** A few of them strike it rich, but most fail miserably. The North American Securities Administrators Association, in a study of day-trading accounts, concluded that 70% of traders "will almost certainly lose everything they invest."

Trading stocks online is cheap, so it may be tempting to try to make some fast bucks with a few quick mouse clicks. But don't quit your day job. Day trading is gambling, not investing.

their ability to take advantage of attractive investment opportunities and are likely to underperform the market.

Whether you choose to invest in a socially responsible fund or stick with an ordinary index fund (and perhaps set aside some money for tax-deductible contributions to your own favorite charities) is a personal decision. If you choose the former route, though, steer clear of any fund that charges a load or has an unusually high expense ratio. You may want to check out the Domini Social Equity Fund (800-762-6814; www.domini.com), a socially responsible index fund with a minimum investment of $1,000 and an expense ratio of under 1%. Vanguard (800-662-7447; www.vanguard.com) is scheduled to offer its own socially conscious index fund in 2000, called the Calvert Social Index Fund. The expense ratio for this fund is likely to be lower than Domini's, but Vanguard requires a $3,000 investment. Nobody ever said that virtue came cheap.

For a free list of socially responsible mutual funds, you can call the Trillium Asset Management Corporation (617-423-6655; www.trilliuminvest.com), an investment firm that publishes a newsletter on socially responsible investing.

BUYING INDIVIDUAL STOCKS

Okay. By now you know that my advice is to stick with mutual funds—specifically index funds. But with the surge in Internet stocks (and the fact that everyone and their mother wants to get in on the next Yahoo!) I feel compelled to offer some advice to readers who want to ignore me and buy individual stocks. Here are some tips:

- **Stick with discount brokers.** There are two main kinds of brokers: **full-service brokers,** who offer investment advice and detailed research to investors, and **discount brokers,** who focus on simply carrying out your trades. A typical transaction that would cost you $15 online at a discount broker could cost $150 at a full-service firm. Full-service brokers claim that their stock-picking expertise is worth the extra cost. But there's no evidence that these would-be experts' advice is worth the steep commissions they charge. And keep in mind that brokers—who are salespeople, not stock analysts—generally make money by getting you to buy or sell stocks. To my mind, you're better off keeping your commissions low and going with a discount broker. Many discount firms, including "deep discount" brokers, reserve their lowest rates for customers who do their trades through the brokers' Web sites.

- **Look at more than just price.** Going with the absolute cheapest brokerage firm isn't always the wisest move. Because of the surge in popularity of discount brokers, many of these companies are overwhelmed by the increased business. Web sites crash. Phone calls go unanswered. And e-mail messages are sometimes not returned. Before you sign up with any firm, make a few random calls (on different days) and make sure you're satisfied with the response that you get.

- **Do some research.** Every summer *Smart Money* magazine (www.smartmoney.com) publishes an excellent ranking of the best discount brokers, based on a variety of factors, including price and service. Read it. Magazines like *Kiplinger's* (www.kiplingers.com) and *Money* (www.money.com) also run articles on this topic from time to time. Finally, check out the brokerage firms' Web sites before you enroll. Two discount brokers that have received high marks in recent surveys are TD Waterhouse (800-934-4448; www.waterhouse.com) and Muriel Siebert (800-872-0444; www.siebertnet.com).

- **Buy stock directly from the company.** Many companies, particularly large ones, allow you to purchase shares directly from the company through something called a **dividend reinvestment plan,** or **DRIP.** DRIPs often have low minimum investment requirements (as low as $100 or less) and charge very low or no commissions. Although some companies do tack on annoying fees (so read the DRIP prospectus carefully before you sign up), for the most part DRIPs can be even cheaper than using a discount broker. One technicality: Some companies require you to buy at least one share of company stock through a broker before they will let you buy shares directly. For a list of hundreds of companies that offer DRIPs, see www.dripinvestor.com (800-233-5922) or www.netstockdirect.com.

FINANCIAL CRAMMING

- The first phase of your investment plan should be to build up an emergency savings cushion equal to at least three months' worth of living expenses. Put these savings in a money market fund.

- Your next move will be to begin investing in stock and bond mutual funds. Your best bet is probably to invest in index funds, since actively managed funds tend to charge higher fees and on average have not performed any better historically.

- Invest only in no-load funds. There's no point in paying hefty fees to invest in a load fund since there's no evidence that they're better investments than no-load funds.

- Don't invest in a mutual fund that charges investors high expenses. As of this writing, expense ratios average about 1.6% a year for stock funds, just under 1.1% for bond funds, and around 0.6% for money market funds. Find a fund that charges you lower expenses.

- Sign up for an automatic investment plan. These plans allow you to have small amounts of money—say, $50 each month—withdrawn from your bank account or paycheck and funneled into a mutual fund. If you invest automatically, some funds will waive the minimum initial investment requirements.

6

LIVING THE GOOD
LIFE IN 2030

Think It's Crazy to Worry Now About Retirement Then? It's Crazy Not To

SUPPOSE YOU set aside $1,000 a year (about $19 a week) from age 25 to 34 in a retirement account earning 8% a year, and never invest a penny more. By the time you turn 65, your $10,000 investment will have grown to $168,627.

But if you don't start saving until you're 35 years old and then invest $1,000 a year for the next thirty years—that's a total investment of $30,000—you'll have only $125,228 by age 65.

You might want to read this example over again, slowly.

The moral of this story (a depressing one if you're in your forties) and the focus of this chapter: If you don't start saving in a tax-favored retirement account while you're young, you'll miss out on perhaps the best investment opportunity of your life. That's because retirement plans offer terrific tax advantages that allow your savings to grow rapidly. In order to maximize the benefit, you should get started right away. The government limits the amount you can set aside each year, so if you fail to contribute now, you won't be able to make it up when you're older (and perhaps wiser).

There's more at stake here than losing out on a juicy tax shelter: you could actually end up living out your golden years in *poverty*.

The Social Security Administration currently predicts that by the year 2014, it will be paying out more than it takes in, and unless Congress finds the money for a complete overhaul by about 2034, there won't be enough money in the fund to pay out full benefits. While Social Security will almost certainly be around in some form when we retire, it will probably provide less support for us than it has for our grandparents.

A less-publicized but equally pressing problem is the transformation that has been taking place in the private pension world. In our parents' era, employees stayed with the same company for twenty or thirty years, and many were rewarded at the end of their work lives with pensions paid for by their employers. Old-fashioned pensions, known as **defined benefit plans,** are rapidly becoming the spotted owls of the employee benefits world as fewer and fewer companies are offering them to new employees. By the time most of us retire, traditional pensions may well be nearing extinction. New types of pension plans have only partially filled the gap left by the decline of the old-fashioned kind.

And because high-tech medical advancements promise to keep us alive anywhere from ten to twenty years longer than our grandparents, we need to stash away even more cash for our old age. Most Americans who reach the traditional retirement age of 65 today can expect to live beyond the age of 80. By the time our generation retires, the figure could well be closer to 90.

Before I go any further, I have a confession to make. Although I was eligible to start contributing to my company's retirement savings plan when I was 24, I waited until I was 26—simply because I didn't get around to it. And I paid dearly. I currently have $52,000 in my 401(k) retirement plan, but would have more than $112,000 if I had started saving when I was supposed to. Learn from my mistake.

This chapter will teach you everything you need to know about retirement accounts but have been too busy to ask. You'll be happy to learn that you don't have to be rich or financially savvy to put some money into an individual retirement account (IRA) or a company plan. And unless you have a massive trust fund or are expecting a giant inheritance from a wealthy old relative, you'd be wise to start doing exactly that—right now.

WHAT ARE RETIREMENT SAVINGS PLANS, ANYWAY?

Back in the early 1970s, when Microsoft was just a glimmer in Bill Gates's eye, Congress decided to give savers a break by creating tax-subsidized retirement savings programs. Today Bill Gates is a billionaire and probably doesn't spend too much time worrying about his retirement savings. But the rest of us are still blessed with those tax-favored plans, called 401(k) plans and individual retirement accounts (IRAs).

Here's a rundown:

- **401(k)s** are retirement savings plans available to employees of most major companies and many small ones. **403(b)** plans (also called tax-sheltered annuities) are offered to employees of public schools and certain religious or charitable organizations. (Since 401(b)s are similar to 401(k)s, I'll refer only to 401(k)s throughout this chapter.)

- **Individual Retirement Accounts (IRAs)** are available to working people (and their nonworking spouses) and are especially attractive for those who work for companies that do not offer retirement savings plans. There are two main types of IRAs: **traditional IRAs** and **Roth IRAs.** I'll get into the details in a minute.

The main tax-saving principle behind all of these retirement savings plans is simple: Uncle Sam agrees not to tax the money in your retirement account while it is accumulating interest and other earnings. That may not sound like such a big deal. But allowing your money to grow untaxed for many years could result in thousands of dollars more for you over your lifetime. The effect of your interest earning interest is known as **compounding.** When money compounds without being taxed for, say, forty years rather than thirty, it not only grows for a longer period of time, but it also grows more quickly, as the example at the beginning of this chapter shows.

CONTRIBUTING TO
YOUR 401(k)

If you're eligible for a 401(k) plan at work, you're lucky. Contributions you make to your 401(k) actually benefit from two tax breaks: one up front, the other in the long term. First, the government allows you to delay paying taxes on the money you contribute to a 401(k) each year. So if you earn $30,000 in a year and you put $1,000 into a 401(k), you're taxed as if you had earned only $29,000 that year. The $1,000 you put into the 401(k) is known as a **before-tax contribution**, and you won't have to pay tax on it until you withdraw it from your account down the road. The other, longer-term benefit of a 401(k) is that you get to delay paying taxes on the *interest* (or other earnings) your retirement account generates over the years.

When you withdraw money at the time of your retirement, you will pay taxes on the whole sum that you withdraw—the amount you contributed plus your earnings. But because the money is able to grow untaxed for many years, paying taxes later rather than sooner could result in thousands of dollars more for you when you retire.

Most companies allow employees to decide what percentage of their salaries they want to contribute to a company retirement plan. In 2000, the maximum amount of *before-tax* income an employee can contribute to a 401(k) is $10,500. (Actually, the maximum you're permitted to contribute may be less, depending on factors such as your salary and your employer's contributions, if any, to your plan.)

One of the biggest benefits of a 401(k) is that many employers match a portion of the amount you contribute with a contribution of their own. Many companies contribute fifty cents for every dollar you put in, up to a fixed maximum (often 3% to 6% of your salary). That's the equivalent of an immediate 50% return on your investment. To take full advantage of this amazing deal, try to contribute at least the maximum amount for which you are eligible to receive matching funds.

Contributions to 401(k)s are siphoned from your paycheck by

your employer. After a while, most people don't even miss the money that's being skimmed off and discover that they're saving money faster than they ever thought possible.

CONTRIBUTING TO AN IRA

The other major type of retirement savings plan is the individual retirement account, or IRA. Unlike 401(k)s, IRAs are not offered by your employer. Instead, they are private accounts set up through brokers, banks, and mutual fund companies. (I'll go into the details of where you should set one up a little later on.)

The maximum you can contribute to an IRA is $2,000 a year, plus an additional $2,000 to your spouse's IRA if he or she doesn't earn any income. If both you and your spouse work, you can each contribute up to $2,000 to your own accounts. These limits apply to your total IRA contribution—whether to a traditional IRA, a Roth IRA, or any combination of IRAs.

The two types of IRAs have different advantages and disadvantages, described below.

Traditional IRAs

At their best, traditional IRAs work much like 401(k)s. You get to subtract, or "deduct," your contribution from your income—that's the upfront tax break. So if you earn $35,000 and contribute $1,000 to an IRA, you can subtract that $1,000 from your taxable income when you fill out your tax forms that year and pay tax as though you had earned only $34,000.

Next, the money in your IRA grows without being taxed for many years—that's the long-term break. Come retirement time, you'll pay tax on all the money in your account as you withdraw it.

Traditional IRAs that offer upfront tax breaks are known as

deductible IRAs. Unfortunately, deductible IRAs are not available to everyone. Whether you are eligible depends on your "adjusted gross income" and whether you're covered by an employer-sponsored retirement plan. (For details on what your adjusted gross income is, see Chapter 9.)

Here are the rules. If your employer does *not* offer a retirement plan, you are almost always allowed to deduct your full $2,000 contribution to a traditional IRA. There is one tricky exception: If you're not eligible for a company retirement plan but are married to someone who *is*. In that case, you can make the full contribution to a deductible IRA only if your combined adjusted gross income is $150,000 or less and you and your spouse file a joint return. So if you stay home to take care of the kids, for instance, and your spouse has a retirement plan at work, you can still open a deductible IRA as long as your spouse earns $150,000 or less.

But what if your employer *does* offer a retirement plan? In that case, your IRA contribution may not be fully deductible. Here are the rules. If you are eligible for an employer-sponsored retirement plan, you can deduct your *full* $2,000 contribution to a traditional IRA if:

- You're single, and your adjusted gross income is $32,000 or less.

- You're married, you file a joint tax return, and together your adjusted gross income is $52,000 or less.

Married people who file separate tax returns, no matter what their incomes, can't claim the full deduction if they are covered by retirement plans at work.

If you don't qualify for a fully deductible IRA, you can still put up to $2,000 a year into a **partially deductible IRA** or a **nondeductible IRA.** To find out what part of your contribution is deductible, consult IRS Publication 590, *Individual Retirement Arrangements.* You can order a copy of this publication by calling the IRS at 800-TAX-FORM, or by downloading it from the IRS Web site at www.irs.gov.

Partially deductible IRAs and nondeductible IRAs don't offer the full $2,000 upfront tax break that makes deductible IRAs so appealing. They also require extra paperwork (you'll have to fill out Form 8606 every year when you file your taxes). These IRAs should be considered only if you can't qualify for a deductible IRA or a Roth IRA and you've put the most you can in your company 401(k).

Roth IRAs

Roth IRAs are a breed unto themselves. Unlike 401(k)s and deductible IRAs, Roth IRAs don't give you an immediate upfront tax break on your contributions. But once your money is in a Roth IRA, it will never be taxed again. Roth IRAs don't just compound tax-free: They stay that way. Forever. When you retire and start taking your money out of a Roth IRA, you won't have to pay federal taxes on it as you would with a traditional IRA or a 401(k). In retirement plan lingo, 401(k)s and deductible IRAs offer *tax-deferred* growth (meaning you delay paying tax on your contributions and earnings), while the Roth IRA offers *tax-free* growth. For many people—especially young people saving over many years—the Roth IRA may be the better deal. (I'll get into the gory details of why in a moment.)

One big advantage of Roth IRAs is that you may be able to open one even if you already have a retirement plan at work, which you may not be able to do with a deductible IRA. That's because the eligibility rules for Roth IRAs are simpler than they are for deductible IRAs. It doesn't matter if you and your spouse are eligible for a retirement plan at work—all that matters is your income.

You can make the *full* $2,000 contribution to a Roth IRA if:

- You're single and your adjusted gross income is not more than $95,000.

- You're married, file jointly, and your adjusted gross income is not more than $150,000.

You can contribute less than the full $2,000 as long as you earn under $110,000 as a single person or $160,000 as a couple filing jointly.

Married people filing separately can never make the full Roth contribution, but can make partial contributions if their adjusted gross incomes are less than $10,000. (Pretty stingy.)

The Choice: Which IRA Is Right for You?

If you want to put money in an IRA, you'll need to decide which kind. Roth IRAs are often considered the better option for younger people. Here are some of the questions you should be asking yourself:

- **Do I qualify for a deductible IRA?** Deductible traditional IRAs have relatively low income limits, so you may not qualify for the full $2,000 deduction. No mystery here: If you can't deduct your full contribution, go with the Roth.

- **Can I afford to make the full $2,000 contribution if I go with a Roth?** Roth IRAs pay off big in the long run, but they may require some belt-tightening today. If you're in the 28% tax bracket and deduct your contribution to a traditional IRA, a $2,000 contribution would give you a $560 tax deduction. So the $2,000 contribution would end up costing you just $1,440. But Roth IRAs are not deductible, which means your $2,000 contribution to a Roth would cost you . . . $2,000. If you can afford to put the full $2,000 in a Roth IRA, you'll be doing your future self a big favor. But if you can only afford to put $1,440 in your account either way, the Roth IRA won't provide you with much financial advantage in the long run. In that case, your decision will be based on other considerations, like the ones in the next three points.

- **Will I be in a substantially lower tax bracket when I retire?** Many people fall into a lower tax bracket when they retire

Figure 6-1
THE IRA DECISION

Richard, single and 26, does not have the option of participating in a 401(k) plan at work. He has never contributed to an IRA but wants to start. Problem is, he hasn't made up his mind whether to go with a deductible IRA or a Roth IRA. At times like this, you have to get down to the numbers. So bear with me as we take a look at two possible IRA scenarios for Richard, each showing why he would probably do better with a Roth.

First, let's say that Richard can only fit $1,000 in IRA contributions into his budget this year. He has two choices: He can simply deposit $1,000 into a Roth IRA; or he can put $1,389 into a deductible IRA and then save $389 in income taxes, by deducting his contribution from his taxable income. (Richard is in the 28% tax bracket, and 28% of $1,389 is $389.) The money in a Roth IRA will never be taxed, but if Richard chooses the deductible IRA, he *will* have to pay taxes when he withdraws the money at retirement. For this example, I've assumed an annual return of 10% on Richard's IRA. If his tax bracket at retirement is the same as it is now—28%—then both IRAs come out the same:

	Deductible IRA	Roth IRA
Contribution to IRA	$1,389	$1,000
Savings from tax deduction	$389	$0
Cost of contribution	$1,000	$1,000
Value of IRA in 30 years	$24,235	$17,450
Taxes paid on withdrawal	$6,785	$0
After-tax value in 30 years	$17,450	$17,450

It's a draw. So why should Richard go with a Roth? Because Roth IRAs have more flexible rules for withdrawals. What's more, Richard won't have to scrounge up the extra $389 and wait to get it back at tax time.

Now, let's say that Richard can afford to make a $2,000 contribution to an IRA this year. If he goes for a traditional IRA, he will be able to deduct $560, but he can't put that money in his IRA, because IRA contributions are limited to $2,000 a year. So he will have to invest that $560 in a taxable account. Here are his options:

	Deductible IRA	Roth IRA
Contribution to IRA	$2,000	$2,000
Deduction	$560	$0
Contribution to taxable account	$560	$0
Cost of contributions	**$2,000**	**$2,000**
Value of IRA in 30 years	$34,900	$34,900
Taxes paid on withdrawal	$9,772	$0
Value of taxable account in 30 years	$5,635	$0
Total after-tax value in 30 years	**$30,763**	**$34,900**

In this example I've assumed that the earnings on Richard's taxable account get hit with a 20% tax every year. But even if those earnings are taxed less, the money in a taxable account will never be able to earn as much as the money in a Roth IRA, which is not subject to federal income tax at all. Richard should get a Roth.

because they stop receiving regular income from their jobs. (Now there's a cheery thought.) Of course, it's hard to predict today what your tax situation will look like thirty or forty years from now. But here's the general concept: Roth IRA contributions are taxed today, while deductible IRA contributions are taxed when you take them out. So if you suspect that you will be in a lower tax bracket when you retire than the one you are in today, a deductible IRA might make more sense.

- **Will I need my IRA money right away when I retire?** Again, no one can be sure about the answer here, but it's worth thinking about. With traditional IRAs, you are forced to start withdrawing your money once you hit the age of $70^1/2$. Roth IRAs have no such requirements, which could be a big advantage if you can afford to delay making your withdrawals. The longer you leave your money in an IRA, the more it can grow.

- **Will I need to withdraw my IRA money before I retire?** You can withdraw the money you have put into a Roth IRA at any time without penalty (though you will have to pay a penalty if you withdraw any of the earnings on that money). Although this is not advisable—once you have taken the money out, it can't be replaced—it does provide more emergency protection than a traditional IRA. (For details on withdrawing money from IRAs, see page 163.)

My advice generally is to put as much money as you can afford in a Roth IRA and leave it there. But if you have reason to believe that a deductible IRA would be better for you, look into the question before you make any decisions. Financial magazines like *Money* (www.money.com) and *Smart Money* (www.smartmoney .com) have run helpful articles on the subject that can be accessed on their Web sites. You should also check out the IRA comparison calculators available at sites like www.financenter.com and www.datachimp.com.

HOW YOUR RETIREMENT
SAVINGS GROW

The money in your retirement plan doesn't just sit there; it's channeled into investments so it can grow. When you sign up for a plan, you're given a choice of investment options. You pick the ones you want and decide how to divide your money among your selections.

Your options will depend on the kind of plan you enroll in. With a 401(k), the employer typically narrows down the investment options for you. Many plans offer a "menu" of about eight alternatives, which might include shares of your company's own stock, a stock mutual fund, a bond mutual fund, a balanced mutual fund (which has a mix of stocks and bonds), and a money market fund. Every time you contribute, the money is automatically divided up according to your initial specifications. However, you may not get to choose how to invest your employer's matching contribution.

IRAs are slightly more complicated because they offer more choices. First you must decide where to open one. Although IRAs are offered by banks and brokerage firms, your best bet is probably a large, low-cost mutual fund company. Here's why: When you open an IRA at a bank, your options may be limited to ultrasafe investments like certificates of deposit (CDs) and money market deposit accounts—neither of which typically offers a high enough rate of return to keep you comfortably ahead of inflation over the long term. Although more and more banks also offer the option of putting mutual funds in your IRA, there's a good chance you will pay a substantial commission on these funds. A full-service brokerage firm may also charge hefty fees. No-load, low-expense mutual funds, such as the ones listed in Chapter 5, do not charge loads or commissions.

Since retirement plans allow your money to grow tax-deferred (or tax-free in the case of the Roth IRA), you should consider the tax advantages (and disadvantages) of putting certain investments in them. For instance, it doesn't make sense to put tax-free bond funds into a retirement plan; stick with taxable investments only. (For a discussion of different investment options and suggestions on the pros and cons of each, see Chapter 5.)

A LESSON IN HOW A LITTLE
ADDS UP TO A LOT

Although he has never earned more than $26,000 a year, Peter, 40, has more than $310,000 in retirement savings. How did he do it? Peter works at a company that allows him to sock away 17% of his salary each year into a 401(k). His starting salary in 1982 was just $10,000 a year, but he immediately began contributing the maximum he could to his company plan (even though his company offered no matching program) and has continued to do so ever since. For the three years he lived with his parents after college (he moved out at age 25), Peter also deposited an additional $2,000 into an IRA each year. Although it's true that Peter profited from the fact that stock and bond funds did very well in the 1980s and 1990s, his real achievement has been his determination to contribute to his 401(k) and IRA every year. If he continues to save the maximum in his 401(k) plan, gets a 3% cost-of-living salary increase each year, and earns 8% a year on his investments, he will have about $750,000 by the time he turns 50. Amazing.

SOME DRAWBACKS (AND WHY THEY DON'T MATTER)

On the surface, IRAs and 401(k)s appear to have a major downside for young people. Once you put money into these accounts, you may have to wait until you reach the age of 59^1/$_2$ to withdraw your money without paying a penalty. If you try to take it out before then, you'll often get hit with a stiff 10% penalty, plus income tax on the amount you withdraw.

These tough rules are meant to prevent savers from raiding their retirement plans, since withdrawals generally can't be replaced. But the rules aren't actually as rigid as they seem. Here are the details.

Withdrawals from 401(k)s

401(k)s are tough to crack. To withdraw money from them, you must prove to your employer that you need it for something important, such as paying medical bills, and that you have nowhere else to turn. But many 401(k)s do offer an escape hatch: They allow you to *borrow* the money at ratesthat are sometimes more favorable than a bank's. When you borrow from your 401(k), you are essentially borrowing money from yourself, and the payments you make—including interest—go right back into your own account.

Borrowing rules vary from company to company, so check the details with your employer. Usually, you can borrow half the amount you contributed to your 401(k) plus earnings. Depending on how long you've worked for the company, you may be able to borrow up to half of your employer's contributions too. Some employers do not permit loans of less than $1,000. Loans usually must be paid back within five years, although if you use the money to buy your primary home, you may be able to pay it back over a longer period.

Even if you can't withdraw or borrow from your retirement plan very easily, it usually still makes sense to invest in a 401(k). The advantage of tax-favored compounding is so great that after about ten years, its benefit could outweigh the 10% penalty you would have to pay for making early withdrawals.

Withdrawals from IRAs

Not surprisingly, the rules for IRA withdrawals differ depending on what kind of IRA you have. Under most circumstances, you will have to pay both income tax and a 10% penalty on IRA money you withdraw before the age 59^1/2. But there are a few exceptions, which can get pretty complicated. Bear with me.

Roth IRAs have the most lenient guidelines: You can withdraw the money you've contributed to them at any time without paying the income tax or the 10% penalty. But that applies only to your *contributions*. You will have to pay both the penalty and the tax if you withdraw the *earnings* on your contributions before you retire.

The government also lets you withdraw money from *any* IRA, without paying the 10% penalty, for any of the following reasons:

- educational expenses for yourself, your spouse, or your children (including tuition, fees, books, and possibly room and board);

- unreimbursed medical expenses if they exceed 7.5% of your adjusted gross income (see Chapter 9 to figure out what that means);

- up to $10,000 in homebuyer costs. This loophole is an especially big deal for Roth IRAs, because it generally lets you avoid paying the income tax on your withdrawal as well as the penalty. (I say "generally" because if your Roth IRA is less than five years old, you will not be spared the tax.) The $10,000 limit is a *lifetime* cap per person, and the exemption is reserved for people who have not owned a house in at least two years.

One last tip: If you need your IRA money for a short period of time, you can *borrow* it once a year, without tax or penalty, as long as you pay it all back within 60 days.

A WORD ABOUT INFLATION AND TAXATION

Personal finance articles and books often offer dramatic examples of the rewards of saving without ever mentioning inflation. So far in this chapter I haven't done much better. It's time for me to come clean.

Although saving over a long period of time really is a good idea, the fact is it won't make you as rich as it might seem from the exam-

DIVIDING YOUR RETIREMENT SAVINGS PIE

Once you sign up for your 401(k), you'll be given a menu of investment choices and asked to divvy up the money in your account. Most experts urge young investors to put the bulk of their retirement money into stocks—and I agree—but unfortunately there is no magic formula you can use to come up with the right mix. For help, you may want to check Financial Engines (www.financialengines.com). This site helps you determine the best investment mix for your retirement money, using a mathematical model developed by a Nobel Prize–winning economist named Bill Sharpe. (As my grandmother used to say, this man is clearly no dummy.) Financial Engines can help you decide how to allocate the money not only in your company 401(k) plan, but in your IRA as well. The service functions as an ongoing subscription and charges $14.95 (per account) every three months. To minimize your costs, consider using the service for just one three-month period each year.

ples given so far. As you may remember from Chapter 5, inflation can drastically reduce the purchasing power of the dollar over time. Consider, for example, the scenario I outlined at the beginning of this chapter; the $168,627 you'd have forty years from now would not buy nearly as much as $168,627 can buy today.*

---

* There's a less obvious way inflation comes into play in this example. If you decided to save for ten years starting at age 25, you'd be making your ten annual $1,000 deposits many years earlier than if you waited until you turned 35 and then invested $1,000 a year for thirty years. Because $1,000 buys more today than it will many years from now, each of the $1,000 deposits you'd make from ages 25 to 34 would buy more than each of the $1,000 deposits you'd make if you waited ten years and saved from age 35 to 65. Thus the benefits of saving early are offset somewhat by inflation.

This doesn't mean you shouldn't save. As the numbers show, you still come out way ahead if you start saving in a retirement account while you're young—even after inflation. When money is allowed to grow for decades without being taxed, the results are extraordinary.

Consider the following example. Suppose you put $2,000 into each of two accounts—a Roth IRA and a taxable account—in 2001. Let's also assume that each account earns 8% a year, the annual inflation rate is 3%, and you're in a 33% tax bracket (including federal, state, and local taxes). After thirty years, the $2,000 in the Roth IRA will have grown to approximately $8,300 (in 2001 dollars). The $2,000 in the taxable account, on the other hand, will have increased to only about $3,950 (again in 2001 dollars). The bottom line: You will have earned more than three times as much ($6,300 versus $1,950) by keeping your money in a tax-favored account than by putting it in a taxable one.

ANSWERS TO SOME COMMON QUESTIONS

Okay. Now you've got the point: You don't want to miss out on the benefits of saving in a retirement plan when you're young. This next section will answer a few questions you want to ask before you get started.

The Facts on 401(k)s

Q: *Am I eligible for a 401(k)?*
A: Ask your employer. You may be required to work for your employer for a year or reach age 21 before you can contribute.

Q: *One of my 401(k) investment options is stock in my company. Should I bite?*
A: Probably not. When you work for a company, you already

THE RETIREMENT PRIORITY BOX

Now that you know more than you ever wanted to about retirement plans, you may be left with one final question: What do I do first? Here's a quick rundown of the rough order you should assign to your various retirement savings options:

1. **401(k) with employer matching.** The best deal around. The matching alone can generate an immediate 50% to 100% return on your money (once you're vested), and the 401(k) provides an upfront deduction and years of tax-deferred growth. Don't put money in any other retirement account until you have reached the limit of what your employer is willing to match.

2. **IRA (Roth or deductible).** The Roth IRA offers years of tax-free growth. The deductible IRA offers tax-deferred growth and an upfront tax break. Both offer a wider range of investment options than 401(k)s. IRAs also allow you to withdraw your money without penalty to buy a home or pay for educational expenses.

3. **401(k)s without employer matching.** If you've already contributed the maximum to options 1 and 2 above, try to max out your 401(k)—even if it's a stretch on your budget.

4. **Partially deductible or nondeductible traditional IRA.** If you have contributed the maximum to your 401(k) and you're not eligible for a deductible or Roth IRA, these accounts offer limited tax advantages—tax-deferred compounding but little or no upfront tax break.

5. **Taxable investment account.** Once you've exhausted your tax-favored savings options—IRAs and 401(k)s—you'll have to save in a regular old taxable investment account. To get the most from your money, open your account at a no-load, low-expense mutual fund company. (See page 142 for details.)

have a huge "investment" in it. If the business runs into difficult times, you are at risk twice: Not only could you lose your job, but you could also see your retirement portfolio plummet. What's more, many employers match employee contributions with shares of company stock, so you may already be heavily invested in your firm.

Q: *My company plan allows me to invest in a guaranteed investment contract. What's that?*

A: Guaranteed investment contracts (GICs), sometimes called stable value funds, are investments that are similar to CDs (certificates of deposit) but are guaranteed by a bank or insurance company instead of the federal government. They are often offered as a choice in 401(k) plans. GICs are considered relatively safe investments. They have rates of return that are generally one or two percentage points higher than those of money market funds. Though I recommend putting most of your long-term savings in higher-yield investments like stock, GICs can be used to balance your portfolio.

Q: *What happens if I change jobs?*

A: If you move to a new company, you can transfer your 401(k) money into an IRA or into your new 401(k) if your new company allows it. But you must be aware of a few annoying rules. It's important that you tell your old employer that you want a **direct rollover** into your new company's 401(k) or into an IRA. Although the rules say the plan can pay out or "distribute" the 401(k) money directly to you, there are several reasons to avoid this method. If you are paid the money directly, the plan must withhold 20% of the amount you are due and send it to the IRS (which will hold on to it until you file your taxes for that year). You are then responsible for making up that 20% from your other savings when you make the transfer into your new plan. If you can't come up with the money in 60 days, you will have to pay tax on that 20%, plus a penalty. (I told you these rules are annoying.)

Another option you have if your account is over $5,000 is to leave your 401(k) money with your old company. Once you leave a company, you're no longer eligible to contribute to its 401(k), but your account will continue to grow if your investments do well. If you like the investment choices at your old company's 401(k) better than the ones in your new company's plan, this may be a good option for you.

No matter what you do, resist the temptation to cash in your 401(k). You will have to pay tax on the money, plus the 10% penalty.

Q: *What happens if I have an outstanding loan against my 401(k), and I quit or I'm fired?*

A: This is a situation you should try to avoid. Most companies will ask you to pay the entire loan back in one lump sum when you leave the firm. If you can't, the amount you owe may be treated as money withdrawn (instead of borrowed) from the plan, and you may therefore owe taxes plus the 10% penalty.

Q: *They tell me I'm vested. What does that mean?*

A: To be **vested** is to have a nonforfeitable right to the money your employer contributed to your retirement plan on your behalf. Most company retirement plans require you to work for the firm for a certain number of years before you become fully vested, meaning you can get 100% of the money your employer contributed for you. Typically it takes about five years. Some companies have a gradual vesting policy. With a gradual schedule, you might be 20% vested after two years at a company, 40% after three years, and so on. Once you become vested, however, it doesn't mean you may withdraw your money without paying the 10% penalty and taxes on your earnings. If you're not vested and you need to get your money when you leave the firm, you can withdraw the money you contributed (plus earnings on those contributions), but you can't keep any of the money your employer contributed for you (or the earnings on those employer contributions). If you're partially vested, you'll get to keep a portion of the money your employer contributed for you, plus earnings. Knowing your company's vesting schedule can help you time a career move. Keep in mind that some companies consider a year of service to be less than a full calendar year (for instance, five months and a day). That's why you should consult your company's employee benefits or human resources department to find out the exact date you'll be vested.

Q: Can *my employer raid my 401(k)?*

A: If the company you work for is facing rough financial times, you may worry whether your boss can dip into the 401(k) to pay his bills. The answer is no. Your employer is not legally allowed to use the 401(k) money for business purposes. What's more, if your employer files for bankruptcy, the 401(k) money is protected, and none of the employer's creditors can touch your account. The person (or company) who is legally responsible for ensuring that no one tampers with your 401(k) is called the trustee. The trustee might be, for example, a bank or the president of your company. And what if your employer decides to end the plan? You'll still be okay, because you'll receive all the money you put in plus any contributions made by your employer on your behalf (as long as you are vested).

The Scoop on IRAs

Q: *Where should I open my IRA?*

A: Find a no-load mutual fund company that offers you the option of investing your IRA in funds with low expense ratios. (See Chapter 5 for details on finding such a company.) At the very least, the company should have a stock fund, a bond fund, and a money market fund.

Also, research the company's rules. Some companies permit IRA customers to make an initial contribution of only $250, while others demand $1,000 or more to open an account. And choose a firm that can establish an automatic savings program linked to your paycheck or your savings or checking account.

Q: *Are there any IRA fees I should watch out for?*

A: Yes. One common practice is to tack on an IRA maintenance fee of between $10 and $30 a year. Sometimes the fund company will waive the fee if you maintain a given minimum amount in your account.

Q: *What's the deadline for contributing to an IRA?*

A: The deadline is April 15 of the *following* year. If, for example, you suddenly realize on January 1, 2001, that you forgot to

A NEW TYPE OF OLD-FASHIONED PENSION

At the beginning of this chapter, I mentioned that old-fashioned defined benefit pension plans were on the verge of disappearing. That's true, but employers have not stopped offering pension plans altogether. The new trend is toward something called **cash balance plans,** and for many younger workers these plans may actually be an improvement over the old versions. (Older workers, unfortunately, may do worse under these plans.) Traditional pensions reward employees for staying with their companies for a long time, and your promised pension spikes up dramatically as you near retirement. But most people today do not plan to spend the rest of their lives at the same company, and cash balance plans address that reality. In practice, they look a bit like 401(k)s, but since it's a pension plan, your company, not you, foots the bill. Your employer simply credits a given amount of money—typically 5% of your salary—toward your pension every year, and you can monitor your "account" to keep track of what you've accumulated in benefits. Once you're "vested," which usually takes about five years, you'll be able to keep those benefits even if you leave your job. Seniority doesn't enter the picture, and that means two things: Younger workers can accumulate benefits earlier than they used to, and they can also move from job to job more easily without worrying about staying at the same company long enough to qualify for substantial benefits. If your employer offers you the chance to switch from a defined benefit plan to a cash balance plan, odds are you should take it.

make your 2000 IRA contribution, you're still okay; you have until April 15, 2001, to contribute to a traditional IRA or Roth IRA for tax year 2000 (and in the case of a deductible IRA, deduct it on your 2000 return).

Q: *Can my parents give me the money to open an IRA?*
A: Yes. But you (or your spouse) have to have *earned* at least as much money during the year as you contribute to the IRA.

IF YOU'RE SELF-EMPLOYED

If you are your own boss, consider opening one of the three basic types of retirement savings plans for self-employed people. The advantage of these plans is that they allow you to contribute (and deduct) much more than an IRA.

The first type of self-employment retirement plan is called a **simplified employee pension,** or **SEP,** sometimes also referred to as a **SEP-IRA.** SEPs work pretty much like IRAs. The main difference is the amount of money you can contribute. You can contribute 15% of your first $170,000 of **net earnings from self-employment** to a SEP. (To figure out your net earnings subtract your business deductions, half of your self-employment tax, and your SEP contribution from your gross income. Consult an accountant to help you figure this out.) So, depending on how much you earn, you can contribute (and deduct) as much as $25,500 annually to a SEP—clearly a more attractive option than a standard IRA. If you don't have employees, a SEP-IRA is easy to set up; if you do have people working for you, you may have to contribute for them as well.

If your self-employment doesn't generate very much income, you might benefit more from the **SIMPLE IRA** than from a SEP. As the name suggests, SIMPLE IRAs are the least complicated kind of self-employment retirement plan. They allow you to set aside (and deduct) up to $6,000 a year—even if that accounts for all of your self-employment income. (You'd have to earn more than $45,000 to deduct that much in a SEP.) You may be able to contribute even more than $6,000, but the rules are fairly complex so you should talk to a tax advisor before making any decisions. One odd catch you should be aware of: If you want to set up a SIMPLE plan, you have to do it before October 1. (By contrast, SEPs can be opened right up to the April 15 filing deadline, more than six months later.) As with SEPs, SIMPLEs—short for Savings Incentive Match Plans for Employees—may require you to make contributions to your employees' accounts as well. They are best for people who earn a small income, generally in a side job like freelance writing or crocheting potholders.

Another option is a retirement plan known as a **Keogh**. A Keogh requires somewhat more paperwork, but it also has advantages. For starters, you might not have to make contributions for your part-time employees. There are also several different types of Keogh plans to choose from; the most popular is called a **profit-sharing plan**. You can contribute up to 15% of your first $170,000 of net earnings (up to a maximum of $25,500 each year) to a profit-sharing Keogh. With this type of Keogh, you can vary your contributions annually, meaning you're not required to contribute a set amount each year. Other types of Keogh plans generally allow you to contribute more money (up to $30,000 a year), but you're locked into contributing a set percentage of your earnings each year.

For more details on all of these options, contact a no-load, low-cost mutual fund company.

FINANCIAL CRAMMING

- Enroll in your company retirement savings plan or open an individual retirement account (IRA) at a no-load mutual fund company—right now.

- Looking for easy money? If your company offers a 401(k), contribute at least as much as your employer will match. A fifty-cent match for every dollar you put in is the same as earning a 50% return on your investment.

- If you're thinking of changing jobs, check your vesting schedule to see whether you've worked long enough to take all your 401(k) money with you when you quit. Staying an extra few months could mean thousands of extra dollars in your pocket.

- Figure out whether a traditional or Roth IRA makes more sense for you. Many younger people have more to gain from Roth IRAs. See page 156 for details and IRA comparison calculators like the ones at www.financenter.com and www.datachimp.com.

- If you work for yourself, check out SEPs, SIMPLE IRAs, and Keoghs. These plans may permit you to sock away far more for your retirement than you could with a traditional or Roth IRA.

7

OH, GIVE ME
A HOME

Advice on Getting an
Apartment or House of
Your Own

A RECORD NUMBER of Americans own homes nowadays, and it's no wonder. The economy has been good, and there has been an explosion in the number of programs that make it easier for people to get a place of their own.

Yet the financial commitment you make when you buy a home is still an enormous one. In fact, in some ways home ownership is a bigger financial burden now than it was for our parents' generation. Today people spend about one-third of their take-home pay on monthly home payments; in the 1970s home payments took up just one-quarter of their paychecks.

This chapter explains everything you need to know about buying a home. It will help you decide how much home you can afford, direct you to special programs, and fill you in on everything from how to qualify for a mortgage to where to find the best rates. If you're overwhelmed by the process—or simply haven't had a chance to figure out whether it makes sense for you to buy or rent— this chapter is for you. And even if you're nowhere near the point where you can consider buying a home, you can benefit from the first section, which offers tips on being a smart renter.

WHAT EVERY RENTER
NEEDS TO KNOW

With home prices in many parts of the country at record highs, you may feel that the odds of your purchasing a home are about as good as your chances of being offered your own talk show. For now you're a tenant, so be a wise one. Here are steps you can take to reduce the cost of renting and eliminate the headaches you're likely to encounter as a tenant. Keep them in mind before, during, and after you sign a lease:

- **Try to negotiate the rent.** I know a lot of people feel squeamish about doing this, but force yourself. When you find a place you like, tell the landlord you're very interested but hadn't planned to spend as much as he or she is asking for. Ask if there's any way you can get a break—say, $25 a month. If you're a desirable candidate (that is, if you have a good credit record and you've been working at the same job for at least a year), there's a decent chance the landlord will make some reduction. If not, nothing is lost. Of course, in cities where there are five renters competing for every apartment, your chances of getting a break are slim to none.

- **Negotiate the terms of your lease.** Though it isn't exciting, it's important that you read your lease, which might be two or three pages long. Look for provisions that seem unfair; they may be illegal. In some states, for example, a landlord can't include clauses banning water beds or demanding excessive penalties for late rent. To find out the rules in your area, call your state or county housing office or office of consumer affairs. These government agencies may be able to provide you with brochures that answer your questions about tenants' rights.

  Also look for clauses that, although legal, may be burdensome to you. You may be able to negotiate them out of the lease *before* you sign. Beware of provisions that give your landlord the right to enter your apartment without your permission or the right to raise your rent if his taxes or operating costs increase. Watch out for provisions that say no one but you can live in the apartment. Look for bans on pets; although you might not have one now, you might want to get one in the future. And think twice before agreeing to any unreasonable stipulation the landlord may have added to the standard lease agreement. I know of one couple in San Francisco who had to agree to wash their landlord's plants every week with soap and water! That meant that they couldn't go away for more than a week without getting someone to take over this ridiculous chore.

- **Negotiate with the real estate broker if you're dealing with one.** In most cities, if you use a broker to help you find an apartment to rent, you don't pay him or her a commission. But in a few places like New York City and certain parts of Boston, renters are sometimes expected to pay brokers as much as 15% of a year's rent to secure a place. If possible, try to avoid dealing with brokers by combing newspaper ads for rentals offered directly by the owner; many local papers also carry these listings in their online editions. If you must use a broker, explain up front that you're a serious customer but are willing to pay a commission of only, say, 10%. If you hunt around, you may find a broker willing to cut a deal.

- **List all your roommates on the lease, and have them all sign it.** Although some landlords won't allow this, it's worth asking about. Having all your roommates listed on the lease ensures that you will all share legal responsibility in case of a problem. It also protects you if one of your roommates suddenly decides to move out before the lease is up.

- **Get everything in writing.** Ask for a written lease instead of a verbal agreement. Also, get any additional promises the landlord makes (such as guarantees to paint walls or fix leaky faucets) included in the lease before you sign.

- **Understand how the security deposit works.** A security deposit is money you give to a landlord to protect him in case you damage the apartment or house. If you don't cause any damage, the security deposit will be returned to you when the lease is up. Most states limit the size of security deposits to one or two months' rent, and many also restrict the ways in which they can be used. In general, the landlord can use the money to fix damages you caused or to cover your rent if you break the lease early, but not for basic maintenance on the apartment or house.

Get a receipt for the security deposit from the landlord. In some states the landlord is required to put your money in an interest-bearing account and pay you the interest at the end of the tenancy. (Even in states that don't require a landlord to pay you interest, many landlords do.) Call your state or local housing office for the rules. When your lease is up and you move out, the landlord must refund your deposit if you did not cause any damage. If you don't trust your landlord, take pictures of how you left the place and have a neighbor (or if possible, your landlord) sign a statement saying that you left the apartment in good condition.

- **If you plan to renew your lease, contact your landlord two months before the lease is up and try to negotiate.** If you live in an area with an abundance of available rentals, your landlord might agree to keep the rent the same or even to lower it. But don't wait too long to bring up the subject; start the negotiations a couple of months before your lease is up. If you wait until the week before your lease ends, the landlord will assume you're bluffing when you say you're thinking of moving out.

- **Know your rights.** The law protects renters in many ways. Here are a few:
    —Federal law prohibits a landlord from refusing to rent to you based on your race, sex, religion, disability, national original, or familial status (meaning whether you're pregnant or have kids under 18). Some cities and states also prohibit housing discrimination based on age, marital status, or sexual orientation. If you think you've been denied housing for any of these rea-

sons, call the Federal Housing Discrimination Hotline at 800-669-9777.

—In many states, you must be told of an impending rent increase before your lease is up. The amount of time you must be given varies from state to state.

—In most states, if you disobey a provision in your lease and your landlord knows but accepts your rent anyway, the landlord cannot kick you out for violating that provision. For example, if your lease forbids overnight guests but your landlord knows you had a friend stay over and accepts your rent check anyway, he cannot evict you later based on your friend's visit.

—In some states you can withhold rent if there has been negligence on the part of the landlord, but the rules are very specific about how to go about this. Again, call your county or state housing office or office of consumer affairs to find out the rules in your area. If you don't receive adequate help from these offices, call the office of the attorney general in your state.

For additional information on your rights as a tenant, try contacting local branches of consumer groups like the Public Interest Research Group (www.uspirg.org) or the Legal Aid Society. And Tenant.net (www.tenant.net) is a useful Web site that features links to renters' rights sites all over the country.

SHOULD YOU RENT OR BUY?

Many people believe that, given the choice, renting is a bad idea. They think it's the equivalent of "throwing money away." But when you're young, it's often smarter to rent than to buy.

Unfortunately, making the decision involves a lot more than simply comparing your monthly rent with the monthly mortgage you'd pay as an owner. A variety of factors must be taken into account, including how long you plan to own the home, how much you think the home will increase in value, or *appreciate*, the tax break you will get for buying, the fees you'll have to pay when you buy, and the rate of return you think you could earn by investing the cash you

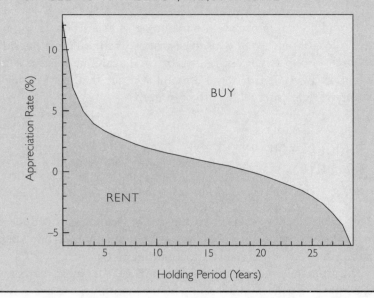

Figure 7-1
THE BUY VS. RENT DECISION

Deciding whether to rent or buy a home can be a complicated and confusing process. In the end, it pays to sit down and consider all the variables that enter into the decision. Let's say you're thinking of buying a $100,000 home. The down payment on the home is $10,000, the interest rate on the mortgage is 8%, and the opportunity cost is 6%. You're currently paying $800 a month in rent. Does it make sense for you to buy a home, or should you just go on renting?

The following graphs may help you to get a feeling of whether you should rent or buy. Here's what to do: Estimate how much the price of the home

SINGLE PURCHASING $100,000 HOME

would save by *not* buying (this is called your **opportunity cost**). (Of course, plenty of emotional factors go into this decision too, but I'll leave those for you to think about.) In all, more than a dozen different financial factors affect the rent-versus-buy decision. You can get a rough idea of what to do by looking at the two graphs in Figure 7-1. Also consider these tips:

you want to purchase will rise each year (the appreciation rate). Next, estimate how many years you will own the home. Select the graph that matches your marital status, and make a dot corresponding to your estimated appreciation rate and estimated holding period. If your dot is above the line, you should buy. If your dot is below the line, you should rent.

Keep in mind that if the assumptions we started with in this example do not fit your own situation, these graphs may not be applicable to you. When you're making your own buy/rent decisions, you might want to check out the simple online calculator at Financenter (www.financenter.com). If you have access to a computer with a Lotus-compatible spreadsheet program, you may also want to look at a program called BUY-RENT.WK1, which you can download online at members.xoom.com/echang80/buyrent.htm.

COUPLE PURCHASING $100,000 HOME

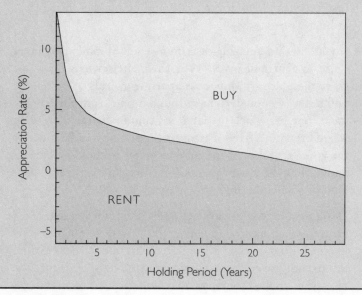

- **If you can't see yourself in the same place for several years, you should probably rent.** Like I said, there are many financial factors (more than a dozen) that can determine whether it makes sense for you to buy or rent. One very important factor is the thousands of dollars in upfront fees you'll pay when you purchase a home. These charges are called **closing costs** because they're paid when you close the deal and sign the final paperwork on a new home. Then, when you sell your home, you can expect to pay thousands more to a real estate broker. If you remain in your new home for many years, these costs won't make much difference, at least in theory; the hope is that your home's selling price will increase by more than enough to cover them. But if you move after a couple of years and your home's value did not appreciate significantly, you may not be able to sell your home for a profit that would cover these costs. In general, our lives change so much when we're in our twenties and thirties that buying is not always smart. This is important to keep in mind. I know many people who purchased studio apartments when they graduated from college and then two or three years later got married and had to sell their places at huge losses.

- **If you have an amazing deal on a rental, it may make more sense to rent and invest your savings elsewhere.** In some cities there are still low-cost apartment deals to be had. If you're lucky enough to have found a **rent-controlled apartment** (one for which the landlord cannot charge more than a fixed rent and fixed increases) that is substantially below the going rental rate, you may be better off holding on to it and putting the money you save in your company retirement plan or some other investment.

- **Don't assume you always get a tax break for buying.** Most of us have at least one relative who prattles on about how buying a home is the best tax break around. That's because the federal government allows homeowners to deduct the mortgage interest they pay, meaning they get to subtract it from their taxable income. If you're buying a low-priced home, however, the tax break may be worth very little.

Consider this example. Say you paid $10,000 in mortgage interest in a year and had an income of $50,000. You would be able to subtract, or *deduct,* the $10,000 worth of interest and bring your taxable income down to $40,000. Assuming your tax rate is 33%, that would translate into a savings of $3,300. But if you got a very small mortgage, you may not get a tax benefit at all. That's because all taxpayers (whether they own a home or not) get a break known as the **standard deduction.** In 2000, the standard deduction is $4,400 for single taxpayers and $7,350 for married taxpayers filing joint returns.

In order to reap a tax advantage from buying, the annual interest you pay on your mortgage (plus other deductions you get) must be *greater* than the standard deduction. If you're buying a low-priced home, this may not be the case. If you don't qualify for a tax break, there's much less of an incentive for you to buy. (For details on other tax breaks that homeowners can receive, see Chapter 9.)

WHAT LENDERS LOOK FOR

The first question most prospective homebuyers ask is, What price home can I afford? The answer, to a great extent, depends on how big a **mortgage** you can obtain. A mortgage is a loan you use to pay for a home. It is said to be "secured" by your home, meaning if you don't pay it back, the lender can take your home. To determine if you can responsibly handle a mortgage and, if so, what size mortgage you qualify for, lenders look at many different aspects of your financial life, including all of the following:

- **Your credit record.** Buyers who don't have a good credit report can find it hard to qualify for a mortgage. Lenders these days are especially concerned with whether you have a history of paying back your loans. To find this out, they will get a copy of your credit report, which is the long-term record of your financial behavior. (See Chapter 3 for details on credit reports.) If you've defaulted on a loan in recent years, been 60 days late on a loan or bill payment within the last two years, or been repeatedly late by 30 days during that time, you may have trouble getting a bank to give you a mortgage.

- **Your ability to come up with the cash.** Generally speaking, lenders will not give you a loan for the full purchase price of a home. They require you to contribute some of your own money up front; this money is called a **down payment.** Lenders tend to require a down payment of 3% to 20% of the price of the home, and coming up with this money is one of the main obstacles for first-time homebuyers. But there are ways around this problem. Many lenders let you use a gift from relatives to cover part or all of the down payment. (And as I'll discuss later on, some lenders do not require any down payment at all.)

  The typical homebuyer also has to pay about 1% to 4% of a home's price in closing costs, which include fees for inspections, appraisals, title insurance, credit checks, land surveys, and legal services. This can add thousands of dollars to the cost of your home. Also, some lenders want buyers to have two to three months' mortgage payments saved up in reserve.

- **Your income.** Lenders want to make sure you earn enough to pay the costs of owning a home. To do this they compare your future monthly housing costs (also known as your **PITI,** which stands for Principal, Interest, property Taxes, and Insurance) to your pre-tax monthly income. The traditional guideline used by lenders is that your PITI costs should not exceed 28% of your pre-tax monthly income. But under special circumstances—if you have a spotless credit history or can pay a very large down payment—lenders may accept PITI costs of up to 42%. (If you buy a condominium or cooperative, the condo or co-op fees are also considered part of the basic monthly housing costs. Thus, the acronym should actually be PITIC.) Figure 7-2 gives you an idea of what price home you can qualify for based on your income.

- **Your debt.** Lenders want to make sure that you aren't already burdened with lots of loans. That's why they look at your current monthly debt commitments, such as auto loan payments, student loan payments, and minimum credit card payments, *plus* your future monthly housing costs, and calculate what portion of your monthly income before taxes will be devoted to these expenses. The percentage they come up with is called your debt-to-income ratio. Lenders like to see a debt-to-income ratio that doesn't exceed 36%, but applicants with especially good credit or high down payments might be accepted with ratios of up to 44%.

- **Your job history.** Lenders like to see that borrowers have a secure job. In general, if you've worked in the same industry for at least two years, they view you more favorably than if you've switched careers during that time.

COSTS OF OWNING A HOME

When you become a homeowner, you will incur a variety of expenses that you may never have even heard of as a renter. Here's a description of each:

- **Principal and interest.** Your monthly mortgage payment consists of two parts: principal and interest. The amount you borrow from the lender is known as the principal. The fee the bank charges to lend you money is called interest, and it is expressed as an annual percentage. Suppose you get a mortgage of $100,000 and you're expected to pay it back over 30 years (that's standard). If the lender charges you an interest rate of 10%, after 30 years you would have paid the lender back the $100,000 in principal plus a total of

Figure 7-2

HOW MUCH HOME CAN YOU BUY?

One of the key factors that will determine how expensive a home you can purchase is your income. To get a ballpark idea of what you can afford, use this table. First, to find out what current home loan interest rates are, call your local bank and ask for the rate on the "fixed, thirty-year mortgage with two points," since that's a typical combination. (For a full discussion of points, see the section on page 202.) Then look in the left column and find your before-tax income. Locate the point where your income and current rate meet. That figure represents the cost of the home you are likely to qualify for.

This table assumes that you have a good job and a good credit report, and that you can make a 10% down payment. It also assumes that 25% of your income is devoted to mortgage payments (principal and interest), 3% to property tax and insurance, and 8% to other debt like student loans.

	INTEREST RATE YOU PAY						
	6%	7%	8%	9%	10%	11%	12%
$20,000	$77,218	$69,587	$63,094	$57,538	$52,755	$48,614	$45,008
30,000	115,828	104,380	94,641	86,307	79,133	72,921	67,513
40,000	154,437	139,174	126,188	115,076	105,510	97,228	90,017
50,000	193,046	173,967	157,736	143,845	131,888	121,535	112,521
75,000	289,569	260,951	236,603	215,767	197,831	182,303	168,782
100,000	386,092	347,934	315,471	287,690	263,775	243,070	225,042
150,000	579,138	521,901	473,207	431,534	395,663	364,605	337,564
200,000	772,183	695,868	630,942	575,379	527,550	486,140	450,085
250,000	965,229	869,835	788,678	719,224	659,438	607,676	562,606
300,000	1,158,275	1,043,803	946,413	863,069	791,325	729,211	675,127

Income (Before Taxes)

Source: National Association of Home Builders, Mortgage Finance Department

$215,926 in interest. (Shocking, isn't it?) In the early years of your loan, you're paying back mostly interest and very little principal. As time goes on, you start to pay back the principal. To soften the blow somewhat, you get to deduct your interest payments if you itemize your taxes. (For a discussion of what this means, see Chapter 9.)

To get a sense of what your monthly mortgage payment would be, check out Figure 7-3.

- **Property tax.** This is an expense you pay to your town, city, or county. It is based on where you live and the official appraised value of your home and the land on which it is built. To get a sense of the property taxes charged for various homes in neighborhoods you're interested in, ask a real estate broker. You can also call the town hall or city hall and ask for the tax assessor's office. One bit of consolation: If you itemize your deductions, you can deduct property taxes. (See Chapter 9 for details.)

- **Insurance.** Most lenders require you to get **homeowners insurance** so that the insurance company will pay the cost of replacing your home if it is destroyed in a disaster, such as a fire. That's because your home is the lender's collateral. If it's completely ruined and you walk away from it (and your loan obligation), the lender is protected by your homeowners insurance. Depending on where you live, you might be required to buy flood insurance also. (For tips on buying insurance, including renters coverage, see Chapter 8.)

  Another type of insurance you might be required to buy if you make a down payment of less than 20% is **private mortgage insurance (PMI)**. PMI protects the lender if you default on your mortgage. Once you've paid off 20% of the loan's principal, many lenders allow you to discontinue PMI coverage. (It's important to ask your lender about this when you obtain your mortgage.) If you obtained your mortgage after July 29, 1999, your lender is legally required to discontinue your PMI obligations once you've paid off 22% of your principal, as long as you have made all your payments on time.

Figure 7-3
GETTING A HANDLE ON YOUR
MONTHLY MORTGAGE PAYMENTS

Based on what you learned from Figure 7-2, locate your house cost in the left-hand column. Now find the current interest rate being charged for thirty-year fixed-rate mortgages. As you can see, you'd have a lower monthly payment with a 20% down payment than with 5% down.

Note that this table includes only principal and interest payments, *not* property taxes, homeowners insurance, or PMI. Use the following rules of thumb to (very roughly) estimate these additional costs: Annual property taxes are typically between 1% to 3% of the cost of your home; PMI amounts to about 0.4% of your mortgage per year; and homeowners insurance can range from $200 to $1,000 a year. These extra costs can vary dramatically depending on where you live and the amount of your mortgage. For more precise estimates, ask a lender or a local real estate agent.

Cost of Home	Down Payment %	$	Monthly Mortgage Payment with Interest Rates of: 6%	8%	10%	12%
$50,000	5%	$ 2,500	$ 285	$ 349	$ 417	$ 489
	10%	5,000	270	330	395	463
	20%	10,000	240	294	351	411
$100,000	5%	5,000	570	697	834	977
	10%	10,000	540	660	790	926
	20%	20,000	480	587	702	823
$150,000	5%	7,500	854	1,046	1,251	1,466
	10%	15,000	809	991	1,185	1,389
	20%	30,000	719	881	1,053	1,234
$200,000	5%	10,000	1,139	1,394	1,667	1,954
	10%	20,000	1,079	1,321	1,580	1,852
	20%	40,000	959	1,174	1,404	1,646
$300,000	5%	15,000	1,709	2,091	2,501	2,932
	10%	30,000	1,619	1,981	2,369	2,777
	20%	60,000	1,439	1,761	2,106	2,469
$400,000	5%	20,000	2,278	2,788	3,335	3,909
	10%	40,000	2,158	2,642	3,159	3,703
	20%	80,000	1,919	2,348	2,808	3,292

Source: Fannie Mae

There are three basic ways you can be charged for PMI. With one type of PMI, you are asked to pay an upfront fee of about 0.5% of the loan amount. (On a $100,000 mortgage, you would pay $500.) After that you are generally charged an annual fee of one-third of 1% per year. With another type of PMI, you don't pay anything up front, but your monthly payment will be higher. With the third kind of PMI, called "single premium" mortgage insurance, you can pay the whole cost up front, either in cash or by adding what you owe to the loan itself.

Many people who take out thirty-year mortgages do not actually expect to keep their homes for that long. That's why you should ask your lender about **lender-paid mortgage insurance (LPMI)**. In LPMI arrangements, the lender pays the mortgage insurance, and you agree to make it up through a higher interest rate. Because the insurance is now absorbed into the mortgage itself, it may be tax-deductible. The downside is that you'll keep paying for your insurance even after the 22% mark, which you would not have to do with regular PMI. But if you are planning to leave your home in less than ten years, that probably won't matter. Ask your lender to run the figures on both scenarios—PMI and LPMI—to see which one is better for you.

- **Condominium and cooperative fees. Condos** and **co-ops** are housing units (usually apartment buildings) that are jointly owned. Each resident owns his or her own unit or apartment, while the common spaces (stairwells, elevators, hallways, lobbies) are owned collectively by all the residents. To pay for the upkeep of these common spaces, residents pay extra fees, known as *maintenance fees* or *common charges*.

  The main difference between a co-op and a condo is the way in which the units are owned. In a co-op, residents do not technically own the apartments; instead they own **shares**, or units of ownership, in the cooperative. The cooperative owns all the units in the building. In order to buy or sell units in a co-op, residents usually must get approval from the

co-op board, which is a group of co-op residents. With a condo, residents have more autonomy; they own their apartments and can usually buy and sell them without getting permission from any board.

SPECIAL MORTGAGE PROGRAMS FOR NEW HOMEBUYERS

Several mortgage options are especially appealing to people in their twenties and thirties. These special loans may not be the first ones offered to you, so make sure you ask your lender if you qualify for any of them.

- **Get a mortgage from your state or local housing agency.** One of the best-kept secrets of home buying is the special mortgage deals offered by state and local housing agencies to first-time homebuyers. The reason you've probably never heard of these programs is that they don't advertise the way banks do. The interest rates on the mortgages offered by these programs tend to be anywhere from one to four percentage points lower than the rates offered by banks. That could mean savings of hundreds of dollars a month on your mortgage payments, and tens of thousands of dollars over the life of your loan. These programs also allow you to make very low down payments, ranging from no money down to 5% of a home's price.

  Details vary from state to state, and many states have a variety of programs to choose from. Typically you can participate in the program if your income is no more than the county or state's median household income and the home you want to purchase costs slightly less than the area's average purchase price. However, some states have low-rate loan programs for buyers whose incomes exceed the state's median income level or who are buying homes that cost more than the local average. For the phone number of your state housing agency, see Figure 7-4. When you call, say that you're a first-time homebuyer looking for a mortgage and ask for a list of lenders that participate in state programs. For more information, check out the Web site of the National Council of State Housing Agencies at www.ncsha.org.

- **Get a "Fannie Mae" or "Freddie Mac" loan.** If you don't qualify for a state-sponsored mortgage, special mortgage programs created by Fannie Mae and Freddie Mac might make it possible for you to afford a home. Fannie Mae and Freddie Mac are two companies that were created by the federal government to help banks and mortgage companies expand their mortgage offerings to all types of borrowers. These companies do not offer loans directly to borrowers; instead, they design new mortgage programs that are offered to consumers by thousands of banks and other lenders across the country.

Lenders often put their own names on these programs. For example, Countrywide Home Loans, a giant mortgage company, offers Fannie and Freddie loans as part of its "House America" program. When you shop around, ask lenders if they participate in Fannie's "Flexible 97" and "Community Home Buyer's Program," or in Freddie's "Affordable Gold" and "Alt 97." They'll know what you mean.

In general, the criteria for qualifying for these Freddie or Fannie mortgages are less strict than they are for traditional mortgages. Your debt can be higher and your income lower than they would ordinarily have to be. Several Fannie and Freddie programs permit down payments as low as 3%, and in some cases they allow you to use gifts from relatives and employers to cover that down payment. Of course, a lower down payment means you'll be taking out a larger loan, which means somewhat higher monthly payments and a bit more interest in the long term. Still, these deals offer help for people who would not otherwise be able to come up with a down payment. (For another angle on low down payment deals, see the box on page 198.)

To participate in most Fannie and Freddie programs, you

Figure 7-4
TELEPHONE NUMBERS OF
STATE HOUSING AGENCIES

Alabama Housing Finance Authority	334-244-9200
Alaska Housing Finance Corporation	907-338-6100
Arizona Department of Commerce	602-280-1365
Arkansas Development Finance Authority	501-682-5900
California Housing Finance Agency	916-322-3991
Colorado Housing and Finance Authority	303-297-2432
Connecticut Housing Finance Authority	860-721-9501
Delaware State Housing Authority	302-739-4263
District of Columbia Housing Finance Agency	202-408-0415
Florida Housing Finance Corporation	850-488-4197
Georgia Department of Community Affairs	404-679-4840
Hawaii Housing Community and Development Corporation	808-587-0567
Idaho Housing Finance Association	208-331-4883
Illinois Housing Development Authority	312-836-5200
Indiana Housing Finance Authority	317-232-7777
Iowa Finance Authority	515-242-4990
Kansas Department of Commerce and Housing	785-296-5865
Kentucky Housing Corporation	502-564-7630
Louisiana Housing Finance Agency	225-342-1320
Maine State Housing Authority	207-626-4600
Maryland Community Development Administration	410-514-7400
Massachusetts Housing Finance Agency	617-854-1020
Michigan State Housing Development Authority	517-373-8370
Minnesota Housing Finance Agency	651-296-7608

Mississippi Home Corporation	601-718-4612
Missouri Housing Development Commission	816-759-6600
Montana Board of Housing	406-444-3040
Nebraska Investment Finance Authority	402-434-3900
Nevada Housing Division	702-687-4258
New Hampshire Housing Finance Authority	603-472-8623
New Jersey Housing and Mortgage Finance Agency	800-654-6873
New Mexico Mortgage Finance Authority	505-843-6880
State of New York Mortgage Agency	800-382-4663
North Carolina Housing Finance Agency	919-877-5700
North Dakota Housing Finance Agency	701-328-8080
Ohio Housing Finance Agency	614-466-7970
Oklahoma Housing Finance Agency	405-848-1144
Oregon Housing and Community Services Department	503-986-2015
Pennsylvania Housing Finance Agency	717-780-3800
Rhode Island Housing and Mortgage Finance Corporation	401-751-5566
South Carolina Housing Finance and Development Authority	803-734-2000
South Dakota Housing Development Authority	605-773-3181
Tennessee Housing Development Agency	615-741-4968
Texas Department of Housing and Community Affairs	512-475-2120
Utah Housing Finance Agency	801-521-6950
Vermont Housing Finance Agency	802-864-5743
Virginia Housing Development Authority	804-782-1986
Washington State Housing Finance Commission	206-464-7139
West Virginia Housing Development Fund	304-345-6475
Wisconsin Housing and Economic Development Authority	608-266-7884
Wyoming Community Development Authority	307-265-0603

Source: National Council of State Housing Agencies

must have a good credit record. If you've been habitually late
paying back student loans or credit card bills in the last two
years, you may not be eligible. Also, many Fannie and Freddie
programs have income limits, so if you earn an above-average
salary, you may not be able to participate in them. But some
programs, like Fannie's "Flexible 97," currently have no
income limit. In 2000, the maximum loan you can get from
any Fannie or Freddie program is $252,700. (In Alaska and
Hawaii, the maximums are 50% higher.) For more details
about these programs, call Fannie Mae at 800-832-2345
(www.fanniemae.com) or Freddie Mac at 800-FREDDIE
(www.freddiemac.com). For a free copy of Fannie's publication *Opening the Door to a Home of Your Own,* call 800-
688-HOME.

- **Get help through the Federal Housing Administration.** FHA
  mortgages are loans made by banks and mortgage companies, and they are insured by the federal government. The
  insurance protects the lender in case the borrower defaults.
  With FHA loans, your debt can be higher and your income
  lower than with traditional mortgages. The FHA requires
  only a 3% down payment, and your credit record does not
  have to be flawless.

  One drawback to FHA loans is that the total cost can be
  higher than the cost of a Fannie or Freddie loan because the
  cost of federal mortgage insurance is somewhat higher than
  the cost of private mortgage insurance. But if an FHA loan
  is the only kind of mortgage you can qualify for, the additional cost may be a worthwhile expense.

  There are no maximum income limits on FHA borrowers.
  Maximum loan amounts vary from city to city. In high-cost
  areas like San Francisco and New York City, the maximum
  loan you can get through the FHA in 2000 is $208,800. In
  other areas the maximums are lower. For more information,
  contact a lender or your local U.S. Housing and Urban
  Development office (which you can find through its Web
  site, www.hud.gov).

- **Get assistance from the Department of Veterans Affairs.**
  Veterans Affairs (VA) mortgages are made by lenders—
  mostly mortgage companies—and are partially guaranteed
  by the Department of Veterans Affairs. These loans generally do not require any down payment at all, although in
  some cases the lender may require one. You pay a one-time
  charge called a **funding fee,** which covers mortgage insurance. As of 2000, the funding fee ranges from 0.5% to 3%
  of the mortgage, depending on the terms of your loan.

  Eligibility is limited to people who have at some point
  enlisted in active duty or who have served at least six years
  in the Selected Reserves or the National Guard. The maximum VA loan amount is $203,000. There are no maximum
  income limits on applicants for these loans. For more information call 800-827-1000 (www.va.gov).

IF YOU DON'T QUALIFY FOR SPECIAL PROGRAMS

Because of income limits or credit history or your inability to come
up with even a 3% down payment, you may not be able to qualify
for the programs I've mentioned so far. Here are some tips for finding a mortgage on your own.

If Your Problem Is the Down Payment

If you don't qualify for low down payment programs, you still have
some options. Here are some ideas to consider with caution:

- **Get the down payment (or part of it) as a gift.** About one in
  four first-time homebuyers receive money from friends or
  relatives to cover their down payment. Some lenders require
  that your down payment consist at least partially of your
  own money. Others permit the entire down payment to come
  from a gift. Some lenders require that the gift come from a

relative; others allow it to come from friends. In most cases, lenders require a letter from the generous friend or relative stating that the down payment money is a gift, not a loan.

Keep careful records if you receive a cash gift. Lenders want to be able to verify that the portion of the down payment that you claim is from a gift is not, in fact, a loan. Some will review your bank records before granting your loan. If they see that a large sum of money was deposited in your account a few months before you tried to get a mortgage, they'll ask you to prove that the money is not a loan. Make copies of any large gift checks you receive (like wedding gifts, for instance). Also, if you sell something valuable (like a car), keep a receipt of the transaction.

- **Look into pledged asset mortgages.** A few banks and brokerage firms will lend you 100% of the cost of a home (meaning you don't have to make a down payment) if your relative will put 20% to 30% of the loan amount into the institution's investments. These loan programs are known as **pledged asset mortgages (PAMs)** because they allow relatives to use their assets as collateral for your mortgage. A PAM makes sense only if it enables your relative to make a worthwhile investment.

- **Borrow money from your 401(k) plan.** Most large companies allow employees to borrow for a first-time home purchase. Your bank will allow you to do this, and it will treat the 401(k) money as your own savings. The bad news is that because this money is a loan, it will increase your debt-to-income ratio. What's more, you will lose out on years of tax-deferred compounding. If you have other options, try them first. (For details on borrowing from a 401(k), see Chapter 6.)

- **Tap into your IRA.** Thanks to recent changes in the law, you can now withdraw up to $10,000 from your IRA to pay for a "first-time" home purchase without paying the usual 10% penalty. That $10,000 is a lifetime limit, and you don't have to use it all up at once; you can spread it out over several home purchases. (To qualify as a "first-time" homebuyer, you don't actually have to be buying a home for the first time; you just can't have owned a home within the past two years.) But there are serious disadvantages to making this kind of withdrawal. You will have to pay tax on the money you withdraw if you have a traditional IRA, though not if you have a Roth IRA that's at least five years old. More serious, IRA withdrawals—unlike loans from a 401(k)—can never be paid back. Because of the miracle of compounding, money in your retirement account is worth more than your other savings. Think twice before you give up that advantage.

- **Start saving.** Okay, so this is an obvious one. But you should run, not walk, to sign up for an automatic savings program. If you save regularly, your down payment will accumulate sooner than you think.

If Your Problem Is Your Tainted Credit History

If your problematic credit record is a barrier, try these options:

- **Find a lender that will overlook your checkered past.** Most lenders require you to have a good credit record (generally meaning no payments 60 days or more past due and not more than one or two payments 30 days past due) for at least a year to qualify for a standard mortgage. If you've messed up in the past by being late on student loan or credit card payments, the best thing you can do once you're on track is to stay timely for at least a year. Some lenders will overlook an occasional late payment if you can prove that you've made timely rental payments for at least a year or you have been in the same line of work for at least two years. If you absolutely can't wait that long to buy a home, you may want to consider what is called a **sub-prime mortgage,** although I don't recommend it. These special mortgages usually require down payments of 20% to 30% (though some lenders allow

A DRAWBACK TO LOW DOWN PAYMENTS

Low down payment mortgages are appealing for people who don't have much money saved up. The danger is that they can tempt you into buying a more expensive house than you can really afford.

Here's an example. Say you have $10,000 saved up for a down payment. In today's market, you could use that money to make a 10% down payment on a $100,000 home, or you could stretch yourself thin and put a 5% down payment on a $200,000 home.

The first problem, of course, is that your monthly payments will be much higher for the more expensive home. Assuming an 8% interest rate on a thirty-year mortgage, you'd pay about $660 a month for the $100,000 home, versus about $1,395 for the $200,000 home. That kind of difference can bust your budget pretty fast.

A less obvious problem is that low down payments can make you more vulnerable if home prices fall suddenly.

down payments of as low as 5%). Most have interest rates that are one to two percentage points higher than the rates on standard mortgages. If you have no choice but to pursue a sub-prime loan, shop around for the best loan you can find. Look into Fannie Mae's "Timely Payment Rewards Program," which offers better rates for credit-impaired lenders than most other sub-prime lenders. Also, consider companies that offer "credit repair" mortgages; these loans hit you with sub-prime interest rates for the first two or three years, then convert to a lower rate if your credit history has improved.

Suppose you buy the $100,000 home, and real estate prices suddenly dive 6%. Your home is now worth $94,000. Since you paid a $10,000 down payment, you have a mortgage of $90,000. If you were forced to sell the house today, for $94,000, you could pay off your $90,000 mortgage and walk away with $4,000 of your original down payment—a $6,000 loss. Bad news, but not devastating.

But what if you own the $200,000 home? If you've paid a $10,000 down payment, then you have a $190,000 mortgage. After the 6% drop in real estate prices, your home is now worth $188,000. In other words, you actually owe the bank $2,000 more than the home is worth. And if you had to sell the house today, you'd take a total loss of $12,000—losing your entire down payment and an additional $2,000.

So while low down payment mortgages can make home buying more affordable, don't let them make you greedy for possessions beyond your means. You could end up regretting it for a long time.

- **Consider hiring a mortgage broker.** Mortgage brokers are people who shop for a mortgage for you. Some specialize in getting mortgages for people who have trouble qualifying because of a problematic credit report or lack of credit history. Because people with shaky financial pasts are considered riskier than those with good credit records, the interest rates on these mortgages can be higher—by two percentage points or more—than the standard rates. But be careful. There are a lot of shady operators who promise to get you a mortgage in exchange for a hefty fee. Before you sign up, find out exactly what you'll be charged for the service. To find a reliable broker, ask friends and relatives for referrals. To ensure that a broker is reputable, check with your state banking department or your local mortgage brokers association. You can also search the Web site of the National Association of Mortgage Brokers (www.namb.org) to find an approved broker in your area.

If Your Problem Is Your Income

If you have a stellar credit record but don't earn enough to qualify for the mortgage you want, look for a lender that is willing to consider other aspects of your financial life. Increasingly, lenders are more flexible with borrowers who have good credit histories. If, for instance, the monthly housing costs of a home you're interested in exceed 28% of your monthly income, your lender may give you some leeway. If you can show that you have been able to handle a monthly rent of, say, 35% or more of your income, the lender might approve your mortgage application.

SHOPPING FOR A MORTGAGE

If you were shopping for a video camera or a car, you wouldn't dream of buying the first one you saw. This should be true when you shop for a mortgage as well. If you're able to lower your interest rate by just half a percentage point, you'll save thousands of dollars over the life of the loan.

You can get a mortgage from several different types of lending institutions. One option is a bank. Credit unions also offer mortgages. Then there are mortgage companies—financial institutions whose only business is granting mortgages. There are no overwhelming advantages to dealing with one type of lending institution over another. Your best bet is to compare the offerings of several different kinds of lenders. (That can take a bit of work, but the Internet can offer substantial help.) This section will highlight what you need to look for—and look out for—when shopping for a mortgage.

Fixed Rate Versus Adjustable Rate

All lenders offer two basic types of mortgages. The most common type is a **fixed-rate mortgage,** which is usually paid back over thirty years. (Your parents probably have this type of mortgage.) A thirty-year fixed-rate mortgage has an interest rate that stays the same over the thirty years you repay it, so the monthly mortgage payment stays the same for the entire thirty years.

The other general type of mortgage is the **adjustable-rate mortgage (ARM)** sometimes known as a variable-rate mortgage. The interest rate on an ARM changes based on what happens to interest rates in the economy. If rates go down, your ARM interest rate decreases, and so does your monthly payment. If rates go up, your interest rate and monthly payments rise. With most ARMs, the lender raises or lowers the interest rate only once a year. And most lenders guarantee that they will not increase (or decrease) an ARM's, interest rate more than two percentage points per year and six percentage points over the life of the loan.

Unfortunately, there isn't an easy answer about which kind of mortgage you should opt for. Your choice will depend on your financial situation and your temperament. It will also depend on one factor that no one can predict: the way interest rates will change in the future.

ARMs are especially appealing to first-time homebuyers because their *initial* interest rate is lower than the rates on fixed-rate mortgages, and sometimes substantially lower. In 1995, for example, the average thirty-year fixed-rate loan charged an interest rate of 7.4%, while the average ARM charged an initial rate of just 5.6%. This lower initial rate can mean lower monthly payments for the first couple of years of the ARM. Because ARMs have lower monthly payments at the beginning, they can be easier to qualify for than fixed-rate mortgages. With an ARM, you could do extremely well if interest rates in the economy do not rise. If rates increase, however, the total cost of the ARM could exceed the cost of the fixed-rate loan. (For tips on evaluating ARMs, see the box on page 204.)

The benefit of fixed-rate mortgages is that your monthly payments will be steady forever. Some people rest easier knowing that their mortgage payments will always be the same. And if you lock in a low rate, you could save hundreds of dollars over what you would pay with an ARM. Even if interest rates in the general economy do take a nosedive, people with fixed rates are not stuck with their deals. Lenders allow borrowers to "refinance"—that is, pay off a mortgage with a new one at a lower rate.

There are many variations on these two basic mortgage types. For example, some special mortgages charge a fixed interest rate for five years and then adjust at the end of the fifth year based on prevailing interest rates. From then on, the loan adjusts annually. This is called a 5-1 mortgage. There are also 1-1, 3-1, 7-1, and 10-1 mortgages. Another hybrid is the 5-25 loan, which is fixed for five years and then adjusts just once to a fixed-rate loan for the remaining 25 years. There's also a 7-23 mortgage. Since the initial rates on these loans will be lower than the rates on thirty-year fixed-rate mortgages, they can be very appealing if you know you will want to sell your home before the loan starts adjusting. But watch out: It's difficult to be absolutely certain today that you'll move in five, seven, or ten years. If you end up staying longer, you may be hit with a big jump in your monthly payments if interest rates have risen by the time your rate adjusts. No matter what type of mortgage you get, read all the provisions extremely carefully to make sure you know exactly what you're committing yourself to.

Rates Versus Points

The most important factors contributing to the cost of a mortgage are the interest rate and the **points.** As you know, the interest rate is the fee, expressed as a percentage of your loan, charged by the bank for lending you money. Points are another type of fee a bank gets for lending you money. Unlike interest, which is paid regularly for the life of the loan, points are paid only once, at the time you close the deal. Points are part of your closing costs. One point equals 1% of the loan. So one point on a $100,000 loan equals $1,000.

Lenders offer various combinations of rates and points. This is true not only from bank to bank, but also within one bank. In general, if you pay more points, you'll pay a lower interest rate. If you pay fewer points, you'll get a higher interest rate.

What combination should you look for? That's determined by how long you plan to live in your home. If you're going to be in your home for many years, it often makes sense to pay more points and get a lower interest rate. The lower monthly payments you'll get with a lower rate will more than make up for the few thousand dollars you paid in points. If you don't plan to stay in your new home for very long, it makes sense to pay fewer points. Of course, if you're low on cash, your only option may be to go with as few points as possible. But if you plan to live in your new home for a long time, you'll ultimately end up paying more.

No matter which rate/point combination you choose, you will want to go with the lender that offers you the most attractive deal. To make it easier for you to shop, the federal government requires lenders to tell you a mortgage's **annual percentage rate (APR)**. The APR is what you'd get if you took most of the charges you're paying on the mortgage (including the interest, points, private mortgage insurance, and certain fees) and expressed them as an annual interest rate. To help you comparison shop, you can compare APRs of the same types of loans. For instance, you can ask each lender for the APR on a thirty-year fixed-rate mortgage for a specific loan amount. Although this is basically a good way to comparison shop, it isn't perfect. That's because the APR doesn't take into account a host of other charges, such as appraisal and document preparation fees. What's more, the APR can be affected by a lender's specific policies. For instance, *refundable* application fees are taken into account when calculating the APR, but *nonrefundable* application fees are not. So in addition to asking for the APR, ask each lender for a list of fees that are not included in the APR. Also, if you're interested in an adjustable-rate mortgage, don't rely on the APR alone; essential factors such as margins and caps are

IF YOU'RE THINKING ABOUT GETTING AN ADJUSTABLE-RATE MORTGAGE

When Nicole and Jimmy found their dream house, they were thrilled to find a lender offering an adjustable-rate mortgage (ARM) with an initial rate of 5%. They assumed that if interest rates in the economy held steady, their rate would remain the same. Unfortunately, that's not the way it always works. In fact, even if interest rates fell slightly, their ARM rate would *increase* to 7% the next year. Here's what Nicole, Jimmy, and all prospective ARM customers need to know:

- **The benchmark the ARM rate is pegged to.** Your ARM's rate fluctuates based on ridiculously named benchmarks like the "One-Year Treasury Constant Maturity" and the "11th District Cost of Funds." Know which one your ARM is tied to.
- **The teaser rate.** Sometimes a lender will offer you an extremely low initial interest rate for the first year. Don't let this rate fool you. In the case of Nicole and Jimmy, 5% was a teaser rate. Their ARM was pegged to the One-Year Treasury

not taken into account when calculating the APR. (For details on finding the best deals, see the section "Making the Process Go Smoothly.")

Fifteen-Year Versus Thirty-Year Mortgages

By far the most common type of mortgage is a fixed-rate loan that lasts for thirty years. Another type of mortgage you might consider

Constant Maturity, which was 5.75% when they got their loan. When their ARM adjusts for the first time, the new rate they pay will be based on the current rate of the One-Year Treasury benchmark plus a fixed number of percentage points (typically three) called a **margin.**

- **The cap.** The annual cap is the maximum amount an ARM rate can increase in any one year. Nicole and Jimmy's ARM has an annual cap of two percentage points. Here's why the cap protects them somewhat. If the One-Year Treasury benchmark falls to 5.25% at adjustment time, the lender will add three percentage points to it, resulting in a new rate of 8.25%. Since their ARM has an annual cap of two percentage points, the lender will increase their rate to just 7% (the 5% current rate plus the two percentage point cap). In year three, if the Treasury benchmark stays at 5.25%, the lender will raise their 7% rate to 8.25% (that's 5.25% plus the 3 percentage point margin). In addition to an annual cap, look for an ARM with a lifetime cap of five or six percentage points. That way you'll know exactly how bad it can get.

is a fifteen-year fixed-rate mortgage. This type of loan is more difficult to qualify for than a thirty-year mortgage, and it often has a lower interest rate than a thirty-year fixed-rate mortgage. Since you pay it off in fifteen years rather than thirty, you're able to build up **equity,** or ownership, in the home sooner. Although some people view a fifteen-year mortgage as a disciplined way to pay off their home loans faster, it's not always the best choice. The monthly payments on a fifteen-year mortgage are higher than those on a thirty-year loan. Depending on your situation, it may make more sense to go with the lower monthly payments of a thirty-year loan and use the cash you're not pouring into your home for other investments. For example, you may be better off putting the money in a 401(k) in which your employer matches your contributions. Also, instead of locking yourself into the higher monthly payment of a fifteen-year mortgage, you may want to get a thirty-year loan that allows you to pay it off faster when you want to. For that reason, get a mortgage that does not include **prepayment penalties,** which are fees for paying off your loan early.

Two Mortgages to Avoid

One type of mortgage you probably should stay away from is the **graduated-payment loan.** Although this type of mortgage looks appealing, particularly to young people, it can be dangerous. With a graduated loan you do not pay all the interest you owe each month; instead, the unpaid interest is added to the unpaid balance of your mortgage. This is attractive because it keeps your monthly payments very low in the early years. Of course, that's because you're not paying off all your interest and you're not paying off any principal—you're just building up more debt. (This process is known as **negative amortization.**) Your monthly payments will gradually increase. Eventually you will end up paying the full interest due each month. At that point you will be deeper in debt than when you first got the mortgage. And if for some reason you have to sell your home at that time, you could find yourself in big trouble.

Another type of mortgage to avoid is a **balloon mortgage.** The way it works is that you make small monthly payments for a fixed number of years—anywhere from one to seven—and then you're required to pay off the remainder of the loan in one large payment. People sometimes opt for balloon mortgages if they plan to sell their home in a few years, or anticipate that they will be getting a chunk of cash—such as an inheritance—before the loan comes due. But if something goes wrong and you can't make the final balloon payment, you could default on the loan if you aren't able to refinance with a lower-rate loan.

MAKING THE PROCESS
GO SMOOTHLY

If you've gotten this far in the chapter, you have a good basic understanding of what you need to know to get a mortgage. When you're
actually ready to begin your search, you're likely to encounter some
hassles. Here are some tips to make your mortgage search as painless as possible:

- **Before you do anything, get a copy of your credit report.**
  Even if you've never been late on a payment, you should do
  this. (See Chapter 3 for details on how.) Credit reporting
  agencies are notorious for making mistakes.

- **Before you start house hunting, call your local bank or mortgage company and say you want to get "prequalified" for a
  mortgage.** Prequalification is a way for lenders to give
  prospective buyers a sense of whether they can qualify for a
  mortgage and, if so, how large a mortgage they can get.
  Prequalification does not mean you have a guarantee of a
  mortgage from the lender. It's an informational service that
  gives you a lender's firsthand impression of what you can
  afford. A growing number of lenders are willing to provide
  this service over the telephone, and some companies with
  Web sites allow you to prequalify online. For a list of personal information you need to have handy when you call,
  see Figure 7-5.

- **Shop around.** There are services that can help you with your
  mortgage shopping. One outfit is HSH Associates. HSH surveys more than 2,000 lenders in 125 major cities and publishes a weekly list of the best deals. To get a copy of the
  latest list, call 800-UPDATES. You'll get the names of about
  five dozen lenders in your area for $20. Some of the listings
  are available for free online at www.hsh.com. Also check the
  local newspapers, which often print weekly listings of mortgage rates.

Figure 7-5
INFORMATION YOU NEED IN ORDER TO APPLY FOR MORTGAGE PREQUALIFICATION

GENERAL INFORMATION

Name and co-borrowers' names	Number of children
Age	Address
Marital status	Telephone number

INCOME

Employer's name and address	Salary
Job title	Bonuses
Date hired	Average overtime or commissions

ASSETS

Total sums in:

Bank (including savings, checking, money market accounts)	Other investments, including real estate
	Retirement accounts
CDs	Cash-value life insurance
Mutual funds	Automobile, including year bought and current value
Stocks	
Bonds	Gifts expected from friends or relatives

DEBTS

Current balances and monthly payments on:

Credit cards	Car loans
Student loans	Other loans

EXPENSES

Monthly cost of:

Rent	Renters insurance
Utilities	

The Internet also offers great opportunities for mortgage shopping. Sites like LendingTree (www.lendingtree.com), iOwn (www.iown.com), and E-Loan (www.eloan.com) will help you sort through the offerings of dozens of major lenders and find the loan that's best for you. You should also take a look at the financial calculators at Financenter (www.financenter.com), which can help you make decisions on a wide range of mortgage-related issues.

• **Once you've shopped on your own, consider enlisting the help of a mortgage broker.** As mentioned above, mortgage brokers are people who shop for a mortgage for you. Although some deal only with clients who have bad credit records, others offer homebuyers with good credit records another shopping alternative. Brokers can sometimes get you a discount on a mortgage because of their relationship with certain lenders. First you should shop around on your own to find the best deal you can. Then see if a broker can beat it. The broker may charge you (or the lender) a fee for this service—often 1% to 2% of the loan amount. So use a broker only if the mortgage he or she finds you, minus any fee you have to pay, is a better deal than the best mortgage you found on your own. Again, you need to be especially careful that the broker you're dealing with isn't part of a fly-by-night operation. Ask friends and relatives for referrals, and check with your state banking department or your local mortgage brokers association.

• **If you find a lender offering a good deal, consider getting a "preapproved" mortgage.** Although "prequalify" and "preapproval" sound similar, their meanings are very different. Preapproval is a process by which the lender does a thorough analysis of your financial situation and commits to offering you a mortgage before you find a home you want to buy. You will be asked to submit all the necessary paperwork, and the lender will look at your credit report and verify your employment information. (Some lenders let you apply for preapproval over the Internet.) If everything

A WORD ABOUT REAL ESTATE AGENTS

First-time buyers tend to trust real estate agents (also known as real estate brokers) a little too much. An agent's goal is to get you to buy the house or apartment he or she shows you, not to get you a great deal. He or she gets a commission of as much as 6% of the home's selling price from the seller. On a $100,000 house, the agent can make $6,000. And the more you pay, the more he or she gets.

If you live in a state that requires an attorney to be present during the closing, use a lawyer you find on your own—not one recommended by the agent. When you're looking for a mortgage, don't ask the advice of your real estate agent; some mortgage companies offer incentives to real estate brokers who steer business to them.

One final suggestion: Comb your local newspaper's real estate listings (they're usually available online as well) on your own without an agent. If you don't use an agent, you may be able to get the seller to accept a lower price.

checks out, the lender will give you a commitment letter that says you are entitled to a loan. The only major snafu can occur if the bank's appraisers deem the home you choose too high-priced relative to its true value. Otherwise you'll usually be able to sail smoothly through the mortgage process.

Lenders sometimes charge $100 or so for this service, but you should try to dispute it. Once you've done your homework and you're convinced a lender is offering a good mortgage deal, get preapproved. A preapproved loan can even be used as a bargaining chip with a homeowner who is anxious to sell. The seller may be willing to knock the price down a bit when he or she discovers that you have a mortgage commitment, because that means the deal can take place immediately.

- **Find out if you can lock in a rate.** Some lending institutions offer programs that allow you to lock in an interest rate while you shop for a home. Often there is a lock-in fee of 1% of the loan amount you are borrowing, but this money will go toward your closing costs when you close on the deal. Some lenders charge as much as $350 to lock in a rate and won't refund the fee; others do not charge at all. These programs protect you if rates soar. (If rates fall, some lenders will not force you to go with the locked-in rate. Try to find a lender that offers this flexibility.) Before you lock in a rate, you should get preapproved by the lender. Also, before you pay extra for a lock-in loan, find out all the details. Ask how long the lock is good for. It often takes about 30 days to do all the paperwork associated with a home loan, so try to find a minimum 60-day lock.

- **Cozy up to your loan officer (or at least shake his hand).** The process of actually getting your mortgage can be time-consuming and frustrating. You can't just fill out your application and keep your fingers crossed. You have to stay on top of it. The basic rule is, be assertive but polite. Call once a week to see how the process is going, and always ask the name of the person you're speaking with. Try to meet the people working on your loan. This might make them less likely to throw your application into a pile and forget about it. If you get your mortgage from your own bank and you maintain a hefty balance in your accounts (usually at least $3,000), you may be able to get a quarter percentage point off the mortgage interest rate. Ask your loan officer.

FINANCIAL CRAMMING

- If you're about to rent an apartment, read the lease carefully. There may be a condition you don't like, such as a provision that allows your landlord to enter your apartment without your permission or a prohibition against overnight guests. Try to negotiate unwanted conditions out of the lease before you sign.

- If you can't come up with the cash to qualify for a mortgage, don't despair. Try your state's housing agency (see Figure 7-4 for a list of phone numbers). Also, ask your local lender about Fannie Mae, Freddie Mac, and FHA mortgages.

- Before you go hunting for a home to purchase, get "prequalified" for a mortgage by your local bank. Prequalification will not guarantee you a home loan, but it will give you an idea of how large a mortgage you can afford. See Figure 7-5 for the information you'll need to give the bank to get prequalified.

- Check with several banks and mortgage companies before you get a mortgage. Call HSH Associates at 800-UPDATES (www.hsh.com) and request a list of lenders in your area offering good deals (the cost is $20). Also consult local newspapers, which often print weekly listings of mortgage rates, and check out Web sites like LendingTree (www.lendingtree.com), iOwn (www.iown.com), and E-Loan (www.eloan.com). Careful shopping can save you thousands of dollars in the long run.

- If you're considering an adjustable rate mortgage (ARM), make sure you know how high your rate could rise—and how high your monthly payments could go. See page 204 for details.

8

INSURANCE:
WHAT YOU NEED AND
WHAT YOU DON'T

Finding the Right Policies and
Forgoing Coverage You Can
Do Without

YOU MAY NOT KNOW IT, but a quiet revolution has been taking place in the insurance world lately. It used to be that people who needed insurance relied on the wisdom of the insurance agents who sold it to them. The agent would quote a price, and people would accept it without much question. Only the most ambitious customers thought to compare costs and find a cheaper insurance policy than they were being offered.

Now, thanks to consumer awareness—and more recently, to the impact of the Internet—the insurance world is changing. You might still consult with an agent or two, but that's just the first step. If you have Internet access, you can make use of services that will comb through dozens of available policies and help you find a better deal. You may even be able to avoid paying commissions by buying your policy directly from an insurance company.

For most of us, there are still two classes of insurance: insurance we have too much of and insurance we have too little of. Into the first category goes the life insurance policy you were talked into buying when you graduated from college and the credit protection you signed up for when you got your Visa or MasterCard. Into the second group goes the renters insurance you never even thought about purchasing and the health insurance you figure you can get by without. This chapter will help you decide how much protection you should have, if any, in each of the basic categories: health, auto, disability, home, and life. It will alert you to types of policies to avoid, show you how to maximize insurance-related benefits you get from your employer, and offer you advice on how to use the Internet to find the least expensive comprehensive policies.

No matter what type of insurance you think you need, begin by reading the first three sections—"Shopping for Insurance," "Checking Out Credentials," and "Making the Most of Your Employer Plan." Then you can skip around and read only the sections on the type of insurance you need.

SHOPPING FOR INSURANCE

The point of insurance is to protect you and your family from financial loss due to illness, accident, or natural disaster. The charge you pay for all types of insurance is called the **premium.** Remember this term. You'll hear it a lot.

Premiums can vary tremendously from one insurance company to the next. Take the case of auto insurance. Studies have shown that insurers in the same city often sell the same policies at premiums that differ by thousands of dollars. The Illinois Department of Insurance found that a 20-year-old male living on the West Side of Chicago could pay as little as $556 or as much as $5,400 for the same amount of auto liability protection! The point is clear: Shop around before you select any kind of insurance policy.

Before I get into the details of the various types of coverage, here are some general tips that will help you save money when you buy insurance:

- **Get the highest deductible you can afford.** With certain types of coverage—health insurance, home insurance, and some auto insurance—you must pay a fixed dollar amount of the costs yourself before the insurance kicks in. This fixed amount is known as a **deductible.** For example, on a health insurance policy with a $200 annual deductible, you must pay the first $200 worth of medical bills you incur each year with your own money. Any expenses you incur above $200 will be paid, at least in part, by the insurance company.

One way to reduce your premium (there's that term again) is to increase your deductible. For example, say you're a 30-year-old single resident of Los Angeles who purchased a health insurance policy from Blue Shield of California. If you opted for a $250 deductible, you'd pay a premium of $254 a month. If you chose a $1,000 deductible, you'd pay just $107 a month—a 58% decrease in your premium. The same principle applies to renters insurance, homeowners insurance, and auto insurance.

This rule isn't right for everyone, of course. It makes sense to choose a lower premium only if you have enough savings to cover the higher deductible. Also, with a higher deductible you'll end up regularly covering certain costs yourself—for example, routine medical checkups and minor car and home repairs. If you tend to go to the doctor a lot or you're prone to car accidents, a lower deductible might make more sense for you. Otherwise, a higher deductible is probably a smart option.

- **Check with a couple of insurance agents.** There are two categories of agents: **Life and health insurance agents** sell life, health, and disability insurance; **property and casualty insurance agents** sell homeowners, renters, and automobile insurance. An increasing number of companies sell insurance in both categories. In general, insurance agents make their money through commissions, so they're understandably eager to make a sale. But don't be shy about shopping around. If an agent is impatient and doesn't want to answer your questions, find another one. And don't feel obliged to buy from an agent just because he or she did some research for you. That's an agent's job.

In theory, agents known as **independent agents** or brokers shop among a handful of insurance companies to find the best deal for you. In practice, if you don't do your homework, you may end up with the policy that pays the highest commission, or **load,** to the agent. Still, it's certainly worth your time to give one of these agents a call. To find one, ask relatives and friends for recommendations. Another type of agent, known as a **captive agent,** tends to sell only the products of one particular company. Why, you may wonder, would you ever go to a captive agent? Well, sometimes the companies they sell for offer very attractive policies. Find the section on the kind of insurance you need for the names and numbers of some captive agents to consider.

- **Contact companies that sell directly to consumers.** There are some insurance companies that sell directly to consumers rather than through agents. These firms can often charge less because they don't have to pay the salaries and expenses for hundreds of agents. The service reps who answer the phones at these companies may not be able to advise you on what to buy, but they can answer basic questions. If you have confidence in your ability to choose a policy (and you should, after you read this chapter), get a price quote from such a firm, typically known as a **low-load** or **direct response** company. See the section on the type of insurance you're looking for to get names and numbers of companies that sell direct.

- **Consider services that will shop for you.** There are several toll-free phone services and Web sites that will scan their multicompany databases and send you a free list of the least expensive policies. If you purchase a policy through one of these outfits, you pay no more than you would have had you purchased the policy from an insurance agent; these services make their money by keeping the commission the agent would have received. One advantage to these firms is that they have access to many more policies than ordinary insurance agents do. Locate the section on the type of insurance you're interested in to get the names and numbers of the appropriate services to contact.

- **Read *Consumer Reports* magazine.** This independent publication frequently publishes surveys of companies that sell auto, health, homeowners, and life insurance. You can find back copies at your local library, or pay a small fee to access articles on their Web site (www.consumerreports.org). Personal finance magazines like *Kiplinger's* (www.kiplinger .com), *Smart Money* (www.smartmoney.com), and *Money* (www.money.com) also periodically run useful reports on insurance.

AUTO INSURANCE: YOU'D BETTER SHOP AROUND

Lainie, 24, was about to move from New York City to Washington, D.C., and had to purchase auto insurance for her 1995 Ford Taurus. After making just three phone calls to insurance companies, she reaped the rewards of shopping around. She gave each company representative the same information: She wanted a $500 deductible; she had a spotless driving record; she wouldn't be using the car to commute to work; and she would be driving only about 2,000 miles a year. One firm quoted Lainie an annual rate of $1,817. Another firm said it charged $1,448 a year. The third firm quoted her an annual rate of just $1,140. An added bonus: When Lainie mentioned that she was about to turn 25, the agent at the second firm said she should call back a month before her 25th birthday, and she'd get a $350 discount on the annual rate. The third firm also promised a discount, but wouldn't tell her how much. The bottom line: In just 20 minutes Lainie saved more than $700 by comparison shopping.

CHECKING OUT
CREDENTIALS

You're not going to spend your life (or even several days of your life) investigating every detail of a particular insurance company or agent, but it does pay to do some legwork. The following tips can at least help you avoid disaster:

- **If you use an agent, ask about qualifications.** When you're buying life, health, or disability insurance, you may want to look for an agent who has the letters "CLU" after his or her name. This stands for Chartered Life Underwriter. If you're looking for auto or homeowners coverage, the designation to look for is "CPCU" (Chartered Property and Casualty Underwriter). Although these credentials offer no guarantee of good service, they do tell you that the agent has passed tough insurance courses and has a certain amount of basic insurance knowledge.

- **Contact your state insurance department.** Figure 8-1 lists the phone numbers of every state insurance department. You should call to make sure the agent you're dealing with is licensed in your state. Some state insurance departments will tell you whether there have been any complaints filed against an agent. You can also ask if there have been any complaints filed against the insurance company you're considering doing business with.

- **Check on the insurer's financial health.** It's a good idea to do business with a financially sound company. Even though states have "guaranty funds," which are supposed to protect consumers (up to certain limits) if insurance companies go bankrupt, you could wait a long time before you collect on a claim. There are four major rating agencies that judge the safety and soundness of insurance companies: A. M. Best, Duff & Phelps, Moody's, and Standard & Poor's. It doesn't hurt to stick with an insurer that gets high grades from two of these firms. But even then, you won't be guaranteed that a company is sound. For instance, A. M. Best gave one insurer an A+ rating just two weeks before it failed. Nevertheless, you may want to make sure that a company you're interested in hasn't received a really low grade from one of these agencies.

If you're dealing with an agent, ask him or her to send you the ratings and the full reports on the companies whose policies you're interested in. If you're not dealing with an agent, a local library or nearby university library should have the ratings books published by these companies. The following firms will give you at least four ratings on the phone for free: Duff & Phelps (312-368-3157, www.dcrco.com), Moody's (212-553-0377, www.moodys.com/insurance/index), and Standard & Poor's (212-438-2000, www.standardandpoors .com/ratings/insurance). You can also get free information online from A. M. Best (www.ambest.com). When you call, it's essential to ask what each rating means. For example, a company that gets a "B" from Moody's is considered to be in poor financial health.

MAKING THE MOST OF YOUR EMPLOYER PLAN

Many large employers pay most of the health insurance premiums of their employees. And many purchase a fixed amount of life insurance and disability insurance for employees. The type and amount of insurance that employees get varies tremendously from company to company. The best way to learn about your plan is to read the information your employer provides. (I know, I know—this is about as much fun as doing your taxes. But the time you spend will be worth it.) Then make an appointment with whoever is in charge of benefits at your company so you can ask questions about your coverage.

In the health, disability, and life insurance sections below, I've listed specific steps that will help you evaluate your employer's offerings. Meanwhile, here are some general rules to keep in mind:

Figure 8-1
TELEPHONE NUMBERS OF
STATE INSURANCE DEPARTMENTS

Alabama	334-269-3550
Alaska	907-269-7900
Arizona	602-912-8444
Arkansas	501-371-2600
California	916-492-3301
Colorado	303-894-7499
Connecticut	860-297-3800
Delaware	302-739-4251
District of Columbia	202-727-8000
Florida	850-922-3130
Georgia	404-656-2056
Hawaii	808-586-2790
Idaho	208-334-2250
Illinois	217-782-4515
Indiana	317-232-2385
Iowa	515-281-5705
Kansas	785-296-3071
Kentucky	502-564-3630
Louisiana	504-342-5900
Maine	207-624-8475
Maryland	410-468-2000
Massachusetts	617-521-7794
Michigan	517-373-9273
Minnesota	651-296-6848

Mississippi	601-359-3569
Missouri	573-751-2640
Montana	406-444-2040
Nebraska	402-471-2201
Nevada	775-687-4270
New Hampshire	603-271-2261
New Jersey	609-292-5360
New Mexico	505-827-4500
New York	212-480-6400
North Carolina	919-733-7343
North Dakota	701-328-2440
Ohio	614-644-2658
Oklahoma	405-521-2828
Oregon	503-947-7984
Pennsylvania	717-787-5173
Rhode Island	401-222-2223
South Carolina	803-737-6160
South Dakota	605-773-3563
Tennessee	615-741-2241
Texas	512-463-6464
Utah	801-538-3800
Vermont	802-828-3301
Virginia	804-371-9185
Washington	360-753-7301
West Virginia	304-558-3394
Wisconsin	608-266-0102
Wyoming	307-777-7401

Source: Insurance Information Institute

- **If your company has a "flexible benefits plan," make the most of it.** A flexible benefits plan (also known as a **flex plan** or a **cafeteria plan**) is a program that gives employees the opportunity to choose among a variety of benefits. Options often include health insurance, life insurance, and disability insurance. With some flex plans you may also be given a choice of noninsurance benefits, such as extra vacation days, group legal services, or additional employer contributions to a 401(k) plan.

  Under a flex plan the employer gives you a fixed number of "credits" to spend on benefits. You get to decide how to use the credits. For instance, you may opt for a top-of-the-line health insurance plan but forgo life insurance because you don't need it. Or if your spouse has a terrific employer-sponsored health insurance plan that covers you, you could forgo your own company's health insurance and opt for extra disability insurance. These plans can be extremely beneficial if you study your choices carefully and spend your credits wisely.

- **If possible, purchase health insurance on a before-tax basis.** If your employer offers this option, it means that you will not have to pay taxes on the portion of your salary that goes toward your premium. This little perk can save you hundreds of dollars a year.

- **If your company offers a flexible spending account (FSA), use it.** An FSA is a special tax-favored account offered by some employers. Don't let the similar names confuse you: A flexible spending *account* is different from a flexible benefits *plan*. (Clearly, employee benefits personnel could use a little help coming up with more creative names.) An FSA is an account in which you can use a fixed amount of your own money—typically anywhere from $100 to $5,000, taken from your paycheck throughout the year—to pay for specific medical expenses that aren't covered by health insurance. What makes an FSA different from a savings account is that you can put the money into the FSA on a before-tax basis, and that money will never be taxed. FSA money is commonly used to pay for eyeglasses, contact lenses, allergy shots, dental care, prescription drugs, and chiropractic sessions. You can also use the money to pay the deductibles on your medical and dental plans. You can't use FSA money to pay for things like cosmetic surgery, electrolysis, or health club memberships. Rules vary from company to company, so educate yourself before you sign up.

There is one drawback to an FSA: If you don't use the money you put into the account during the year, you'll lose it. That's why you should put in only an amount you're certain you will spend. And if you do find yourself nearing the end of the year with cash in your account, remember to spend it before it's too late.

HEALTH INSURANCE

Everyone should have health insurance. If you're lucky, you're covered through your job. Although you probably have to cover some portion of the annual cost, the amount you pay is much less than what you'd pay if you had to purchase insurance on your own. If you don't have an employer that provides coverage for you—if you freelance, run your own business, work for a small company that doesn't provide insurance, or are unemployed—you're responsible for your own coverage. Because individual coverage is so expensive, it may be tempting to go without it. (One in four people in their twenties do just that.) Don't. If you get into an accident and you're hit with thousands of dollars in medical bills, you could lose every penny you have and find yourself in deep debt.

The Two Basic Types of Health Insurance

The jargon used in the health insurance industry is confusing enough to make anyone feel sick. But you need to learn the essential terms, even if you have group coverage through your employer. The two main types of health insurance are called **indemnity plans** and **managed care plans.**

Indemnity offers freedom at a price. Its main appeal is that it allows you to see any physician you choose. That means you can stick with your current doctor (or choose another) and visit specialists you select when necessary. But indemnity plans are typically expensive. Your employer will probably pay the bulk of your monthly premiums, but you are required to pay an annual deductible that can be anywhere from $100 to $2,500 a year. Once your medical bills exceed the annual deductible, the insurer will start chipping in. Usually the insurer will pay 70% to 80% of your medical expenses that exceed the deductible, and you'll pay the remaining 20% to 30%, known as a **co-payment** (also known sometimes as **co-insurance**). There are often annual caps on the total amount you will have to pay yourself and lifetime ceilings on the amount the insurer will pay for you.

Just a few years ago, indemnity coverage was a standard employee benefit. Today, fewer than 20% of companies offer it. The most common health insurance arrangement these days is managed care, which costs less but can limit your choices. Under managed care, you are given a list of doctors who participate in your plan. This list is called a **network.** If you stick with doctors in your network, your costs will be much lower than if you use a doctor outside the network. Compared to indemnity plans, managed care plans have lower premiums and co-payments (generally $10 per doctor's visit), and may not require any deductible.

There are three main types of managed care programs. The most restrictive type is the **health maintenance organization (HMO).** In an HMO you usually have to get permission from your primary doctor—your "gatekeeper," in industry lingo—if you want to see a specialist. Also, your choice of physicians is limited to your HMO's network. If you prefer to see a specialist outside the network, you'll usually have to foot the whole bill yourself. The benefit of HMOs is their low cost: You won't have to pay any deductible, so your total cost per doctor's visit is usually limited to your $10 co-payment.

With another managed care plan, called a **preferred provider organization (PPO),** you don't need permission from a gatekeeper in order to see a specialist in your network. But this freedom will cost you. Most PPOs require you to pay an out-of-pocket deductible, typically $250, before your coverage kicks in. PPOs also give you the option of seeking treatment outside your network, but you will have to shell out higher co-payments for the privilege. Instead of the flat $10 you'd generally pay for a visit inside the network, you will have to pay 20% to 30% of the total cost of your treatment, up to an established maximum (usually $2,000). One thing to beware of: A few PPOs require 10% to 20% co-payment even for in-network treatment.

The least common kind of health plan is the **point-of-service (POS) plan,** which is a kind of hybrid between HMOs and PPOs. With point-of-service plans, you have a choice: You can save money by staying within your network and going through a gatekeeper when you need special treatment, as with an HMO; or you can go outside the network and pay a deductible (usually $250) and a 30% co-payment (up to a preset ceiling of about $2,000), as with a PPO.

The details of your company's health insurance options may differ somewhat from what I've sketched above, but you can use these descriptions as a general guide.

If Your Employer Offers Health Insurance

Even if your employer does not let you choose your health plan, you'll need to be smart about your coverage. Here are some suggestions:

- **Evaluate your managed care options carefully.** Though managed care plans can be less expensive than indemnity plans, there are some serious trade-offs to consider. You may have to wait several days, if not weeks, to see a specialist. You may find that your doctor is less apt to prescribe expensive lab tests than doctors you have visited in the past. As I mentioned earlier, you may have to get permission from your primary physician before you can see a specialist, like an allergist or dermatologist. And in the case of HMOs, if you want to see an out-of-network physician, you will have to cover all or much of the cost yourself.

Some companies allow employees to choose between an HMO and a PPO or POS plan. If your company offers different plans, speak to a few of your coworkers about their experiences before you make a decision. If you already have a regular doctor, find out if he or she belongs to any of the networks your company offers.

- **Know what is covered by your plan.** Some plans cover everything from therapy sessions to chiropractic adjustments; others cover a more limited range of services. You'll want to know the details. Ask, for example, whether you are covered for prescription drugs. For about six months I didn't know that all I had to do was show my company insurance card at the drugstore to get my prescription medication for just $5. Not too swift.

  You'll also need to understand your plan's reimbursement policies. Many plans cover 70% to 80% of what they consider "reasonable and customary" out-of-network charges. If your doctor charges $100 for a checkup but your plan specifies that $60 is the reasonable and customary charge for a doctor in your area, the plan will reimburse you for $48 (80% of $60), leaving you to pay the remaining $52 yourself. If you know this in advance, you can explain the situation to your doctor and ask for a discount. Some doctors are surprisingly flexible.

- **Ask about waiting periods or exclusions when you start a new job.** If you have any chronic medical problems, known as **preexisting conditions,** find out if your company insurance plan will cover you for these ailments immediately. Some indemnity plans have a waiting period of six months before they cover you. In general, HMOs do not have such a waiting time. If you are transferring from a job where you had health insurance, the waiting period probably will not apply to you, thanks to the Health Insurance Portability and Accountability Act of 1996 (HIPAA).

BEFORE YOU LEAVE YOUR JOB, ASK ABOUT YOUR HEALTH COVERAGE

If you work for an employer with twenty or more employees, in most cases your company must offer you the option of continuing your health coverage for 18 months—whether you're fired or you quit. (Actually, if you're fired for doing something truly heinous, like embezzling company funds, you probably won't be eligible for this extension.) Under the Consolidated Omnibus Budget Reconciliation Act of 1985 (COBRA), your employer must offer you the same health insurance you had as an employee, but you will have to pay for this coverage. The law says the employer can charge you 102% of the cost. (If your employer pays $300 a month to cover you, you will pay $306 a month.) Still, this may be less expensive than the rate you would pay for a policy of your own with the same type of coverage.

- **Find out the cost of covering pregnancy.** If you are considering having a baby, find out about maternity benefits and pediatric care. Many managed care plans offer excellent deals. Usually you get a package that covers the cost of prenatal doctor visits, delivery, hospital stay, and well-baby care for a very small fee. (I know someone who paid just $5 for all her pregnancy needs!) Set up an appointment with your health benefits officer and get the details. Before you sign up for a managed care plan, ask if you (or your partner) can meet with the obstetrician in the HMO.

What to Look For in an Individual Health Policy

If you don't have coverage through a group plan, you'll have to purchase insurance on your own. An individual policy is often expensive, but if you know what you're looking for and do some research, you can find a decent deal. Your goal is to find coverage that will help you pay for a major medical problem. Policies that cover anything more will almost certainly be prohibitively expensive, depending on where you live. You may find it necessary to pay for routine medical services with your own money and rely on your health insurance to protect you only in case of a medical catastrophe.

Of course, you don't want a policy that offers such skimpy protection that it is worthless. Try to find a policy that meets these conditions:

- **It covers at least 80% of your hospital, surgery, and in-hospital doctor bills once you meet the deductible.** Ideally, you'd be able to find a policy that covers 100%, but unfortunately this type of coverage can be prohibitively expensive. With a policy that covers 80% of these costs, you'll have to pay the remaining 20% out of your own pocket. To avoid getting hit with tremendous medical expenses, look for a policy that caps your annual co-payments at $1,000 to $2,000.

- **It has a maximum lifetime benefit of at least $1 million.** A lifetime cap is the dollar limit the insurance company will pay over the course of the policy. Anything substantially less than $1 million isn't enough.

- **It isn't riddled with exclusions and limits.** Some individual policies limit coverage to $25,000 for AIDS or fail to cover preexisting conditions like asthma or recurring knee problems. Others won't cover these ailments for the first year or so of the policy. Pay attention to these kinds of details.

If you had insurance at your last job, you are probably entitled to individual coverage, even if you have developed an illness or condition that would otherwise make you uninsurable. That's because your right to be insured is protected by HIPAA, the Health Insurance Portability and Accountability Act of 1996. For more information about your rights, contact the Department of Labor at 800-998-7542 (www.dol.gov/dol/pwba) and ask for its free booklet *Recent Changes in Health Care Law.* The gist of it is this: As long as there is an insurer in your state that sells individual insurance, you are entitled to **guarantee issue individual coverage (GIIC).** The premiums for GIIC can be very high, but some states will subsidize them. Call your state insurance agency (see Figure 8-1) for more information.

Before You Buy an Individual Health Policy

Depending on your current situation, you may have some alternatives to buying an expensive individual policy. Here are a few to consider:

- **See if you're covered by your parents' plan.** If you're a student, you may still be covered by your parents' policy. Some employer-sponsored plans allow children of employees to be covered until age 26 if the children are still in school. If you're not in school, chances are your coverage has stopped already. If it hasn't, there is a way to extend it. Under federal law, you can continue to receive your parents' coverage for 18 months if your parents make the request soon after they receive notice that your coverage is about to lapse. You will have to pay for this coverage, but the price will probably be less than the price of a similar policy you could get on your own.

- **Join a group plan.** Groups get better deals than individuals. See if there's a professional association, religious organization, or any other group that will offer you coverage. If you're a lawyer, try your local bar association. If you're a real estate or travel agent, call your local trade association. If you're an artist, contact a community artists league. If you're currently doing temp work, look for a temp agency that offers health benefits; some agencies offer employees the chance to purchase group coverage.

• **Get temporary coverage.** If you're out of work but seriously hunting for a job, look into a temporary insurance policy. This type of policy lasts up to six months and can be renewed once. After twelve months you will hopefully have found a job with health benefits. The advantage of these policies is that they are cheap. The disadvantage is that you probably won't be covered for any preexisting conditions. You should also consider a temporary policy if you start a new job and your employer requires you to be with the firm for several months before you receive health insurance.

How to Find an Affordable Individual Health Policy

Unfortunately, locating a low-cost individual health insurance policy isn't easy. Here are some tips that may help you in your search.

• **Consider an HMO.** Only about 25% of HMOs in the country allow individuals to sign up. What's more, the premiums on an individual HMO membership may be higher than those of individual indemnity policies. Still, if you think you'll be needing many visits to the doctor and you like the particular HMO, this is a worthwhile option. To find one, call your state insurance department.

• **Try Blue Cross and Blue Shield.** These are the largest managed care and indemnity providers in the United States. In some states, Blue Cross and Blue Shield companies have open enrollment policies, which means they provide coverage to everyone who applies. As a result, the premiums may be higher; as a young, healthy person you may do better with a company that picks and chooses its customers. Still, it's worth a call to find out about rates, or a visit to their Web site at www.bluecares.com.

- **Contact your state insurance department.** If you have a pre-existing condition that makes it difficult for you to get insurance, call your state insurance department and ask about "high-risk" insurance policies. Some states sponsor such policies. If yours doesn't, it may be able to point you toward a private insurer that does.

- **Ask about special deals for people with good health.** Some insurers and HMOs offer discounts to people with healthy lifestyles. If you're in great shape, ask whether you can get a discount. Keep in mind that smokers pay about twice as much as nonsmokers for health insurance.

- **As a last resort, consider catastrophic coverage.** If you have very little money to spend on health insurance, look into **catastrophic coverage.** This kind of policy charges low monthly premiums in exchange for very high deductibles and out-of-pocket limits. This kind of coverage will protect you from financial ruin if you develop a major illness or get into a serious accident, but it won't do you much good for less serious medical problems.

- **Try these firms for quotes.** InsWeb (www.insweb.com) offers quotes from five of the largest health insurers. You should also call Quotesmith (800-556-9393; www.quotesmith.com), a service that will scan its multicompany database and send you a free list of its least expensive offerings.

AUTO INSURANCE

Auto insurance covers harm done to you, your car, other people, and other people's property. The total amount of coverage you need depends on the health insurance you have, the condition of your car, the value of the assets you must protect in case you're held responsible for an accident, and the rules in your state. Unfortunately, this coverage is especially expensive for young people. Single men under

25 years old often pay two or three times what men over 25 pay; single women under 25 might pay one and a half to two times more than women over 25. For married people, the rates are lower.

Three Basic Auto Coverages

Auto insurance consists of three separate kinds of protection: auto liability coverage, medical payments coverage, and collision and comprehensive coverage. Here's a rundown of each:

- **Auto liability coverage.** If you cause an accident with your car and injure someone or damage something, auto liability insurance will pay your legal expenses and the injured person's medical and repair expenses. Of the three major components of auto insurance, auto liability—which is technically known as **bodily injury liability** and **property damage liability**—can make up more than half of your auto premiums.

  Some states, known as **no-fault states,** require drivers (and their insurance companies) to pay for their own medical costs in a car accident, regardless of who was responsible for the accident. But even if you live in a no-fault state, you still need liability protection. That's because each no-fault state has a threshold above which a person who causes an accident can be sued. For example, in some no-fault states drivers can be sued for causing severe physical injury to other drivers.

  Most states require car owners to purchase some liability protection. You probably should buy more auto liability insurance than your state requires. Even if you don't have many assets, you need liability protection in case a court decides to garnish your future wages. Insurance analysts are hesitant to say what the "right" amount of liability protection is, but when pressed, they offer this as a reasonable guideline: If you don't have much savings and you don't own a home, get coverage of at least $100,000 per person, $300,000 per accident, and $100,000 for property. If you own a home and have some money saved, consider purchasing an umbrella liability policy, which is coverage above and beyond any auto or homeowners liability protection you have. (For details, see the home insurance section.)

- **Medical payments coverage.** This insurance covers your medical and hospital bills (up to a certain dollar amount) if you are injured in a car accident. It also covers the medical and hospital bills (again, up to specific limits) of any passengers in your car. If you live in a no-fault state, you probably will be required to buy a minimum amount of medical payments coverage, typically called **personal-injury protection** or **no-fault insurance.** No-fault insurance covers your medical and hospital bills (and in some states, your loss of income if you're disabled) regardless of who is to blame for an accident.

  If you live in a "fault" state, you're usually not required to purchase medical payments coverage, but you may want to anyway. Accidents in which no one can be proven negligent won't be covered by liability insurance, and liability insurance will not cover your own injuries in accidents that you have caused. If you already have good general health insurance, you won't need medical payments insurance to cover your own medical bills, but you may still want to consider purchasing it if you often have passengers in your car.

- **Collision and comprehensive coverage.** Collision insurance pays for damage to your car if it bangs into something, like a tree or your garage door or another car. Comprehensive insurance covers damage caused by fire, flood, theft, tornado, and just about any other physical damage that's not covered by collision. In all states, both of these coverages are optional. However, if you took out a loan to buy your car or if you're leasing, the lender or dealer will require that you purchase collision and comprehensive coverage.

  The maximum amount an insurance company will pay under a collision or comprehensive policy is, at least in theory, the cost of replacing the automobile with a comparable

used car. (Unfortunately, some insurers aren't this generous.) After your car is about five years old or you've paid
off your loan, you may want to consider dropping your collision and comprehensive coverage. To determine whether
it makes sense for you to continue your collision and comprehensive coverage, consider the value of your car minus
the deductible. Compare the answer to your annual premium. You can find information on the current value of
your car at the Kelley Blue Book Web site (www.kbb.com).

An additional type of insurance you may decide to purchase is
uninsured motorists coverage. This coverage, which is required in
some states, protects you if an uninsured driver crashes into your
car and you're injured. You may also want to consider getting **under-
insured motorists coverage,** which will protect you if the driver who
crashes into your car has some, but not enough, insurance to cover
your costs.

If You Rent a Car, Cover Your Assets

One type of coverage you'll want to have when you rent a car is liability protection. If you own an automobile, your standard auto liability coverage may cover you when you rent a car. Check to make

---

BABY, YOU CAN'T DRIVE MY CAR

It may seem like no big deal, but when someone asks to borrow your car, you should think twice before you say yes. If you
permit someone to drive your car and he or she has an accident, *your* insurer is likely to pay for the damage (less any
deductible you have to pay). That means your insurance company could raise your premium just as if you had caused the
accident.

sure this is the case. If you don't own a car but you do rent cars, purchase car renter's liability insurance at the car rental counter. If you rent often, it may be cheaper to purchase a car renter's liability policy from an insurance company.

How to Reduce Your Auto Insurance Costs

Your premiums are based on factors such as your age, where you live, the type of car you drive, your gender, your driving record, and how much driving you do. The following suggestions can reduce your premiums by as much as 25%:

- **Drive safely.** Some insurance companies charge less for drivers who have no violations or accidents. If you have a clean record, point it out when you are pricing policies.

- **Don't drive much.** Some insurance companies charge less if you drive less. For instance, one major insurer charges lower premiums for customers who commute fewer than 30 miles a week. If you join a car pool or start taking public transportation, alert your agent.

- **Choose your car carefully.** Certain types of cars are harder to damage or are stolen less often than others. Insurers use this information when setting rates. You can reduce your collision and comprehensive coverage by as much as 45% if you buy a new or used car that is a low-risk model, like a Volvo. Ask your agent for a list of such cars, or look at the car safety ratings from the Highway Loss Data Institute (www.hldi.org) or the Insurance Institute for Highway Safety (www.highwaysafety.org).

- **Get good grades.** If you're currently a student with a B average or better, on the dean's list, or in the top 20% of your class, tell the insurance agent. Good grades can reduce your premium by up to 25%. In some cases college graduates are eligible for these discounts until they either reach age 25 or get married.

• **Grow up.** Some insurers lower a single woman's rates once she reaches age 25. A single man's rates get lowered at age 30. A married woman of any age gets the discount, but a married man receives it once he's age 25. As long as you have a good driving record, most insurance companies will reduce your rates when you hit these landmark birthdays. Call your insurer with a reminder.

• **See if you're entitled to a household, or "multicar," discount.** If you're married and both you and your spouse have cars, see if you can save money by getting auto coverage from one company. Insurers often offer discounts of up to 20% if both of your cars are insured on the same policy. If you live at home with your parents, you might be able to get a similar discount if your car is insured under your folks' policy.

• **Get your home and auto insurance from the same company.** Some auto insurers give you a better deal if you insure the rest of your earthly possessions with them.

• **Get insured through an "affinity group."** As with other kinds of insurance, you can sometimes get a break on car insurance by belonging to a certain group, like an alumni association or a trade union. One insurer even offers insurance discounts to people who purchase Ford cars.

• **Check with your state's insurance department.** Some state insurance departments publish lists of companies and prices for residents looking for auto insurance. (See Figure 8-1 for phone numbers.)

• **Call these firms for quotes.** The *Consumer Reports* Auto Insurance Price Service (800-695-5459) charges $12 to find 25 of the best policies for your specific situation. If you'd rather shop around on your own, try Geico (800-841-3000; www.geico.com) and Amica (800-242-6422; www.amica .com), two companies that sell directly to consumers. USAA (800-531-8080) offers auto insurance to anyone who is either an active-duty or retired military officer or a dependent of one. Also contact your local agent for State Farm (www.statefarm.com), Allstate (www.allstate.com), and The

Hartford (800-843-7824; www.hartford.com), three of the country's largest auto insurance providers.

DISABILITY INSURANCE

What would happen if you had a horrible skiing accident and couldn't work for ten months?

At the time of this writing, only Puerto Rico and five states— California, Hawaii, New Jersey, New York, and Rhode Island— require employers to provide any income to disabled employees who get hurt off the job. And federal disability benefits from Social Security are extremely difficult to get; the majority of people who apply are rejected.

Your only real protection is likely to be private disability insurance. Although you may never have heard of it, it is something you should have. Ideally, you should have coverage that would pay you about 60% to 70% of your income following an accident that left you unable to work. For many young people, disability coverage is more important than life insurance.

If you work for a large company, you may already have some disability insurance under a group policy. If you do, it may be all you need. If you don't work for a company that offers disability protection, consider buying an individual disability policy. Unfortunately, disability insurance can be very expensive, especially for people who have physically risky jobs, like construction workers or firefighters.

If Your Employer Offers Disability Insurance

Disability protection is different from workers compensation. **Workers comp,** as it is known, protects you if you are injured while performing your job. Disability insurance, sometimes known as **income protection,** covers you for any injury or illness, whether it happens at home, on vacation, or on the job. If you're lucky enough to work for an employer that provides you with disability insurance, you should assess exactly how well you're protected. Here are some tips to help you understand your coverage:

- **Find out what percentage of your income you'll receive if you're disabled.** Large companies with more than 500 employees often provide disability insurance that will pay 60% of your income—usually up to $5,000 a month—if you suffer a long-term disability. If you earn more than $100,000 a year, you may want to supplement your employer coverage with an individual policy. The same goes if a significant part of your income comes from bonuses and other special compensation, which most insurers do not consider to be part of your salary.

- **Ask about waiting periods and benefit periods.** Typically you start receiving benefits within six months of becoming disabled. This period is known as the **waiting period** or **elimination period.** (I guess that's because during it, any savings you have are eliminated!) The period of time during which you receive disability payouts is known as the **benefit period.** Should you ever become disabled, you will not continue to pay premiums. Many companies offer policies that pay disability benefits until the employee reaches age 65.

- **Take advantage of your flexible benefits plan.** If you have a choice, opt for disability protection rather than life insurance if you're single and have no dependents.

What to Look for in an Individual Disability Policy

Insurance companies offer all kinds of confusing extras attached to their disability policies. Below are the basics you will need:

- **Illness and accident coverage.** Most disability policies provide both. Make sure the one you're considering does.

- **Guaranteed renewable.** With a guaranteed renewable policy, you can renew your policy each year without undergoing a medical exam, and the insurer can't single you out for a rate increase just because you've made a lot of claims. Only general rate increases will affect you. This is an important feature.

- **Noncancelable policy.** With a noncancelable policy, the insurer can't cancel your current policy or raise your premium for any reason. This attractive feature is being phased out by many insurers, however.

- **Residual benefit protection.** If you're partially disabled, some policies will pay you a portion of your disability benefits, known as residual benefits. This is extremely important coverage in case you become partially disabled and can work only part time.

How to Reduce Your Disability Insurance Costs

The problem with individual disability coverage is that it's not cheap. For example, a 27-year-old paralegal who earns an annual salary of $30,000 might pay about $800 a year for a top-of-the-line policy that protects him for about 70% of his income. Here are ways to keep your costs down:

- **Consider a step-up, or gradual-payment, policy.** This type of policy allows you to pay lower premiums when you're young and higher ones when you're older. With this plan, the paralegal might pay only about $500 a year for the first five years and $900 or so from then on.

- **Buy through your employer.** Not all employers pay for their employees' disability coverage. But a growing number of employers now have systems in place to let employees *buy* individual coverage on a voluntary basis. These arrangements can cost significantly less than what you might pay for a policy on your own, especially if you're a woman. Believe it or not, women can generally expect to pay up to 30% more than men for individual disability insurance. But if they buy their policies through their jobs, they are protected by workplace equality laws. Check with your human resources department to see whether you have this option.

• **Increase your elimination period.** The elimination period is the time you must wait to receive benefits after becoming disabled. One way to reduce your annual premium is to increase the elimination period to, say, six months. Stretching your elimination period from 90 to 180 days can reduce your premium by 30% or more. This option makes sense if you have enough savings to tide you over during the additional delay, if your employer is likely to continue paying you a salary in the early months of your disability, or if it's the only way you can afford coverage.

• **Decrease your benefit period.** Relatively few disabilities last more than five years. In fact, most last less than two years. If you are willing to accept the risk, you can save up to 50% of your premium by reducing your benefit period to five years, instead of receiving benefits until you retire.

• **Limit yourself to emergency coverage.** If you can't afford a full-scale disability policy, look into coverage that will kick in only in a worst-case scenario, such as a debilitating accident or a catastrophic illness like a heart attack or a stroke. These no-frills disability policies have very short benefit periods (typically two years) and generally cost about $250 a year.

• **Try these firms for quotes.** A handful of insurance companies specialize in disability coverage. Two of the largest are Unum (800-843-3426; www.unum.com) and Northwestern Mutual Life (800-672-4341; www.northwesternmutual.com).

HOME
INSURANCE

If you own a home, you probably have some homeowners insurance; you were required to get coverage on the building by the lender that gave you a mortgage. But if you're like a lot of homeowners, you don't have enough coverage—or you're paying too much. And if you rent, you probably never even thought about buying any coverage.

Three Basic Coverages If You Own a Home

Homeowners insurance covers the cost of rebuilding or repairing your home (and surrounding structures such as a detached garage) if it's destroyed or damaged by disasters such as fire, theft, snow, or windstorm. It covers the *contents* of your home up to a fixed dollar amount in the event of many of these same disasters. And it can also protect you if you are held liable for injuring people or damaging property. Here's a more detailed rundown of each type of protection.

- **Your home's structure.** You need to buy enough insurance to cover the full cost of rebuilding your home. To figure out approximately how much it would cost to rebuild, contact a mortgage lender or insurance agent and find out the building cost per square foot in your area. (These professionals will not charge you for this information. A real estate appraiser can also answer the question but may charge a fee.) Multiply the number of square feet in your home by the local square foot building cost. This will give you an idea of how much it would cost to rebuild your home.

- **The contents of your home.** Standard homeowners policies usually cover the contents of your home—your "personal property"—for 50% to 75% of the amount you insured your home's structure for. So if you insured the structure for

$100,000, your home's contents would be insured for $50,000 to $75,000. You can increase the amount of coverage you have for a fee. Make sure your **personal property insurance** covers you for **replacement cost,** not **actual cash value** of your home's contents. Coverage for replacement cost gives you enough money to buy new comparable items to replace your belongings. Coverage for actual cash value pays you the amount of money you could get to repair or replace the items, *minus* the depreciation on the items.

To figure out how much personal property insurance you need, make a list of everything you own and estimate how much it would cost you to replace these items. This is a hassle, but it's worth doing. Write down the purchase date and purchase price of all your belongings, including furniture, rugs, televisions, VCRs, stereos, CD players, computers, dishes, pots and pans, glasses, artwork, and major appliances. Also list your suits, dresses, shoes, and coats. (Don't forget the expensive stuff like a wedding dress or a tuxedo.) Gather as many receipts as you can to back up your list. Write down the serial or model numbers for appliances. When you make major purchases, save the receipts. Take pictures of your more valuable belongings. This inventory will come in handy if you ever need to file a claim. Keep a copy of the list, along with the receipts and photos, at work in a safe place. Also give a copy to a trusted friend or relative. (Don't leave a copy lying around your apartment. It's a great road map for a burglar. For the same reason, don't give the list a revealing file name on your home computer.) Most people never get around to doing this exhaustive inventory, but at the very least, take pictures or a videotape of your valuables and store the photos or tape in a safe place.

- **Damage you do to other people and other people's property.** Homeowners policies include liability protection that covers you for damage you cause accidentally inside or outside your home. If you leave a pair of boots in the middle of your kitchen floor and your neighbor trips on them and breaks her leg, your liability insurance will probably cover your legal costs, as well as her medical bills and other costs, if you're held responsible for the injury. If you run a shopping cart over someone's foot in a supermarket, your liability coverage may pay for his or her medical expenses if you're found liable. If you have a pet, your policy will often cover you for damage the pet does to people or property.

Many homeowners policies come with a standard amount of liability insurance of $100,000 per accident. In these litigious times, this may not be enough. There is no perfect way to figure out how much you need. To get a rough idea, tally up all your major assets including your home, your car, your possessions, and your investments (don't forget about your retirement savings). The amount of liability insurance you get should exceed this amount.

Choose a Policy That Covers the Most Disasters

Your possessions and your home's structure are protected against losses caused by **perils**. The perils covered by homeowners insurance can include fire, lightning, windstorm, riots, vandalism, and even civil commotion. Your insurance options here are vaguely reminiscent of high school chemistry—you can choose HO-1, HO-2, or HO-3. (This odd code is used in nearly all states.) Insurance agents sometimes refer to these three classifications as basic (HO-1), broad (HO-2), and special (HO-3) coverage. If you can afford it, buy HO-3. It doesn't cost much more than the others, and it covers a much wider range of perils.

Certain perils, such as earthquakes and floods, aren't covered by any of the standard homeowners policies—not even by HO-3. If you live in a region threatened by earthquakes, consider buying earthquake insurance. If your area is prone to flooding, get flood insurance through the National Flood Insurance Program (800-427-4661; www.fema.gov/nfip).

If you live in a co-op or condo, you will need to purchase a special policy known as HO-6. If you rent, the policy you need has the designation HO-4.

What's Covered and What's Not

Though policies vary, there are limits on what most homeowners policies cover. For example, many policies provide only $1,000 of theft coverage for jewelry and $5,000 for computers. If this isn't enough to replace your jewelry and computer equipment, purchase extra protection by adding an **endorsement,** sometimes referred to as a **floater.** This is simply an amendment to your insurance policy to protect a specific item. With an endorsement, you can, for example, increase the coverage on your computer from $5,000 to $10,000 if the computer is worth that much. The cost for this increase in coverage would range from $15 to $100 per year.

Many homeowners policies include **off-premises** protection, which covers your possessions outside your home—whether you're robbed while on vacation or mugged on your block. If, for example, your portable computer or luggage is lost or stolen when you're trekking around Europe, your homeowners insurance should cover the loss. Check your policy carefully. If you live in a high-crime area, you may have to pay extra for this coverage.

Most policies include some **loss of use** protection. If your home is damaged and you're forced to live elsewhere for a while, this coverage will pay the cost of your hotel bills, meals, and other basic living expenses as long as they are reasonable. Don't expect the policy to pay for lavish hotels or restaurants. A typical amount of coverage is 20% of the total amount of insurance you bought for your home's structure.

If you work at home, your home office equipment is usually not covered by your homeowners policy. If the business is small, you can get additional coverage by purchasing an endorsement. For larger businesses, you will have to purchase a separate policy. Ask an insurance agent for details.

If You Rent, Get Insurance

If you rent an apartment or house, the idea of buying **renters insurance,** also known as **tenants insurance,** may not have crossed your mind. You may figure that because you have few valuables and little or no savings, you don't need it. But you're wrong. The first and most obvious reason to buy it is to protect your personal property. If all your possessions were stolen or ruined in a fire, including your clothes, jewelry, stereo equipment, television, VCR, computer, camera, sofa, and bike, a renters policy would cover you up to a fixed dollar amount.

In addition to protecting your possessions, a renters policy offers some liability protection inside and outside your home. If someone slips and falls in your apartment, your renters policy may cover that person's medical bills if you're held liable. If you accidentally leave the tap running when you go to work, ruin the floor, and are held responsible, your renters insurance may pay for the cost of repairs. And if you knock over a sculpture in an art gallery, your renters policy may cover the expense, up to a set maximum.

How to Reduce Your Homeowners or Renters Insurance Costs

The first step (as with health insurance) is to get a high deductible so you can keep your annual premiums low. Remember that this makes sense only if you have enough savings to cover the higher deductible. Here are three other suggestions that apply whether you own a home or rent.

- **Ask if you're eligible for any discounts.** If you have deadbolt locks on your doors or live in an apartment building with a doorman, you may be able to get a discount of as much as 10% on your premium. If you have a security alarm, a fire extinguisher, and/or a smoke detector, you can often get a discount of anywhere from 2% to 20%, depending on the type of system you have.

- **Consider moving your automobile coverage and homeowners or renters coverage to the same insurance company.** Some companies offer a dual-policy discount of up to 15%.

- **Check with your state's insurance department.** State insurance departments sometimes publish lists of companies and the premiums they charge for homeowners insurance. (See Figure 8-1 for phone numbers.) This information can help you shop around.

- **Call these firms for quotes.** Try Amica (800-242-6422; www.amica.com), which sells directly to consumers. USAA (800-531-8080; www.usaa.com) offers home owners insurance to anyone who is either an active-duty or retired military officer or a dependent of one. Also contact State Farm (www.statefarm.com) and Allstate (www.allstate.com), which sell through captive agents and are two of the largest homeowners insurance providers. InsWeb (www.insweb.com) is another good resource.

CONSIDER AN UMBRELLA LIABILITY POLICY

If you have a lot of assets—or have the potential to earn a lot—you should consider getting an **umbrella liability policy.** This special type of policy expands the liability protection provided by your auto and homeowners coverage. It also protects you if you're sued for something unrelated to your car or home, such as slander. The cost for a $1 million umbrella liability policy in 2000 was about $200. Umbrella policies are usually a better deal than purchasing more auto liability and home liability coverage separately.

LIFE
INSURANCE

If you've never received a friendly letter from a life insurance agent, just wait. In the next few years, you'll probably get at least half a dozen trying to sell you life insurance. Throw them out. There's a good chance you don't need it.

The purpose of life insurance is simple: If you die, it protects the people who rely on your income. The rules are easy. If you have kids (or anyone else financially dependent on you), you need it. If you're married without kids and your spouse could handle the basic housing and living expenses without you, you don't need it. If you're single and you aren't financially responsible for anyone but yourself, you don't need it. (Of course, there always are exceptions, but these are good guidelines for most people.)

Two Types of Life Insurance

The most basic form of life insurance is **term life insurance.** It's called that because it protects you for a specific period of time (a term)—typically up to thirty years. When the term runs out, you can usually renew the policy and begin another term. If you die, the insurance company will pay out a specified amount of money to your beneficiaries. This payment is called the **death benefit.**

When you're young, the premium you pay for term insurance is very low. For a death benefit of $100,000, a 25-year-old nonsmoker would pay about $120 a year. Your premium may stay the same for many years or increase slightly from year to year, depending on which type of term policy you get.

Term life insurance gives you the most coverage for your money when you're young. But don't be surprised if insurance agents discourage you from purchasing it. Agents often don't like to sell term insurance because the commissions on such policies are much lower than the commissions on other types of life insurance policies.

Most life insurance agents will urge you to buy a "permanent" insurance policy, often called a **cash value policy.** (For a sampling of some of their most common pitches, see the box on page 250.) With a cash value policy, the insurance company takes your annual premium and deducts sales and administrative charges, the cost of death protection, and a margin for profit. The remainder goes into a kind of savings account for you, generally called your cash value. The most common forms of cash value policies are called **whole life, universal life,** and **variable life.** With whole life and universal life policies, the insurance company invests your cash value in bonds and various bond-like investments. With variable life policies, the insurance company offers you a choice of mutual fund–like investments to choose from, and you decide how to invest the cash value. Because of special rules in the tax law, the money in the savings account of a cash value life insurance policy grows tax-deferred.

The cost of a cash value policy is usually much higher than that of a term policy for a young person. Even if you can afford it, it probably makes sense to avoid cash value policies and buy term if you need life insurance. That's because the commissions on most cash value policies are very high; they can be more than 100% of your first year's premium, and renewal commissions in subsequent years can be 5% to 8%. You're better off buying term insurance and investing the money you save on premiums in a tax-favored retirement savings plan like an IRA or a 401(k). What's more, many term policies can easily be converted into cash value policies years down the line, if you ever change your mind.

There is one set of circumstances under which it's smart to buy a cash value life insurance policy. If you need life insurance and you're already putting the maximum allowable amount into a tax-favored retirement savings plan, you may want to consider a **low-load** cash value policy. Such policies have very low sales and administrative charges. Low-load companies that sell cash value life policies include Ameritas (800-552-3553; www.ameritas.com), USAA (800-531-8000; www.usaa.com), Paragon (800-685-0124; www.paragonlife.com), and Southland (800-872-7542; www.southlandlife.com). Keep in mind that not all of these insurers sell policies in all states. An up-to-date list of low-load insurance companies can be found on the Web site of "fee-only" insurance consultant Glenn Daily, www

.glenndaily.com/bookstore.htm. ("Fee-only" consultants are generally considered unbiased because they do not get commissions from the insurance or investments that they recommend.) If you're trying to decide between two or three different cash value policies, consider comparing them through the "rate of return analysis service" offered by the Consumer Federation of America (202-387-0087; www.consumerfed.org).

How to Shop for Term Insurance

By now it's probably clear that you're best off purchasing term. There are two basic types of term policies to choose from. **Annual renewable term** is coverage that doesn't require you to take a medical exam each year to renew it. Each year when you renew, your premium will usually increase somewhat. A **level premium policy** lasts for a fixed number of years (commonly, ten or twenty years) and allows you to lock in a premium for a set period. Some level premium deals guarantee you twenty years at the same premium; others may guarantee the coverage for twenty years but the same premium for only five or ten years. After your coverage period ends, you usually must pass a medical exam in order to renew at attractive rates; otherwise, your premium will increase dramatically.

Although annual renewable policies may cost less at the beginning, level premium policies may be less expensive in the long run. You should definitely consider a level premium policy if you're able to afford it today. Look for a policy that guarantees the premium for at least ten years, and compare the cost to an annual renewable term policy.

One final tip: Look for a term policy that will allow you to convert to a low-cost cash value policy at any time, regardless of your health. As mentioned above, you may decide when you're older (and maxxing out on your retirement plan contributions) that you want to purchase a cash value policy.

You have many options when shopping for term insurance. Try calling individual firms that sell low-load policies, like USAA (800-531-8000; www.usaa.com) and Ameritas (800-552-3553;

WHY THE PITCHES DON'T MAKE SENSE

Perhaps you've heard the saying that life insurance isn't bought, it's sold. That sentiment comes from the fact that life insurance agents can be aggressive and extremely persuasive. Who can blame them? The commission an agent gets from selling a cash value policy can be substantial. If you've ever met with a life insurance salesperson, you've probably heard one of the following pitches.

The pitch: "Maybe you don't need life insurance now, but you should buy today when you're young and healthy to protect your insurability in the future."

The reality: The odds of your developing a health problem that renders you unable to qualify for life insurance before you reach age 35 are very low. Since you have limited funds now, why spend your money on insurance you don't need?

The pitch: "Even though you're single, you need life insurance to pay your funeral costs and your debts."

The reality: Your parents, other relatives, or friends will probably be willing to pay for your funeral in the unlikely event you die with no assets. As for your debts, unless you co-signed a loan with parents, partners, or friends, no one else will be responsible for paying them. If you have any assets, the credi-

www.ameritas.com). In addition to getting quotes from agents, check out Web sites that will let you compare quotes from different firms side by side. One highly regarded site is Term4sale (www.term4sale.com); other good sites are SelectQuote (800-343-1985; www.selectquote.com) and Quotesmith (800-556-9393; www.quotesmith.com).

tors will sell them to pay your debts. Otherwise, the creditors will simply take the loss.

The pitch: "If you have a child, you should buy a policy to cover his or her life."

The reality: A child is the last person who needs a life insurance policy. Parents need life insurance. Buying coverage on your child's life is a waste of money despite what late-night infomercials may claim.

The pitch: "Cash value life insurance offers tax-favored growth and is a great forced-savings plan."

The reality: This is true, but you can get the same tax-favored growth by putting money in a retirement plan, without paying a commission to an agent—as well as additional benefits like upfront deductibility with a 401(k) or deductible IRA, and tax-free earnings with a Roth IRA. (For details, see Chapter 6.)

The pitch: "Buying term insurance is like renting. Buying cash value insurance is like buying. When the term is up, you don't have anything to show for it. But look how much money you'll have in twenty years if you buy a cash value life insurance policy."

The reality: Life insurance companies are notorious for using extremely attractive, overly optimistic future rates of return when selling cash value policies. There's no guarantee that your returns will be as good as an agent says.

How Much Death Benefit Do You Need?

You need enough life insurance to enable your dependents (spouse and kids) to carry on a decent lifestyle if you die prematurely. If you have young children, that means you need to figure out how much they would need to live for at least the next fifteen to twenty years. One rough rule of thumb says you should buy a policy that will pay six to eight times your annual before-tax income if you die, but many people need more than that—especially if they have many kids. If you have high aspirations for your kids—for example, if you want to send them to expensive private schools—or if your spouse doesn't work, you will certainly need more.

If Your Employer Offers Life Insurance

Many large employers provide some life insurance for employees. Your company might pay for a term policy with a death benefit of $50,000—more than enough if you're single and have no dependents. If you need more, you might be better off buying directly from an insurance company rather than through your employer. Policies you get through work may be hard to convert if you switch jobs. Moreover, some employers charge all employees the same rate for life insurance, regardless of age. If that's the case with your employer, you would be paying the same premium as a 60-year-old, which would be much higher than what you could be paying. Find out about your employer's offerings and also price several term policies on your own.

INSURANCE YOU PROBABLY DON'T NEED

It's very tempting to buy quickie insurance on impulse. After all, it seems so cheap—just $10 a day to get collision coverage at the rental car counter or $25 for $50,000 worth of life insurance at the airport. Before you throw money at this kind of coverage, evaluate it carefully. In most cases, you don't need it.

- **Rental car collision protection.** If you've ever rented a car, you were probably asked if you wanted to buy the **collision damage waiver.** Next time, do a little research in advance. Review your credit card agreement to see if you are auto-

WHY YOU MAY NEED A WILL

Since we're on the topic of life insurance, this is as good a time as any to discuss the subject of wills. The truth is, I don't know anyone my age who has a will. But that doesn't mean you don't need one.

If you're single, for example, you may want to leave all your possessions (even if that's just a car and a small savings account) to a friend or sibling, but without a will, your property will be distributed to your closest relatives according to state law. If you're married, you may think that your spouse will get everything in the event of your death. But depending on the state in which you live, your parents may be entitled to a share of whatever you leave behind. If you're a parent, you may not want to think about what would happen to your children if you're no longer around, but without a will, a probate court will select a guardian for them. You get the picture.

The easiest way to tackle this task is to get a lawyer to draw up a will for you. If you don't have much in the way of assets and your situation is straightforward, this should cost between $100 and $200. If you can't afford the lawyer's fee, your situation is uncomplicated, and you're willing to spend the time, you can write your own will. One book that can help is *Nolo's Will Book* (Nolo Press, about $25). You may also want to check out Nolo Press's WillMaker 7.0 software, which costs about $40 when you order it directly from the Web site (www.nolo.com). Keep in mind that if you start earning and accumulating more assets (or more dependents) you'll need to update your will. But having one today is a precaution worth taking.

matically protected when you charge a car rental on the card. Most gold and platinum cards carry this perk. And if you already have collision and comprehensive insurance on your own car, find out if your policy extends to rented cars. Warning: Collision damage waivers are different from rental liability insurance, which you will need if you don't own a car or your auto policy doesn't cover rented cars.

- **Flight insurance.** If you need to insure your life, the cheapest way to do it when you're young is to buy a term life insurance policy. If you don't need to, you shouldn't waste money by buying life insurance at a vending machine in the airport. Sure it's tempting (this type of insurance plays on your fear of flying) and it also seems cheap, but it doesn't make sense. Your chances of slipping and killing yourself on the ground are much greater than your chances of dying in an airplane crash. Besides, you might already be covered; some credit card companies give you automatic flight insurance if you charge your tickets on their card.

- **Credit protection insurance.** Credit card companies have been stuffing their envelopes with invitations to buy "credit insurance," which is supposed to pay your credit card bills should you die, lose your job, or become disabled. Supposedly this insurance will protect your credit report from damage during periods when you can't make ends meet. In reality, it mainly protects the lenders—you're shelling out extra money to make sure that they keep getting their payments on time. Needless to say, this insurance should be avoided. It costs much more than it tends to give back and offers little or no protection that would not already be covered by your regular homeowners, life, and disability insurance.

FINANCIAL CRAMMING

- If you work for a company that offers a flexible benefits plan, evaluate your options carefully. If you're single without any dependents, for instance, it probably makes sense to forgo the life insurance offered by your employer and opt instead for better health insurance or more disability coverage.

- Don't go without health insurance, even if you're healthy. To find affordable coverage, see if there's a group you can join like a trade association or religious organization that offers group insurance. If you're between jobs, purchase low-cost temporary coverage. (For general tips on shopping for an individual policy, see page 230.)

- Check with several agents and the few companies that sell directly to consumers when shopping for auto insurance (see page 236). And think twice before allowing a friend to drive your car. If there's an accident, *your* insurance record will be tainted, not your friend's.

- Get disability insurance to protect yourself in case you can't work due to injury or illness. Ideally, you should have coverage that would pay you 60% to 70% of your income if you become disabled. (For advice on reducing the cost of your coverage, see page 239.)

- Purchase renters insurance if you rent a house or an apartment. It protects your possessions if they're ruined in a fire or stolen, and it also offers you some liability coverage inside and outside your home.

- If you own a home, make sure you have adequate insurance for it. Insure your home's structure for the entire cost of rebuilding it.

Catalog the contents of your home, and verify that your personal property insurance covers you for replacement cost.

• If you have children or anyone else dependent on your income, buy term life insurance for yourself. If you don't have dependents, you probably don't need any life insurance at all.

9

HOW TO MAKE YOUR LIFE LESS TAXING

Put More Money in Your Pocket and Less in Uncle Sam's

YOU CAN RUN from many financial subjects, but you can't hide from taxes. If you're like most people, you find the rules complex, the forms confusing, and the Internal Revenue Service (IRS) intimidating. But whether you're a highly paid professional or a hardly paid grad student, you need to know the basics.

This chapter will help you get over your fear of filing. It describes exactly what kind of taxes you pay, explains how to figure out which tax bracket you're in, offers tips on filing your taxes online and off, and, most important, outlines specific strategies that can save you money. Although exploring the intricacies of the tax code isn't anyone's idea of a good time (except for an accountant I once dated), taking the time to understand the basics could save you hundreds of dollars each year. Whether you do your own taxes—something I recommend you try at least once—or hire someone to do them for you, knowing the rules ensures that you won't miss out on any money-saving tax breaks.

One quick note: Although this chapter will give you a good overview of what you need to know about taxes, you should keep in mind that tax law is constantly changing. And while I've made every effort to provide accurate, up-to-date information on the tax code's latest twists and turns, you'll need to check the current rules when you fill out your tax return.

WHY IS YOUR PAYCHECK SO SMALL?

At some point in your life when you received your first paycheck, it became painfully clear that your before-tax salary was an illusion. Your take-home pay, or **net wages**, was much smaller. The reason, you soon figured out, was that your employer subtracted Social Security tax, Medicare tax, and federal, state, and local income tax from your paycheck.

Your employer subtracts or "withholds" tax because the U.S. tax system uses a "pay-as-you-go" method, meaning we pay tax on the money we earn as we earn it. If you're a freelancer or self-employed, you're responsible for making sure you pay enough tax each quarter. If you're an employee, your employer withholds income tax from each paycheck based on salary and the information on the **Form W-4** that employees fill out when they're hired. On a worksheet attached to the W-4, you were asked some basic questions to help you calculate the number of **withholding allowances**. A withholding allowance represents an estimate of the exemptions and deductions you believe you are entitled to in the coming year. (You'll learn more about exemptions and deductions later on.) The more allowances you take, the less income tax your employer withholds from your paycheck; the fewer allowances you take, the more tax is withheld. The number of allowances you're eligible for can depend on a variety of factors, including whether you're single or married, whether you have kids, and whether you own a home.

THE TAXES YOU PAY

Here's a list of the major ones:

- **Income tax.** The federal government, and some state and local governments, require you to pay tax on your **earned income**, which is the income you receive for work you do.

The federal government, and some state and local governments, also require you to pay tax on income you receive from investments. Such **unearned income** includes the interest you get from a savings account and the dividends or capital gains you receive from mutual funds, stocks, and bonds. The total of your earned and unearned income is known as your **gross income.**

- **Social Security and Medicare payroll tax (FICA).** Everyone who works must contribute a portion of his or her wages to a fund that provides retirement income for people 65 and older (that's the Social Security part) and health insurance for this same crowd (that's the Medicare part). Together, these two contributions make up your FICA tax, named for the Federal Insurance Contributions Act. In 2000, as an employee of a company, the Social Security tax you pay is 6.2% of your income, up to a maximum income of $76,200. The Medicare tax is 1.45%, with no maximum. Your total employee contribution to Medicare and Social Security is 7.65% of your income, and your employer matches that amount. If you work for yourself, you have to cover the full 15.3% (the 7.65% employee contribution plus the 7.65% employer contribution) to pay for Social Security and Medicare; this 15.3% is also known as the **self-employment tax.** Some states also impose state unemployment and disability insurance taxes.

- **Property tax.** Some state and local governments require residents to pay tax on certain types of property. In Virginia and Connecticut, for example, residents must pay **personal property tax** on the value of their cars each year. And if you own a home, you might have to pay real estate tax, also known as **real property tax,** to your municipality and/or county based on the value of your home and the land on which it is built.

- **Sales tax.** Most states and many cities and counties impose tax on the items you buy (sofas, potato chips, sneakers) and the services you use (dry cleaning, haircuts, lawn care).

TAXES AND INHERITANCE

When Rebecca's uncle Al died, she received $13,000 in cash from his estate, which she put in her bank savings account in January. She was thrilled by this windfall, but she worried about whether she would owe tax on the money. Here's how it generally works: You do not owe income tax on money you receive as an inheritance, but if you put that money in a bank account you will have to pay tax on the interest. So Rebecca had to pay tax on the $520 that her uncle's money earned her in interest that year.

Some states have inheritance taxes, and a federal estate tax generally kicks in for estates larger than $675,000 (by 2006 the exemption will rise to $1,000,000). But the executor—the person in charge of sorting through a will and distributing the money to beneficiaries—is responsible for making sure the applicable inheritance taxes are paid. If you have any concerns about whether these taxes were paid, check with the executor.

- **Capital gains tax.** Your profit or gain when you sell an investment is subject to a special tax called capital gains tax. Gains from financial assets (like stock mutual funds) that you've held for a year or less are taxed at your regular income tax rate. But gains from investments that you've held for more than one year are considered **long-term capital gains,** and are generally taxed at a lower rate than other kinds of income. The highest possible tax rate for long-term capital gains in 2000 is just 20%—even if you are in a higher tax bracket for the rest of your income. And if you are in the 15% tax bracket for ordinary income, you only have to pay 10% on long-term capital gains.

FIGURING OUT
YOUR TAX RATE

When people talk about their tax bracket or tax rate, they're usually referring to their federal income tax bracket or rate. Federal income taxes probably make up the largest share of your total tax bill. Your federal income tax rate depends on how much income—including wages, bonuses, tips, and earnings from investments—you received over the course of the year. (It also depends on the tax breaks you're eligible for, but I'll tell you more about those later on.)

The federal government has a "graduated" tax system that requires people with higher incomes to pay a higher percentage of their incomes in taxes. A range of income levels is grouped together in what is called a **tax bracket.** A **tax rate** is assigned to each tax bracket. To figure out your tax bracket, you first need to calculate your **taxable income,** which you can do by following the step-by-step instructions on your tax return. For example, if you were single and your taxable income was between $0 and $26,250 in 2000, you would be in the 15% tax bracket. The dollar amounts that fall within each bracket are adjusted for inflation every year. Every few years, the president, with the help of Congress, changes the number of brackets and adjusts the range of incomes in each bracket in order to win friends and influence people. As of this writing, there are five brackets and therefore five rates: 15%, 28%, 31%, 36%, and 39.6%. But figuring out the tax you owe involves more than finding out which rate corresponds to your income.

Take a look at the tables in Figure 9-1. If you are single and have a taxable income of $26,000, that would put you in the 15% tax bracket. Simple. But say your income was $30,000. Here's where it gets complicated. Not all your income will fall into the same bracket. The first $26,250 will be taxed at the 15% rate, but the remaining $3,750 will be taxed at the 28% rate. In this example, 28% is known as your **marginal tax rate,** the rate at which the "last dollar you earn" gets taxed. The marginal rate is the highest rate at which any of your money is taxed. Knowing your marginal rate will help you evaluate the merits of making certain investments.

Figure 9-1
2000 TAX RATES

Filing Status	For taxable income that is:	Marginal rate is:
Single	Not over $26,250	15%
	Over $26,250 but not over $63,550	28%
	Over $63,550 but not over $132,600	31%
	Over $132,600 but not over $288,350	36%
	Over $288,350	39.6%
Married Couples Filing Jointly	Not over $43,850	15%
	Over $43,850 but not over $105,950	28%
	Over $105,950 but not over $161,450	31%
	Over $161,450 but not over $288,350	36%
	Over $288,350	39.6%
Married Couples Filing Separately	Not over $21,925	15%
	Over $21,925 but not over $52,975	28%
	Over $52,975 but not over $80,725	31%
	Over $80,725 but not over $144,175	36%
	Over $144,175	39.6%

Depending on where you live, you probably have to pay state and local income taxes too. On average, you can expect your state and local tax to be roughly 5%. (Some states charge no state income tax at all, however, and others impose a tax on only certain types of income.) Add 5% to your federal marginal rate to get a rough idea of your combined federal, state, and local marginal rate. To calculate your federal, state, and local marginal income tax rate more precisely, consult your state's tax booklet to find out your true state and local marginal rate. You can get a copy by calling your state's department of taxation (or reaching them online via www.taxsites.com). Inside you will find tables to help you figure out your state and local rates.

Remember, your marginal rate does not indicate what percentage of your income will go toward tax. In the example above, if your annual taxable income was $30,000, most of your money would be taxed at a rate of 15% rather than at the marginal rate of 28%. Your overall rate, known as your **effective tax rate,** is a blended, or weighted, average of the tax rates that apply to your income. In this case it's a weighted average of 15% and 28% that results in an effective tax rate of about 17%.

FILING YOUR
TAX RETURN

The term **filing** simply means filling out your tax forms and sending them to the IRS, the government agency responsible for collecting taxes. Although your employer subtracts money for taxes from your paycheck during the year, the amount withheld generally is not the exact amount of tax you actually owe. By filling out tax forms, you learn whether you still owe the IRS some money or whether the IRS owes you a refund.

April 15 is usually the last day you can file a tax return and pay tax for the previous calendar year without having to pay interest or a penalty. (If that date falls on a Saturday or Sunday, the IRS allows you to file up until the following Monday.) If you owe the IRS money and miss the April 15 deadline, you may have to pay interest and a penalty on the money you owe.

Start getting your paperwork together early in the year. By the end of January, your employer will have sent you a **W-2** form that shows your gross wages and the amount of tax that was withheld from your paycheck over the course of the previous year. Your bank, mutual fund company, and/or brokerage will each send you a **1099**

PAPER-FREE FILING

Waiting in long lines at the post office on April 15 may soon be a thing of the past. Many people now find it easier to file their returns by telephone or by computer.

Filing by phone, which the IRS calls **TeleFile,** is incredibly easy. Unfortunately, it is limited to people who would otherwise file a 1040EZ form. (To learn more about the different forms you can file, see page 283.) In order to qualify for TeleFile, you must have filed a 1040EZ form (or used TeleFile) the year before, and you can't have changed addresses since then. If you fit this description, a form (TEL-1) will be sent automatically to your house telling you what number to call and giving you an identification code to use when you do. After filling out part of the form, you call the IRS and enter your information through your Touch-Tone keypad. When you're done, hold on to your TEL-1 form as a record. If you do not owe the IRS any money, you don't have to send them any paperwork; if you do, you'll have to send them a check or money order along with Form 8855-V (which will be included with the TeleFile tax package the IRS sends you).

form, which lists the interest, dividends, or capital gains you earned during the year. If you've done freelance work, you will probably receive a 1099 from the companies you did the work for. Compare your pay stubs and financial statements to your W-2 and 1099s to make sure the figures are accurate. Save these forms in a folder marked "Tax Returns," and create a new folder for each tax year. You'll need them when you fill out your tax return.

Although this chapter deals mostly with federal taxes, don't forget that your state and local taxes are also due on April 15.

If you don't qualify for TeleFile, look into filing your returns electronically. This is known as **e-filing,** and it can be done in several ways. If you use a preparer to figure out your taxes, he or she will probably file your return electronically, free of charge. If you do your taxes using a computer program or a Web site like TurboTax (www.turbotax.com), you will have the option of filing electronically (at no extra cost) or printing out your tax forms and filing them by mail. If you file electronically, you still have to send in a signature card (IRS Form 8453), as well as any W-2 or 1099 forms from your employer. And if you owe the IRS money, you'll have to send them a check or money order as well.

TeleFiling and e-filing are especially advantageous for people who will be getting refunds back from the IRS. Refunds ordinarily arrive about six weeks after you file your taxes. But with TeleFile or e-filing, you can expect a refund within about three weeks. And if you sign up for direct deposit, your refund will probably be deposited straight into your bank account within 14 days.

Who Has to File a Tax Return?

If you're single and are not claimed as a dependent on your parents' tax return, you must file a tax return if your gross income is at least $7,200 (as of 2000). For married couples who file a joint return, the 2000 minimum income for filing is $12,950.

If you're a full-time student and you're under 24, your parents can claim you as a dependent. Even so, you might still have to file your taxes if you exceed certain income limitations. The rules for these limits can be found in IRS Publication 17, *Your Federal Income Tax,* and they are incredibly convoluted; it would probably take longer for you to sort through them than to fill out a simple tax form. My advice: File a tax return, even if you're not entirely sure you need to.

When Should You File?

If you're expecting a refund, send in your tax forms to the IRS as soon after January 1 as possible so that you can get your refund sooner. If you owe money, mail your forms and your check made out to the IRS in early April, so you can hang on to your cash as long as possible. But try not to wait until the last minute.

If you're expecting a big refund or making a big payment to the IRS, or if you're filing close to the April 15 deadline, you may want to send your return via certified mail so that you have a record. If the IRS claims it didn't get your return, you will have proof that you mailed it in.

A NOTE TO STUDENTS

Scholarships that pay for tuition, course-related fees, books, and supplies are not considered taxable income if you are working toward a degree. But if you received a scholarship to, say, study abroad for a year, and the course work is not related to your getting a degree, you must count the money you receive as income. And whether you're working toward a degree or not, the portion of a scholarship used to pay for room and board is considered taxable income. For details contact the IRS at 800-TAX-FORM (www.irs.gov) and get a copy of *Scholarships and Fellowships,* Publication 520.

If you simply can't get it together in time, you can file for an automatic four-month extension by filling out Form 4868, and send in your full tax forms later. But if you think you owe money, you must estimate how much you owe and send in a check to the IRS by April 15. If you have not sent all that you owe by April 15, the IRS may charge you interest on the unpaid amount, plus a penalty if you've paid less than 90% of the amount due.

If You Can't Pay

Even if you don't have enough money to pay the IRS the tax you owe, you should file your return by April 15. If you don't, you will be charged a monthly penalty of 5% of the amount of tax you owe, up to a maximum penalty of 25%. You'll also have to pay interest. To avoid the bulk of these nasty charges, you can request to pay the IRS in installments by filling out Form 9465 and sending it in on

IF YOU CHANGE YOUR NAME, TELL SOCIAL SECURITY

If you get married and change your last name, contact the Social Security Administration. The IRS checks to make sure that the name and Social Security number you list on your tax return match the records of the Social Security Administration. If you change your name without alerting the Social Security Administration, the IRS may delay sending you the refund check you are due. What's more, you might not get credit for the money your employer deducts from your paycheck and sends to Social Security. Call 800-772-1213 or visit www.ssa.gov to get a copy of Form SS-5, which you will have to fill out to register your new name.

time with your completed return. Within 30 days, the IRS will tell you if you've been accepted for the installment plan. The IRS will still charge you a monthly late payment charge of 0.5% of the balance due, up to 25%, plus interest and a one-time charge of $43. To get a copy of Form 9465, call 800-TAX-FORM (www.irs.gov).

If You're Single

If you're not married but have children or dependent relatives living with you, you may be able to file as a **head of household.** This status generally allows you to pay less tax than an ordinary single person. To see if you qualify, check the instruction booklet that comes with your tax forms.

MAXIMIZING YOUR TAX BREAKS

Although the government wants citizens to pay their fair share of taxes, it does offer taxpayers ways to reduce the amount of their income that is subject to tax. This section will discuss the various tax breaks for which you may be eligible.

Exemptions and Deductions

One type of tax break available to most taxpayers is an **exemption,** a specific amount ($2,800 in 2000) that can be subtracted from your taxable income. If you're single and have no children (and are not being claimed as a dependent on someone else's tax return), you are allowed one personal exemption. If you're married and you file a joint return, you and your spouse are each entitled to a personal exemption. You also get an additional exemption for each child you have. If you earn a very high income, however, you may not be entitled to any exemptions.

The other type of tax break is a **deduction.** Deductions are specific expenses that the government allows you to subtract from your income, thus reducing the amount of tax you pay. (For an example of how this works, see the box on page 270.) Uncle Sam offers deductions for certain expenditures. For instance, to encourage people to buy homes, the government allows taxpayers to deduct the interest they pay on their mortgage.

There are two distinct ways to take advantage of deductions. The simpler way is to take the **standard deduction,** which all taxpayers are permitted to do. The standard deduction is simply a fixed dollar amount that Congress allows all taxpayers to subtract from their income. Even if you don't participate in activities that are deemed deductible by the government, you still get the standard deduction. (Technically, you subtract your standard deduction from a figure known as your **adjusted gross income,** or **AGI.** Your AGI is basically your gross income minus special deductions known as "adjustments." Don't get bogged down in the technical details of how to determine your AGI now. When you fill out your tax form you'll be able to calculate it.) In 2000, the standard deduction for a single person is $4,400. For a married couple filing a joint return, the standard deduction is $7,350. These figures are adjusted each year for inflation.

A more complicated but potentially more rewarding method is to **itemize** your deductions. Itemizing means listing the specific "items" that are deductible according to current tax rules, and then subtracting their cost from your AGI. If you choose to itemize your deductions, you cannot take the standard deduction.

Whether you should itemize or take the standard deduction depends on the specifics of your financial life. The following two sections describe some potential itemized deductions. Once you read them over, make your own list of the itemized deductions that are relevant to you. If the total of your itemized expenses is greater than the standard deduction, you should itemize. If the standard deduction is greater, you should take the standard deduction. If you do itemize, make sure you can substantiate the amounts you claim. If you are audited, this is the part of your return that the IRS is likely to scrutinize carefully.

Before you read the following lists of possible deductions, I should add a disclaimer. The rules concerning deductions, even the

---

FIGURING OUT THE VALUE OF A DEDUCTION

Your tax bracket plays a major role in determining just how much a deduction is worth. Suppose you obtained a mortgage to buy a home. Assume that in the first year the interest payments you made on the mortgage totaled $10,000. You would be able to subtract, or deduct, that $10,000 from your adjusted gross income for that year. If you're in the 15% tax bracket, that would mean a savings of $1,500 (15% of $10,000). But if you are in the 28% tax bracket, the $10,000 deduction would be worth $2,800 (28% of $10,000).

---

more straightforward ones, can be very tricky. They also change frequently. Use this list only as a starting point. Consult a current tax guide to make sure specific deductions are still valid. Also, if you earn more than $128,950 in 2000 (whether you are single or married filing jointly), you may not be eligible to take full advantage of itemized deductions.

Some Straightforward Itemized Deductions

To see whether it makes sense for you to itemize, read the following list of possible deductions:

- **State and local income tax.** On your federal tax form you can deduct the state and local taxes you paid (including amounts withheld from your paycheck) during the year. Because most of us pay these taxes, you're likely to be eligible for this tax break.

- **Property tax.** If you own a home, you can deduct the property taxes (also known as real estate taxes) you pay. If you live in a co-op, it pays property taxes for you as part of your monthly maintenance fee; find out what your share of these taxes is.

- **Donations to charities.** If you make a contribution to a group that is considered a "qualified tax-exempt organization" by the IRS, you can deduct it. Qualified organizations include most churches, synagogues, charities, and educational organizations. If you're unsure whether a particular organization qualifies, ask before you make a donation. Contributions you make to your college's alumni association, for example, might be deductible.

  If instead of cash you donate clothes, furniture, or household items to the Salvation Army, for instance, you get to deduct their current market value. Write down a description of each item you donate and how much each is worth (basically that means how much you estimate you could get if you sold them at a garage sale). Also, you can deduct some of the expenses you incur when you do volunteer work. If you volunteer at a senior center on weekends, you can deduct some of your transportation costs to and from the center, for example.

  To deduct donations of cash or property of $250 or more, you'll need a receipt from the charity. For noncash donations worth more than $500 (like clothing or books), you'll have to fill out a special form (Form 8283) when you file your tax return. If your noncash donation is worth more than $5,000, you'll need to get a professional appraisal.

  If you get any "benefit" (theater tickets, a tote bag, a meal) in exchange for a contribution, you can deduct only the amount of your donation that exceeds the value of the benefit. Say you pay $100 to attend a fund-raising dinner for the Save the Leapfrogs Society sponsored by the Boy Scouts of America and the actual value of the dinner is $25; you can deduct $75 on your tax return. The receipt you get from your charity should specify any such "benefits" you have received.

- **Housing costs.** If you own a home, you can deduct the interest you pay on your mortgage. (You cannot deduct the

portion of your mortgage payment that goes toward paying off the principal.) Also, in the year you buy a home,
you may be able to deduct the points, even if these points
were actually paid by the seller of the home. (See Chapter
7 for an explanation of points.) If you live in a co-op building, the co-op may pay interest on a mortgage for the building. If it does, find out what your share of the interest is;
you may be able to deduct it.

Some Trickier Itemized Deductions

Certain expenses are deductible only in specific situations. Here are
some of those deductions. Again, remember that some are not available to taxpayers with very high incomes. Check a current tax guide
for details.

- **Job-related expenses and other miscellaneous deductions.**
  This broad category includes a variety of expenses. The basic
  rule is that these expenses must be related to producing
  income. You can deduct the combined total of these
  expenses that exceeds 2% of your adjusted gross income
  (AGI). Here's how that works. Suppose your AGI is
  $30,000. You could not deduct the first $600 (2% of
  $30,000) of your "job-related and miscellaneous expenses,"
  but you can deduct expenses beyond $600. Below are exam-
  ples of job-related expenses. For more details contact the IRS
  at 800-TAX-FORM (www.irs.gov) and get a copy of
  Miscellaneous Deductions, Publication 529.

    — *Work-related home computers, cellular phones, and
    other equipment.* If your employer requires you to pur-
    chase any equipment, you may be permitted to deduct
    up to $20,000 of the amount you spend in 2000
    ($24,000 in 2001). You must be able to prove that you
    use the equipment more than 50% of the time for busi-
    ness and that your employer told you the item was nec-
    essary for your job. Ask your boss to write a letter to

that effect, and file it away in case you need to show it to the IRS some day.

—*Job-search expenses.* The IRS allows you to deduct costs related to a job search as long as you're looking for a job in your *present* occupation. If you're trying to change professions—say, you're a lifeguard looking to break into investment banking—you don't get the deduction. If you're currently out of work, the kind of job you did most recently is considered your occupation. If you're looking for your first job, you don't get the tax break. The expenses you can deduct if you qualify include the fees of career counseling and employment or placement agencies; the cost of preparing, printing, and mailing your resumé; phone calls; and transportation costs (including 50% of the cost of meals while traveling) for a long-distance job search.

—*Work-related educational expenses.* If you take a course that helps you maintain or improve the skills you use to perform your current job, you may be able to deduct your unreimbursed tuition expenses. Also, if a course is required either by your employer or by law in order for you to keep your job, you may be able to deduct its cost. If, however, you take a course that will qualify you for a new line of work or that enables you to meet the minimum educational requirements of your profession, you can't deduct the tuition. So a financial analyst who is taking a cooking course can't deduct the cost of the class. A paralegal can't deduct the tuition costs of law school, and an accountant can't deduct the costs associated with taking the CPA exam. However, a financial analyst who goes back to school to get an MBA may be able to deduct tuition expenses.

—*Mandatory uniforms for work.* Suits and ties aren't deductible, but nurses' uniforms, firefighter uniforms, letter courier uniforms, police officer uniforms, safety shoes and glasses, hard hats, and work gloves are. (If you're a computer programmer who wears a hard hat to work for kicks, it doesn't count.) If your employer reimburses you for these expenses, you can't deduct them.

— *Unreimbursed business travel and entertainment expenses.* If you pay these costs yourself, there are very specific rules about how much you're allowed to deduct. In general, you must keep a detailed log of your trips and be prepared to prove the business purpose of each expense.

— *Union dues and initiation fees, professional and business association dues, and job-related subscriptions to trade magazines and professional journals.* Make sure to deduct these expenses if you are not reimbursed for them by your employer.

— *Tax preparation fees.* Even though these aren't directly related to work, you can deduct the cost of tax-related software and tax publications. You can also deduct money you pay to a tax preparer.

• **Medical expenses.** You can deduct out-of-pocket medical and dental expenses, for yourself or any dependent, that are greater than 7.5% of your adjusted gross income. You can include premiums you pay for medical insurance, co-payments for doctor visits, the cost of birth control pills or cigarette-quitting programs, prescription medicines not covered by your health plan, and transportation needed for medical care.

• **Losses due to theft and disasters.** You're allowed to deduct the cost of items you lose in a burglary, fire, or other disaster that exceed 10% of your adjusted gross income. The first $100 of losses above the 10% threshold is not deductible.

Deductions You Can Take Without Itemizing

Most deductions have to be itemized, and their sum total must be bigger than the standard deduction for them to be of any use. But there are exceptions to that rule. Here are three of the most important deductions you can take even if you don't itemize:

- **Contributions to a traditional IRA.** The money you contribute to a traditional IRA—though not a Roth IRA—may be deductible if you aren't eligible for an employer-sponsored retirement plan or if your income falls below a certain level. (See chapter 6.) If you're in the 28% tax bracket, a deductible $2,000 IRA contribution will save you $560 on your tax bill. (The math: $2,000 times 28% equals $560.) There is a place on the tax form that will prompt you to take the deduction. One nice feature of the IRA deduction is that you technically don't have to make your contribution during the tax year in question: the deadline for contributing to an IRA is same as the deadline for filing your taxes that year. So, for example, you can deduct an IRA contribution for tax year 2000 as long as you make the contribution before April 15, 2001.

  Although you do not have to pay income tax on the money you contribute to an employer-sponsored retirement savings plan like a 401(k), you do not list 401(k) contributions on your tax return. That's because your employer has already subtracted your contribution from your gross salary. Thus, the net salary on your W-2 already reflects your contribution.

- **Student loan interest payments.** You are entitled to deduct the *interest* payments you make on your student loans during your first 60 months of repayment, up to a maximum of $2,000 in 2000. (This maximum deduction will grow to $2,500 in 2001.) You cannot deduct money that goes toward repaying the principal. Eligibility for this deduction phases out for incomes between $40,000 and $55,000 (for singles) or $60,000 and $75,000 (for married couples filing jointly). For more information, contact the IRS at 800-TAX-FORM (www.irs.gov) for Publication 970, *Tax Benefits for Higher Education.*

- **Alimony payments.** If you're divorced and pay alimony to your former spouse, you might be able to deduct it. But certain conditions apply. You can only deduct money that you are legally required to pay your ex-spouse by the divorce or separation decree. You can deduct only payments that you make in cash (including checks and money orders), not in property. And child support is *not* deductible. For details, check Publication 504, *Divorced or Separated Individuals.*

Making the Most of Your Tax Credits

Tax credits are special breaks that are subtracted directly from the tax you owe. (That's different from a deduction, which reduces the amount of your income that is subject to taxation.) Here are some credits that you should take advantage of:

- **Hope Scholarship Credit.** If you're paying your way through college, you may be eligible for a tax credit of up to $1,500 in each of the first two years of school. A full 100% of the first $1,000 you spend on tuition can be claimed for the Hope credit, plus 50% of the next $1,000. The credit phases out for incomes between $40,000 and $50,000 (single) or $80,000 and $100,000 (married filing jointly). To find out more, contact the IRS at 800-TAX-FORM (www.irs.gov) and get a copy of *Tax Benefits for Higher Education,* Publication 970.

- **Lifetime Learning Credit.** If you haven't claimed the Hope credit in a given year, a "lifetime learning credit" worth up to $1,000 a year may be available. Unlike the Hope credits, a lifetime learning credit can be taken in any year of college or graduate school. The credit covers up to 20% of the first $5,000 of qualified tuition and related expenses. (It is scheduled to double to 20% of the first $10,000—up to $2,000 a year—after 2002.) Phase-outs begin at the same income levels as the Hope credit. For details, check out IRS Publication 970, *Tax Benefits for Higher Education*. There is no limit to the number of times this credit can be claimed, making it a real boon to perpetual grad student types.

- **Child Tax Credit.** It pays to have kids: You can take a tax credit of up to $500 in 2000 for each dependent child who is under 17 at the end of the tax year, including stepchildren and foster children. The credit begins to phase out for singles with incomes over $75,000 and married couples earning over $110,000. You can find more about this in IRS Publication 17, *Your Federal Income Tax.*

- **Earned Income Credit.** In 2000, if you're at least 25 and earn less than $10,380 (and no one can claim you as a dependent), you may be eligible for this special tax break. If you have a child, you must earn less than $27,413 to qualify; if you have two or more children, you must earn less than $31,152. To find out more about this credit, see the instruction booklet that comes with your tax forms, Schedule EIC.

- **Child Care Credit.** If you pay someone to take care of your child while you (and your spouse, if you're married) work, you may be a candidate for the child care credit. This credit can be as high as 30% of your child care expenses (up to $2,400 of expenses for one child, or $4,800 for two or more). Even if you earn a high income, you may be allowed to receive 20% of these expenses. For details call 800-TAX-FORM (www.irs.gov) and ask for *Child and Dependent Care Expenses,* Publication 503. In order to get the credit, you will have to make sure that the required employment taxes, such as Medicare and Social Security, are paid for your child care worker. For details, contact 800-TAX-FORM (www.irs.gov) and get a copy of the *Household Employer's Tax Guide,* Publication 926.

TEN TAX MOVES THAT COULD
SAVE YOU MONEY

Here are some additional tips to consider:

1. **Bunch your deductions into one year.** If you don't have
   enough deductible expenses to make it worth your while to
   itemize this year or if you don't meet the minimums for certain deductions, take the standard deduction and put off additional deductible expenditures until next year. For example,
   make your charitable contributions next January rather than
   this December.

2. **See if you can deduct your moving costs.** If you moved to a new
   place for a full-time job, you may be able to deduct moving
   expenses, such as transportation, packing, and shipping costs.
   You don't have to itemize in order to get this deduction. But
   rules governing who gets this deduction are tricky, so read the
   following description of the 2000 rules slowly. The distance
   between your *new job* and your *old house* must be at least 50
   miles more than the distance between your *old job* and your
   old house. (I know. It's outrageously complicated.) You must
   also stay in your new job at least 39 weeks. Special rules apply
   if you are self-employed. If you recently graduated and didn't
   have a job at school, your moving expenses may be deductible
   if your new job is at least 50 miles from your college residence
   (on or off campus). You will need to fill out and attach Form
   3903 to your tax return to deduct these costs. For details, consult *Moving Expenses,* IRS Publication 521.

3. **Figure out if you'd save money by filing jointly or separately.**
   If you work and your spouse doesn't, it generally pays to file a
   joint return. Of course, there are few young married couples
   who fit this description. If you and your spouse both work,
   you should figure your tax on both a joint return and on separate married returns to see which way saves you money. Filing
   separate married returns may make sense, especially if you

have many deductible expenses that are subject to an "adjusted gross income threshold." Say you and your spouse each earns about the same amount of money but you have exceptionally high medical bills. If you file a joint return, your medical bills would have to exceed 7.5% of your *combined* adjusted gross income in order to be deductible. If you file separately, you can deduct medical costs that exceed 7.5% of your *own* adjusted gross income. It may also make sense for you to file your state return separately, so try filling it out both ways. And make sure to do this carefully: Many tax benefits— notably those concerning IRAs—have low phase-out ranges for couples who file separately.

4. **Check your withholding.** You filled out a W-4 when you started your job. Changes in your personal life, as well as changes in the tax law, may result in your having too little or too much tax withheld from your paycheck. If you get married, buy a home, have a baby, or experience any other major financial life change, you should reevaluate your withholding.

   If you receive a big refund from the IRS, you should probably increase the number of withholding allowances you take. Although receiving a cash windfall from the IRS feels great, it isn't a smart financial move. A refund occurs after you've given the IRS too much money during the year. The problem is, the IRS doesn't pay you interest for the additional money withheld from your paycheck during the year. And although some people say that over-withholding is a good "forced savings program," I don't agree. You're better off withholding the right amount and funneling small amounts of cash into an automatic savings program throughout the year. (See Chapter 4 for details.) That way you get forced savings plus earnings.

   There are other ways that adjusting your withholding can help you. If you just graduated from college, for instance, and you'll be working for less than 12 months this calendar year, request a special withholding method known as a part-year option. Then your employer will calculate your withholding based on the number of months you actually earn money this year, rather than basing the withholding on your annual salary. This will prevent overwithholding.

A warning: Don't claim more allowances than you deserve. This will result in your employer's withholding too little tax during the year. If you don't pay at least 90% of the tax you owe during the current year or 100% of the tax you paid during the prior year, you may be charged interest and a penalty. (At high income levels you may have to pay more than 100% of your previous year's payments.)

5. **Take advantage of state and local deductions.** Read your state's and your town's tax instructions carefully. Some states allow you to deduct some of your federal income tax on your state return. Some states allow you to deduct all or a portion of the license fees for your car. And most states give a tax break to homeowners who pay local property taxes.

6. **Consider taxes when you invest.** If your tax rate is 28% or higher, look into investments that offer some tax advantages, such as tax-free money market funds. While it doesn't make sense to choose an investment solely for the tax break, it is one factor to consider. (See Chapter 5 for a simple formula that will help you determine whether tax-free investments are right for you.)

7. **Consider taxes before you choose a date to get married.** Okay, call me unromantic, but the two of you might save hundreds of dollars if you marry in January rather than December. That's because you may owe more in taxes by filing a joint return than by filing two single returns. Say you each earn $30,000, and you take the standard deduction. As a single person in 2000, you would each pay $3,420 in taxes, for a total of $6,840. As a married couple filing a joint return, you would pay $7,474. So if you put off your nuptials until January, you'll save $634—which may be enough to pay for the champagne and wedding cake. The general rule is that if you and your betrothed earn about the same income, you will probably save money by marrying after the first of the year. If one of you

earns much more than the other, it's generally better to get married before the end of the year and file jointly.

The fact that married people sometimes pay more tax than singles is known as the "marriage penalty." Congress has been promising to abolish it for years. In fact, by the time you file your taxes this year the marriage penalty may no longer exist—in which case you should feel free to plan your wedding whenever you like.

8. **Take advantage of tax-favored employee benefits.** If you work for a company that offers you the chance to use a flexible spending account (FSA) to pay for child care or for medical expenses that aren't covered by your insurance, use it. (For details, see Chapter 8.) And, of course, contribute the most you can to your 401(k).

9. **If you're a self-employed performer, see if you're eligible for a special tax break.** Whether you itemize deductions or not, you may get your first big break on your tax form. That's because you're allowed to deduct business-related expenses (the cost of acting classes, headshots, costumes, etc.) if your AGI is $16,000 or less before this deduction. The rules about who can deduct these expenses are complex, so check the details in *Miscellaneous Deductions,* IRS Publication 529.

10. **Consider refinancing high-rate credit card debt with a home equity loan.** The interest you pay on a home equity loan up to $100,000 is deductible. The interest you pay on credit cards is not. (For details, see Chapter 3.)

IF YOU'RE SELF-EMPLOYED

If you work for yourself—that includes anyone who has his or her own company or who does freelance work—you have certain responsibilities and are eligible for some special deductions.

If you're self-employed, the companies you do work for probably will not withhold taxes from their payments to you. But you can't simply wait until the end of the year to pay the IRS. Instead, you probably will have to pay income tax quarterly. Consult IRS Publication 505, *Tax Withholding and Estimated Tax.* You must also be sure to pay enough self-employment tax. For details get a copy of *Self-Employment Tax,* Publication 533. Even if you're desperately afraid of tax-related reading, call for these booklets and attempt to read them. After reviewing them, if you still find it difficult to determine your estimated quarterly tax or if you're unsure whether you need to pay self-employment tax at all, seek the help of a tax preparer.

As a self-employed person, you are eligible for many additional deductions. You can deduct half the Social Security and Medicare tax you pay. In 2000 you are also allowed to deduct 60% of your medical insurance premiums, which is scheduled to rise to 70% in 2002 and 100% in 2003. You can also deduct business travel expenses, whether or not they exceed 2% of your adjusted gross income. And you may be able to deduct the cost of office supplies and equipment. Contact the IRS at 800-TAX-FORM (www.irs.gov) for the *Tax Guide for Small Business,* Publication 334.

You may also be able to deduct your home office expenses. Keep in mind, however, that the IRS has very strict rules regarding home offices. You must use the space that you designate as your home office exclusively for business and on a regular basis. If your desk is in your living room, for example, you will have trouble proving that you use that portion of your home exclusively for work. Consult a tax guide or preparer. Also, get a copy of *Business Use of Your Home,* Publication 587, from the IRS.

As a self-employed person, one of the smartest tax (and savings) moves is to open an IRA. But the most you can contribute to an IRA is $2,000 each year. If you have more money to put aside, consider contributing to a retirement plan known as a Keogh, or to a special type of IRA known as a Simplified Employee Pension (SEP-IRA) plan. You may be able to set aside (and deduct) up to $25,500 a year in a SEP or $30,000 a year in a Keogh (in 2000), depending on how much you earn. You might also be able to put away up to $6,000 in a SIMPLE IRA. The rules are laid out in IRS Publication 590,

Individual Retirement Arrangements. (For details on IRAs, SEPs, SIMPLE IRAs, and Keoghs, see Chapter 6.)

GETTING YOUR TAX LIFE IN ORDER

Probably the most daunting part of the tax process is getting your paperwork in order. This section offers a rundown of the various tax forms. It also includes a checklist to help you avoid drowning in paperwork.

A Rundown of the Tax Forms

Beginning in February, most post offices and libraries leave stacks of tax forms lying around. But beware: These places often run short as the deadline approaches, so make sure to get your forms well in advance. You can also get forms by calling 800-TAX-FORM, but it generally takes seven to fifteen business days to receive them. The quickest way to access them is online, at www.irs.gov. Here are the basic forms you'll have to choose from:

- **1040EZ.** The IRS's 1040EZ, which wins in the category of most cleverly named form, is also the easiest to fill out. It's generally for single people, or couples filing jointly, with total taxable income of less than $50,000. To use this form, you must also earn less than $400 in taxable interest. You can't itemize your deductions on the EZ; it's meant for people who are better off taking the standard deduction. Two good reasons *not* to use the EZ: You can't deduct your student loan interest payments or your contribution to a deductible IRA.

- **1040A.** This form is almost as simple as the EZ form. To use it, your total taxable income must be less than $50,000, but your taxable interest and dividends can be more than $400.

This form does not allow you to itemize, but it does permit you to claim tax credits and take deductions for deductible IRA contributions and student loan interest payments.

- **1040.** If you think the value of your itemized deductions is larger than the standard deduction, this form is for you. You'll be *required* to fill out the 1040 if, say, your taxable income is $50,000 or more, or you receive certain types of income like rent or capital gains. In order to itemize on the 1040, you must fill out an additional form called Schedule A, which will help you figure out the value of your itemized deductions. The tax instruction booklet that you get in the mail or by calling 800-TAX-FORM (www.irs.gov) will tell you which schedules you need. (For an example of how itemizing on the 1040 can work to your advantage, see Figure 9-2.)

Of course, you'll probably also need to send in your state and local tax forms by April 15. Like federal forms, these should be available at your local post office or library. You can also download them online by visiting www.taxsites.com, which features links to all the state tax forms you may need.

What to Keep and What to Chuck

Good record keeping is important when it comes to filing your taxes. If you use a tax preparer and he or she must spend hours sifting through shoe boxes full of your receipts and documents, you will be charged extra. By keeping neat, accurate records, you will save time and money. Below are the names of tax-related file folders you should set up.

- **Tax Returns: 2000, 2001, 2002, etc.** Each year add a new folder to hold your most important tax documents, including a copy of your tax return, income statements from your employers (W-2s), and income statements from your bank and mutual fund company (1099s). Save each year's folder for at least three years after you file; if you are audited, the IRS can request up to three years' worth of your tax records.

Figure 9-2
WHAT, ME ITEMIZE?

A lot of young people think they don't earn enough to itemize. But consider the case of Jennifer, who recently left her job at a small architecture firm in Denver to work for a design company in New York City. (Moving costs: $700.) Her salary is $38,000, and she rents a studio apartment. She just bought a computer ($2,500) and a fax machine ($500) so she can do more work at home; her boss told her to buy them so that he could fax her work from his summer house. Jennifer uses the computer and fax exclusively for work. Before moving, she donated a couch, a dresser, and a bed to the Salvation Army. She also donated three shopping bags full of old clothes. (Total value of her donations: $2,000.) She has also paid out $2,200 in interest on her recent student loans, of which $2,000 is deductible. To see why it makes sense for her to itemize her deductions on the 1040 rather than take the standard deduction on the 1040A or EZ, take a look at the table below.

	1040EZ	1040A	1040
Total Income	$38,000	$38,000	$38,000
(minus) Student loan interest payments	0	2,000	2,000
(minus) Moving expenses	0	0	700
ADJUSTED GROSS INCOME (AGI)	38,000	36,000	35,300
Personal exemption	2,800	2,800	2,800
Charitable contributions	0	0	2,000
State and local taxes	0	0	3,466
Miscellaneous and business expenses*	0	0	2,294
Other itemized expenses	0	0	0
Total itemized deductions or standard deduction (whichever is greater)	4,400	4,400	7,760
EXEMPTION PLUS DEDUCTIONS	7,200	7,200	10,560
TAXABLE INCOME (AGI minus personal exemption and deductions)	30,800	28,800	24,740
FEDERAL TAX OWED	5,212	4,652	3,711

* Here's how you get $2,294 in miscellaneous and business expenses in the 1040 column. First, you calculate that 2% of Jennifer's AGI ($35,300) is $706. Then you subtract that amount from the $3,000 ($2,500 for the computer and $500 for the fax machine) in total miscellaneous and business expenses.

Source: Ernst & Young LLP

(If you've underreported your income by 25% or more, the IRS can ask for returns from six years back. And if you've committed fraud, there's no time limit.) After three years, throw out your supporting paperwork, but hold on to a copy of the return, your attached W-2s and 1099s, and any other IRS forms you filed. If you've sent money to the IRS, keep the canceled check (or a copy of it); if ten years from now the IRS claims you never filed your 1999 return, you'll want to be able to prove that you did.

- **Business-Related Expenses (Unreimbursed).** Save appropriate credit card receipts, entertainment and meal receipts, and receipts for tolls, taxis, parking, gas, car maintenance, tips, union dues, and subscriptions. If you plan to deduct the cost of a computer or cellular phone, in addition to receipts you must keep records that detail when you use the equipment for work and when you use it for leisure activity. If you're self-employed, save all receipts from business-related travel. Also, keep a detailed spending diary when you go on business trips, and file it in this folder.

- **Charitable Contributions.** Keep lists of property you've donated and receipts from the organizations you contribute to. If you contribute money, file the canceled checks and receipts from the charity here.

- **Child Care/Dependent Care Expenses.** Hold on to documents indicating the dates and amounts of various fees you paid to an individual or a center to take care of your child or other dependent while you worked. (Sorry, but the money you pay a baby-sitter to watch your child so you can go to a movie is not deductible.) Also keep track of the cost of meals and lodging expenses paid to a child care worker who lives in your home. To be able to claim the child care credit, you must make certain that the required employment taxes—Social Security, Medicare, and unemployment—are paid for your employee. Keep records that prove these taxes were paid.

- **Home Improvements.** A home improvement, known as a **capital improvement,** is a renovation that increases your home's value. If you own a home, save all receipts related to home improvements. Although you can't deduct these expenses now, you can add them to the original purchase price of your home when you're ready to sell; this reduces the reported gain you get, and therefore the amount of tax you pay, if you sell the house at a profit. Routine repairs like painting don't count, but adding a new room, putting on a new roof, installing a new toilet, paneling walls, or adding new tile do.

  If you sell your home, you currently don't have to pay tax on up to $250,000 of capital profit if you're single or $500,000 if you're married and filing jointly. You can qualify for this tax break as long as the home has been your principal residence for at least two of the previous five years. Some people say that these high exemptions mean that you no longer have to keep a file on your home improvements, since few couples will see a profit of more than $500,000 on the sale of their homes. But since there is no telling how these laws will hold up in the future, I say keep the file. (For details consult a tax book or *Tax Information for First-Time Homeowners,* IRS Publication 530.)

- **Home (Purchase).** Keep the closing statement and any other paperwork related to the purchase of your home. You may need these documents for tax purposes when you sell your home.

- **Individual Retirement Accounts.** Keep papers that indicate when your IRA contributions were made, the amount you invested, the date you opened the IRA, and the source of any money you rolled over from an employer retirement plan into your IRA. This documentation will be useful when you withdraw the money upon retirement. It's especially important to hold on to copies of IRS Form 8606, which you'll need to file each year if you make nondeductible contributions to an IRA. When you withdraw money from a nondeductible IRA, you won't be taxed on the money you contributed but only on the earnings. Also, hold on to a copy of the special form (Form 5329) that you file if you make a penalty-free withdrawal from your IRA, as described in Chapter 6.

- **Medical Expenses (Unreimbursed).** If you pay any medical costs that your health insurance doesn't reimburse you for, keep the receipts. If at the end of the year these expenses exceed 7.5% of your adjusted gross income, you can deduct the portion that is over the threshold.

- **Miscellaneous Deductions.** This catch-all folder should include receipts for financial publications, tax preparation, job search activities, and certain education expenses.

- **Mortgage Interest Payments.** If you own a home, keep your 1098 form in this folder. A 1098 is an annual statement from your lender indicating how much interest and principal you paid on your mortgage. It may also tell you how much property tax you paid. Co-op owners generally receive a 1098 indicating the portion of the interest they paid on the building's mortgage.

- **Mutual Funds.** Many funds provide a year-end statement that indicates how many shares you bought and sold during the year (including purchases you made through a reinvestment plan) and the price of those shares. Hold on to these statements. You'll be taxed on any gain you made from selling shares, and you'll get a tax break on any loss. You'll need the statements to figure out what your gain (or loss) was. There are several different methods you can use to calculate your gain—and some are more beneficial than others. In order to weigh the advantages of the various methods, you need to keep careful records of what you paid for the shares. (For details on the different methods used to calculate the tax owed on mutual fund gains, get *Mutual Fund Distributions,* Publication 564.) If your fund doesn't send you a comprehensive statement of your transactions, call and request one.

- **Property and Real Estate Tax.** The monthly mortgage payment you make to your lender generally includes the amount you owe to your local government for property taxes. Lenders typically forward the tax to your local taxing authority. At the end of the year, you'll receive a statement from your lender informing you of the amount of property tax you paid for the year. These payments are deductible, so hold on to these statements.

- **Police Reports, Insurance Claims.** With any luck, you won't need this file. But if you've been burglarized, save these documents. If you suffered major losses, you may be able to deduct the value of uninsured items.

- **Stocks and Bonds.** If you own individual stocks and bonds, keep the statements you get from the brokerage firm or the company that issued them. Also hang on to any stock or bond certificates, preferably in a bank safety deposit box.

DO YOU NEED A TAX PREPARER?

One of the best ways to learn about your financial life is to prepare your own tax return. If you've had your taxes prepared professionally in the past, use the records from that year to help guide you in the right direction. If you've never done your own taxes, you may be surprised to learn how easy it is—especially if you use a good tax book or software package. But if you're dead set against doing it yourself, at least take the time to find a decent preparer.

If You Don't Use a Preparer

The general instruction book that the IRS produces is quite well written and easy to understand. It's also free. Call 800-TAX-FORM (www.irs.gov) and ask for *Your Federal Income Tax,* Publication 17.

This guide, with more than 300 pages, is full of relevant details, including a list of other IRS publications you may need.

If you intend to itemize your deductions, you should also invest in one of the big fat tax guides available in any bookstore. Some good ones are *J. K. Lasser's Your Income Tax, Taxes for Dummies,* and *The Ernst & Young Tax Guide.* Make sure you buy the correct book for the current year; you would use the 2001 guides to fill out your 2000 taxes. These books usually cost less than $20 and are well worth the expense.

You should also consider using your computer to help you do your taxes. Quicken's TurboTax Web site (www.turbotax.com) allows you to fill out your tax forms online and file them electronically, for $10 to $20 depending on your return. (If you have a very low income and an uncomplicated return, they may let you file for free.) You can do your state taxes there too. If you have a computer but don't have Web access, you can purchase software (for about $35) that provides you with the forms and instructions. Two popular programs that get high marks from users are: TurboTax (or MacInTax for Macs) and TaxCut.

There are several advantages to doing your taxes on your computer. First of all, you won't have to spend time digging through tax books for details; the tax program knows all the rules and will guide you through the process. What's more, your chances of making a mistake on your tax forms are much smaller when your computer does the math for you. And if the IRS owes you a refund, you'll get it substantially faster if you file your return electronically instead of by mail. For more information about electronic filing, see the box on page 264.

If You Use a Preparer

The most obvious choices are big-name chain tax preparers such as H&R Block and smaller mom-and-pop shops in your neighborhood. The advantage of these services is that they're usually inexpensive. If you're sure you aren't eligible for many deductions and that the standard deduction is for you, a storefront preparer is fine.

RAPID RIP-OFFS

When David, a teacher in New York City, walked into a local tax preparation office, he had a suspicion he might qualify for a pretty big refund that year. He was right: The IRS owed him almost $500. His tax preparer told him that he could file electronically and get his refund in a couple of weeks—or sign up for a special "rapid refund" program that would get his refund to him almost immediately. David jumped at the chance to get the money right away. But when his refund check arrived a few days later, he found that he had been charged $34 for the extra speed.

What David didn't understand is that he had actually signed up for a **refund anticipation loan.** Many tax preparers offer this service to customers who are eager to get their refunds as quickly as possible. Basically, the preparer loans the customer the amount of his or her refund, then pockets the actual refund when it comes from the IRS. But refund anticipation loans offer almost no benefit to the customer, especially now that electronic filing and direct deposit make it possible to get your refund within two weeks anyway. The fees for these loans are truly outrageous. The $34 that David paid to get his refund a couple of weeks earlier works out to an annual interest rate of over 200%. If your tax preparer tries to foist a refund anticipation loan on you, don't take it. If you need money right away, just about any other way of getting it—even cash advances on your credit card—will be cheaper.

Keep in mind that the level of knowledge can vary dramatically. Look for a tax preparation business that operates year-round rather than one that's open just a few months a year. Ask friends and family members to recommend specific preparers. Most chain preparers allow you to request a specific person.

If you have a somewhat more complicated return (for example, if you are self-employed or have received a large inheritance), you may want to find a preparer with some additional education. One of the top credentials is **CPA**, which stands for **Certified Public Accountant.** CPAs have to meet the toughest requirements to get licensed; they also can be expensive. Another, usually cheaper option is an **enrolled agent;** the title refers to any preparer who has worked for the IRS as an auditor or in some similar job for five years or who has passed a difficult two-day exam. At the very least, find a preparer with a minimum of three years' experience filing returns. **Tax attorneys** are typically the most expensive alternative and are necessary only if you are in serious trouble with the IRS.

Be sure to ask what the preparer charges; there may be different rates for different preparers at the same company. You can often find an enrolled agent at a chain preparer like H&R Block; if possible, ask to work with one. Preparers usually file your return electronically, so if you are due a refund, you will get it faster than you would if you mailed in your return.

Finally, if you have someone fill out your forms, look the forms over carefully. *You* are responsible for making sure all the information on your return is true and correct.

FINANCIAL CRAMMING

- Fill out your tax forms as soon after January 1 as possible. If you're owed a refund, file right away; the quicker you mail in your forms, the faster you'll get your check. If you owe money, file in early April so you can hang on to your cash as long as possible.

- If you're expecting a refund, file electronically and sign up to have your refund deposited directly to your bank account. Your refund will arrive weeks faster than it would if you mailed in your tax return.

- If you received a big refund from the IRS, fill out a new W-4 form to adjust your withholding. Since the IRS doesn't pay you interest on the money you overpay during the year, you're better off keeping this money in a bank account or money market fund.

- If you owe the IRS money but you can't afford to pay, send in your return along with whatever payment you can afford by April 15 anyway. You'll have to pay a penalty, but it won't be as stiff as the penalty for late filing.

- Take full advantage of the tax credits available to you if you have children or educational expenses, as described on page 276. These credits are like money in your pocket.

- Look at the list of deductions on page 270. If you're eligible for some of them, fill out the 1040 form to see if itemizing saves you money. You can take some deductions—like those for deductible IRA contributions or student loan interest payments—whether you itemize or not.

- If you're taking the standard deduction this year, postpone making charitable donations and home office–related purchases until after January 1. That way you could get credit for the deductions if you itemize next year.

- If you're self-employed, understand that you can't simply wait until the end of the year to pay Uncle Sam. You may be required to pay your taxes quarterly. For details, get a copy of *Self-Employment Tax,* Publication 533.

FURTHER READING

If you've read through this entire tome, congratulations! You have all the basic information you need to have a prosperous financial life. If you are a glutton for punishment, below are some very selective recommendations. These are the books I would tell my friends to read if they wanted to know more about various topics. Also included are magazines, software, and pamphlets that may interest you. Some of the publications listed here are mentioned in the individual chapters; others are not.

BOOKS

Investing

Evans, Richard E., and Burton G. Malkiel. *The Index Fund Solution*. New York: Simon & Schuster, 1999. A thorough and readable explanation of indexing and its advantages.

Malkiel, Burton G. *A Random Walk Down Wall Street*. New York: Norton, 1999. This updated classic is a must-read for anyone who wants to lean more about investing.

Tobias, Andrew. *The Only Investment Guide You'll Ever Need*. San Diego: Harvest Books, 1998. An excellent (and witty) overview of key investment concepts.

Insurance

Taylor, Barbara. *How to Get Your Money's Worth in Home and Auto Insurance.* New York: McGraw-Hill, 1991. Out of date, but still a great book for anyone who wants to know more about home and auto coverage.

Taxes

The following four books are excellent tax guides. Make sure to get the most current edition!

Bernstein, Peter W., ed. *The Ernst & Young Tax Guide.* New York: Wiley, 1999.

Eiss, Eliot, et al. *J. K. Lasser's Your Income Tax.* New York: Macmillan, 1999.

Esanu, Warren H., et al. *Consumer Reports Guide to Income Tax.* New York: Consumers' Union, 1999.

Tyson, Eric, and David J. Silverman. *Taxes for Dummies.* Foster City, Calif.: IDG Books, 1999.

General Personal Finance

Quinn, Jane Bryant. *Making the Most of Your Money.* New York: Simon & Schuster, 1997. Although its 900-plus pages may be a bit overwhelming, and some of it will be irrelevant to people in their twenties and thirties, this encyclopedic guide is one of the best.

Miscellaneous

Chany, Kalman A., with Geoff Martz. *Paying for College Without Going Broke.* New York: Random House/Princeton Review, 1999. A comprehensive primer on college financing issues.

Clifford, Denis. *Nolo's Will Book.* Berkeley: Nolo Press, 1997. A good resource if you're thinking of writing a will.

PERSONAL FINANCE MAGAZINES

Kiplinger's
Money
Smart Money
Worth

PAMPHLETS AND COMPANY PUBLICATIONS

Debt

Choosing and Using Credit Cards, available from the Bureau of Consumer Protection, Office of Consumer and Business Education, Federal Trade Commission, Sixth and Pennsylvania Ave., NW, Washington, DC 20580. 877-FTC-HELP, www.ftc.gov.

Consumer Handbook to Credit Protection Laws, available from the Bureau of Consumer Protection, Office of Consumer and Business Education, Federal Trade Commission, Sixth and Pennsylvania Ave., NW, Washington, DC 20580. 877-FTC-HELP, www.ftc.gov.

Credit and Divorce, available from the Bureau of Consumer Protection, Office of Consumer and Business Education, Federal Trade Commission, Sixth and Pennsylvania Ave., NW, Washington, DC 20580. 877-FTC-HELP, www.ftc.gov.

Credit Cards, available from the Bureau of Consumer Protection, Office of Consumer and Business Education, Federal Trade Commission, Sixth and Pennsylvania Ave., NW, Washington, DC 20580. 877-FTC-HELP, www.ftc.gov.

Credit Problems, available from the Bureau of Consumer Protection, Office of Consumer and Business Education, Federal Trade Commission, Sixth and Pennsylvania Ave., NW, Washington, DC 20580. 877-FTC-HELP, www.ftc.gov.

Credit Repair, available from the Bureau of Consumer Protection, Office of Consumer and Business Education, Federal Trade Commission, Sixth and Pennsylvania Ave., NW, Washington, DC 20580. 877-FTC-HELP, www.ftc.gov.

Equal Credit Opportunity, available from the Bureau of Consumer Protection, Office of Consumer and Business Education, Federal

Trade Commission, Sixth and Pennsylvania Ave., NW, Washington, DC 20580. 877-FTC-HELP, www.ftc.gov.

Fair Credit Billing, available from the Bureau of Consumer Protection, Office of Consumer and Business Education, Federal Trade Commission, Sixth and Pennsylvania Ave., NW, Washington, DC 20580. 877-FTC-HELP, www.ftc.gov.

Fair Debt Collection, available from the Bureau of Consumer Protection, Office of Consumer and Business Education, Federal Trade Commission, Sixth and Pennsylvania Ave., NW, Washington, DC 20580. 877-FTC-HELP, www.ftc.gov.

How to Dispute Credit Report Errors, available from the Bureau of Consumer Protection, Office of Consumer and Business Education, Federal Trade Commission, Sixth and Pennsylvania Ave., NW, Washington, DC 20580. 877-FTC-HELP, www.ftc.gov.

Keys to Vehicle Leasing, available from the Federal Reserve, Publications Services, MS-127, Board of Governors of the Federal Reserve System, Washington, DC 20551. 202-452-3244, www.federalreserve.gov/pubs/leasing.

Your Legal Guide to Consumer Credit, available from the Public Education Division, American Bar Association, 750 North Lake Shore Dr., Chicago, IL 60611. 800-285-2221, www.abanet.org.

Investing

Planning for College, available from the Investment Company Institute, 1401 H St., NW, Suite 1200, Washington, DC 20005-2148. 202-326-5800.

Mortgage

Choosing the Mortgage That's Right for You, available from Fannie Mae Consumer Education Group, 3900 Wisconsin Ave., NW, Washington, DC 20016-2899. 800-688-4663, www.fanniemae.com.

The Mortgage Money Guide, available from the Federal Trade Commission, Sixth and Pennsylvania Ave., NW, Washington, DC 20580. 202-326-3650.

Mortgage Servicing, available from the Bureau of Consumer Protection, Office of Consumer and Business Education, Federal Trade Commission, Sixth and Pennsylvania Ave., NW, Washington, DC 20580. 877-FTC-HELP, www.ftc.gov.

Opening the Door to a Home of Your Own, available from Fannie Mae Consumer Education Group, 3900 Wisconsin Ave., NW, Washington, DC 20016-2899. 800-688-4663, www.fanniemae .com.

Retirement

Pension Education Clearinghouse Publication Listing. Send a self-addressed, business-size envelope with 55 cents postage to Pension Education Clearinghouse, P.O. Box 19821, Washington, DC 20036.

Protecting Your Pension Money. For information, write to Pension and Welfare Benefits Administration, Department of Labor, 2000 Constitution Ave., NW, Room N-5656, Washington, DC 20210. www.dol.gov/dol/pwba.

Tax

Guide to Free Tax Services, available from the Internal Revenue Service. 800-829-1040, www.irs.gov.

Your Federal Income Tax, Publication 17, available from the Internal Revenue Service. 800-TAX-FORM, www.irs.gov.

SOFTWARE

BUY-RENT.WK1, a spreadsheet that allows you to figure out whether you should rent or buy a house. For information, contact Ed Chang through his Web site, members.xoom.com/ echang80/buyrent.htm.

CarWizard, a program that allows you to do lease-versus-buy analysis for auto costs. You can download the programs along with a companion book, at www.carwizard.com, or order it by calling 800-838-8778.

Kiplinger TaxCut, a tax-preparation program from Kiplinger and H&R Block. Available in computer stores or at www.taxcut.com.

Microsoft Money, a general personal finance program by Microsoft. Available in computer stores or at www.microsoft.com.

Quicken, a general personal finance program by Intuit. Available in computer stores or at www.quicken.com.

TurboTax (MacInTax for Macs), a tax-preparation program by Intuit. Available at computer stores or at www.quicken.com.

Willmaker 7.0, a will program from Nolo Press. Available at computer stores or at www.nolo.com.

ACKNOWLEDGMENTS

The following is a list of the hundreds of people who generously gave of their time and expertise to make this book possible. If anyone has inadvertently been left out, I apologize.

INTRODUCTION

Larry Cohen, SRI International; Carmen Denavas, Census Bureau; Neal Fogg, Center for Labor Market Studies at Northeastern University; Stephanie Schlandt, Payment Systems; Andrew Sum, Center for Labor Market Studies at Northeastern University; David Tong, SRI International.

CHAPTER 2: TAKING STOCK OF YOUR FINANCIAL LIFE

Durant Abernethy, National Foundation for Consumer Credit; Kent Allison, Price Waterhouse; Kent Brunette, American Association of Retired Persons; Anthony Burke, Internal Revenue Service; Peg Downey, Money Plans; Steven Enright, Enright Financial Advisors; Wilson Fadely, Internal Revenue Service; Ross Levin, Accredited Investors; Bill Moss, American Express Company; Edward L. Neumann, Furash & Company; Glenn Pape, Ayco Company; John Pfister, Chicago Title and Trust Company; John Rogers, Bureau of Labor Statistics; Steve Sanders, Sanders Investment Advisors; Ken Scott, Ken Scott Communications; William Speciale, David L. Babson & Company; Kristyn Stout, The Ryland Group.

CHAPTER 3: DEBT AND THE MATERIAL WORLD

John Abadie, NationsBank Corporation; Fiona Adams, Student Loan Marketing Association (Sallie Mae); Jonathan Adkins, Debt Counselors of America; Deb Adler, New York State Credit Union League; Deborah Ankrom, Student Loan Marketing Association (Sallie Mae); Stephanie Babyak, Department of Education; Bill Banks, Chemical Bank; Gary Beanblossom, Department of Education; Monica Beaupre, American Express; Ed Block, Automotive Lease Consultants; Elene Cafasso, Oakbrook Bank; Glenn Canner, Federal Reserve Board; Dennis Carroll, National Center for Education Statistics; Nancy Castleman, Good Advice Press; Kalman Chany, Campus Consultants; Tim Christensen, Department of Education; Karen Christie, Bankrate.com; Larry Cohen, SRI International; Paul Combe, Knight College Resource Group; James Daly, Credit Card News; Linda Del Castillo, Student Loan Marketing Association (Sallie Mae); Dr. Richard F. DeMong, McIntire School of Commerce, University of Virginia; Gerri Detweiler, Debt Counselors of America; Claire Diamond, AT&T Universal Card Services; Rachel Edelstein, Department of Education; Liz Eischeid, Trans Union Corporation; Marc Eisenson, Good Advice Press; Fritz Elmendorf, Consumer Bankers Association; Brad Fay, Roper Organization; Susan Forman, Visa USA; Gerhard Fries, Federal Reserve Board; Jean Frohlicher, National Council of Higher Education Loan Programs; Luther Gatling, Budget & Credit Counseling Services; Jane Glickman, Department of Education; Linda Goldberg, CarSource; Edward Gonciarz, Goldberg, Gonciarz & Scudieri; David Graubard, Kera & Graubard; Jeffrey Green, Faulkner & Grey; Rod Griffin, Experian; Keith Gumbinger, HSH Associates; Robert Hall, Corestates Dealer Services Corporation; Charles Hart, Chart Software; Dayna Hart, General Motors Corporation; Ed Harting, Auto Lease Guide; Paul Havemann, HSH Associates; Robert Heady, Bank Rate Monitor; Stephen Henson, Kelley Blue Book; Stuart Himmelfarb, Roper Organization; Jeanne Hogarth, Federal Reserve Board; Wendy Huntington, Student Loan Marketing Association (Sallie Mae); Dr. Robert Johnson, Credit Research Center, Purdue University; Dr. Jim Jurinski, University of

Portland; Mike Kidwell, Debt Counselors of America; Jacqueline King, The College Board; Dottie Kingsley, Department of Education; Ross Kleinman, Student Loan Marketing Association (Sallie Mae); Laura Knapp, The College Board; Paula Knepper, National Center for Education Statistics; Janis Lamar, TRW Information Systems & Services; Tony Langan, The Chase Manhattan Bank; Phyllis Laubacher, MasterCard International; Roberta Lazarz, Credit Union National Association; Anna Leider, Octameron Associates; Jean Lesher, American Bankers Association; Gail Liberman, Bank Rate Monitor; Ronald S. Loshin, Bank Lease Consultants; Chris Lynn, Oakbrook Bank; John Maciarz, General Motors Corporation; Norm Magnuson, Associated Credit Bureaus; Drew Malizio, National Center for Education Statistics; Garry Marquiss, Bank One Corporation; John Marsh, Wachovia Bank of Georgia; Coleen Martin, Trans Union; Nancy Mathis, Congressman Joseph Kennedy's Office; Randall McCathren, Bank Lease Consultants; Robert B. McKinley, RAM Research Corporation; David Melancon, Visa USA; Maria Mendler, Citibank; Ed Mierzwinski, U.S. Public Interest Research Group (PIRG); Scott Miller, Student Loan Marketing Association (Sallie Mae); Bill Moss, American Express Company; Nancy Murphy, Student Loan Marketing Association (Sallie Mae); Bob Murray, USA Group; Martin Neilson, Seafirst Bank; Jim Newell, Student Loan Marketing Association (Sallie Mae); Michael O'Brien, MasterCard International; Kit O'Kelly, European American Bank; Bussie Parker, Debt Counselors of America; Travis Plunkett, Consumer Federation of America; William Redman, European American Bank; Ruth Lammert Reeves, Georgetown University; Bruce Reid, AT&T Universal Card Services; Andrea Retsky, Congressman Joseph Kennedy's Office; Paul Richard, National Center for Financial Education; Ben Robinson, Congressman Joseph Kennedy's Office; Marcello Rojtman, Department of Education; Denise Rossitto, Student Loan Marketing Association (Sallie Mae); Stephanie Schlant, Payment Systems; Dick Schliesmann, Wells Fargo Bank; Hans Schumann, AT&T Universal Card Services; Tom Sclafini, American Express; Nick Sharkey, Ford Motor Credit Company; Sheila Shekar, Visa; Lewis Siegel, Pirro, Collier, Cohen, Crystal & Bock; Jenny Smith, Oakbrook Bank;

Henry Sommer, Miller, Frank & Miller; Art Spinella, CNW Marketing Research; Jennifer Spoerri, Nolo Press; Virginia Stafford, American Bankers Association; Amy Sudol, The Chase Manhattan Bank; Dr. Charlene Sullivan, Credit Research Center, Purdue University; Marcia Sullivan, Consumer Bankers Association; Terry Sullivan, General Motors Corporation; Ruth Susswein, Bankcard Holders of America; Greg Tarmin, American Express Company; David Tong, SRI International; Francine Van Nevel, Credit Union National Association; Dr. Elizabeth Warren, Harvard Law School; Gail Wasserman, American Express Company; Craig Watts, Fair, Isaac and Company; Laura Weiss, Consumers Union; Sharlene Weldon, Bankrate.com; Dr. Jay Westbrook, University of Texas at Austin Law School; Lance Wilcox, J. D. Power & Associates; Jeff Wischerth, European American Bank; Labat Yancey, Equifax; Anissa Yates, Experian; Steve Zeisel, Consumer Bankers Association; Steve Zwillinger, Department of Education.

CHAPTER 4: BASIC BANKING

Heatherun Allison, Federal Reserve Bank; Kent Allison, Price Waterhouse; Karen Altfest, L. J. Altfest & Co.; Lew Altfest, L. J. Altfest & Co.; Caryl Austrian, Federal Deposit Insurance Corporation; Peter Bakstansky, Federal Reserve Bank of New York; David Barr, Federal Deposit Insurance Corporation; Richard Beebe, Bank of America; Brian Black, Bank Administration Institute; Alexander Bove, law offices of Alexander Bove, Jr.; Dan Brennan, Federal Reserve Bank of St. Louis; Jim Bruene, Online Banking Report; Neal Chambliss, Furash & Co.; Diane Coffey, The Dreyfus Corporation; Jeff Comerford, The Equitable; Elda Di Re, Ernst & Young; Lorna Doubet, Wells Fargo Bank; Fritz Elmendorf, Consumer Bankers Association; Steven Enright, Enright Financial Advisors; John Hall, American Bankers Association; Jennifer Harlan, Society Bank; Kathlyn Hoekstra, Federal Deposit Insurance Corporation; Gunnar Hughes, Twentieth Century Services; Sheldon Jacobs, The No-Load Fund Investor, Inc.; Caroline Jervey, Bauer Communications; Jerry Karbon, Credit Union National Association; Cathy Keary, Merrill Lynch & Company; Ken Kehrer, Kenneth

Kehrer & Associates; David Klavitter, Credit Union National Association; Tom Klipstine, General Motors Corporation; Dina Lee, Ernst & Young; Ross Levin, Accredited Investors; Gail Liberman, Bank Rate Monitor; Jane Mahoney, The Equitable; Joyce Manchester, Congressional Budget Office; Brian Mattes, The Vanguard Group; Diana Mehl, BanxQuote; Michael Moebs, Moebs $ervices; Anne Moore, Synergists Research Corporation; Edward L. Neumann, Furash & Company; Steve Norwitz, T. Rowe Price Associates; Karen Oetzel, Credit Union National Association; Obrea Poindexter, Division of Consumer & Community Affairs; Barbara Raasch, Ernst & Young; Christopher Renyi, Forrester Research, Inc.; Ellen Ringel, Price Waterhouse; Kevin Roach, Price Waterhouse; Richard Robida, Speer & Associates; Mark Rodgers, Citibank; Jay Rosenstein, Federal Deposit Insurance Corporation; Mimi Rossetti, Payment Systems; Dr. John Sabelhaus, The Urban Institute; Pam Sabin, checkfree.com; Judith Saxe, Kronish, Lieb, Weiner & Hellman; Dr. Janice Shields, Center of Study for Responsive Law; Dr. Jonathan Skinner, University of Virginia; Barton Sotnick, Federal Reserve Bank of New York; Chrissy Snyder, Janus Capital Corporation; William Speciale, David L. Babson & Company; Virginia Stafford, American Bankers Association; Ellen Stuart, Chemical Bank; Michele Stuvin, Executive Enterprises; Jack Tatom, Federal Reserve Bank of St. Louis; Paul Thompson, Credit Union National Association; Joseph Votava, Nixon, Peabody Attorneys at Law; Sandra Weiksner, Cleary, Gottlieb, Steen & Hamilton.

CHAPTER 5: ALL YOU REALLY NEED TO KNOW ABOUT INVESTING

Camilla Altamura, Lipper, Inc.; Lew Altfest, L. J. Altfest & Company; Marc Beauchamp, North American Securities Administrators Association; Jennifer Bright, R. L. Polk and Co.; Jim Cain, Lehman Brothers; Lisa Cholnoky, Smith Barney; Peter Cinquegrani, Investment Company Institute; Mark Coler, Mercer; John Collins, Investment Company Institute; Bob Connor, Smith Barney; Pete Crane, IBC Financial; Kim Crawley, Morgan Stanley & Company; Don Criniti, Fidelity Investments; Diane Cullen, Dalbar Financial

Services; Jon M. Diat, Standard & Poor's; Holly Duncan, Financial
Engines, Inc.; Richard Erickson, USAA; Dominic Falaschetti,
Ibbotson Associates; Georgina Fiordalisi, Duff & Phelps Credit
Rating Company; Nick Gendron, Lehman Brothers; Lynne Goldman,
Cerulli Associates; Trista Hannan, Morningstar; Rowena Itchon, T.
Rowe Price Associates; Sheldon Jacobs, The No-Load Fund Investor,
Inc.; Paula Kahanek, Ibbotson Associates; Dawn Kahler,
Wiesenberger/Thomson Financial; Charles Kassouf, Mercer; Teri
Kilduff, Fidelity Investments; Russ Kinnel, Morningstar; Patrice
Kozlowski, The Dreyfus Corporation; Keith Lawson, Investment
Company Institute; Marilyn Leiker, Lipper Analytical Services; Mark
N. Lindblom, Morgan Stanley & Company; Stephanie Linkous,
United Services Advisors; Pam Livingston, E*Trade; Jeanine Magill,
Morningstar; John Markese, American Association of Individual
Investors; Brian Mattes, The Vanguard Group; Patrick McVeigh,
Frnaklin Research & Development; Norbert Mehl, BanxQuote; Bob
Mescal, Institute for Econometric Research; Marilyn Morrison,
Fidelity Investments; Chip Norton, IBC/Donoghue; Steve Norwitz, T.
Rowe Price Associates; Roger Nyhus, Frank Russell Company; Glen
King Parker, Institute of Econometric Research; Chris Phillips, Frank
Russell Company; Teri Redinger, IBC/Donoghue; Matthew Scott,
Domini Social Equity Funds; Mo Shafroth, Charles Schwab; Rami
Shalaan, Wiesenberger/ Thomson Financial; Kimberly Stamel,
Morningstar; Tom Taggart, Charles Schwab & Company; Thomas
Tays, United Services Advisors; Jon Teall, Lipper Analytical Services;
Lukasz Thieme, Lipper, Inc.; Robyn Tice, Fidelity Investments;
Maurice Turner, Working Assets Capital Management; Julie Ann
Urban, Ibbotson Associates; Michael Van Dam, Morningstar; Andrea
Vassallo, Financial Engines, Inc.; Ken Volpert, The Vanguard Group;
Bob Waid, Wilshire Associates; John Worth, The Vanguard Group;
Mark Wright, Morningstar.

CHAPTER 6: LIVING THE GOOD LIFE IN 2030

Kent Allison, PricewaterhouseCoopers; Ted Barna, Pricewaterhouse-
Coopers; Harvey Berger, Grant Thornton; Andrea Bierstein, Western
New England College School of Law; Joanetta Bolden, American

Association of Retired Persons; Jack Bonné, Gateway Asset Management; Kent Brunette, American Association of Retired Persons; Anthony Burke, Internal Revenue Service; Heather Chappel, PricewaterhouseCoopers; Steve Ciolino, Ernst & Young; Joe Conway, Towers Perrin; Gloria Della, Department of Labor; Steven Enright, Enright Financial Advisors; Wilson Fadely, Internal Revenue Service; Karen Ferguson, Pension Rights Center; Martin Fleisher, pension consultant; Phil Gambino, Social Security Administration; Jerry Gattegno, Deloitte & Touche; Hal Glassman, Department of Labor; Mary Ann Green, MBL Life Assurance Corporation; Tom Hakala, KPMG Peat Marwick; Ed Hansen, Mercer; Cindy Hounsell, Pension Rights Center; Richard Koski, Buck Consultants; Ross Levin, Accredited Investors; Tom Margenau, Social Security Administration; John Markese, American Association of Individual Investors; Mike Packard, Pension Benefits Guaranty Corporation; Glenn Pape, Ernst & Young; R. Michael Parry, American Planning Group; Carolyn Pemberton, Employee Benefit Research Institute; Stephanie Poe, Mercer and Associates; Mark Puccia, Standard & Poor's; Tangela Richardson, Social Security Administration; Robert Runde, American Planning Group; Christine Seltz, Hewitt Associates; Greg Spencer, Bureau of the Census; Susan Stawick, Internal Revenue Service; David Strauss, Pension Benefit Guaranty Corporation; James Velten, Coopers & Lybrand; Paul Westbrook, Westbrook Financial Advisors; Caryn Zappone, Hewitt Associates.

CHAPTER 7: OH, GIVE ME A HOME

Gopal Ahluwalia, National Association of Home Builders; Rick Beebe, Bank of America; Mark Berman, The Townsend Consulting Group; David Berson, Federal National Mortgage Association (Fannie Mae); Katherine Billings, Federal Home Loan Mortgage Corporation (Freddie Mac); Mary Burt, National Association of Mortgage Brokers; Raschelle Burton, Federal National Mortgage Association (Fannie Mae); Kevin Bussell, Rent.net; Mark Calabria, National Association of Realtors; Michael Carliner, National Association of Home Builders; Andrew Carswell, National Association of Home Builders; Ed Chang, Interet; Brian Chappelle,

Mortgage Bankers Association of America; Laura Clavier, Merrill
Lynch & Company; Wayne Collett, Countrywide Funding
Corporation; Nancy Condon, Federal Home Loan Mortgage
Corporation (Freddie Mac); William A. Connelly, Department of
Housing & Urban Development; Josh Dare, Federal National
Mortgage Association (Fannie Mae); Michelle Elliott, National
Association of Home Builders; Robert Engelstad, Federal National
Mortgage Association (Fannie Mae); Jon Ferchen, Norwest; Mark
Ferrulo, Florida PIRG; Monica Gallagher, Hewitt Associates; Joe
Gilvary, Bureau of the Census; Vince Gisonti, Deloitte & Touche;
Keith Gumbinger, HSH Associates; Kevin Hawkins, Federal National
Mortgage Association (Fannie Mae); Mollie Hightower, NAMB; Liz
Johnson, National Association of Realtors; Ted Jones, Real Estate
Research Center; Cathy Keary, Merrill Lynch & Company; Sam
Khater, National Association of Realtors; Alfred King, Federal
National Mortgage Association (Fannie Mae); Andrew Kochera,
National Association of Home Builders; Doug Krug, Norwest; Toni
Langkau, New York State Housing Authority; John Lewis, G. E.
Capital; William Lloyd, Norwest Mortgage; Dick Manuel,
Department of Housing & Urban Development; Howard Marder,
New York State Housing Authority; Laura Maxwell, Deloitte &
Touche; Ken McKinnon, Department of Veterans Affairs; Naomi
McLean, Department of Veterans Affairs; Ed Mierzwinski, U.S.
Public Interest Research Group (PIRG); Paul Mondor, Mortgage
Bankers Association of America; Larry Montague, Deloitte &
Touche; Trish Morris, National Association of Realtors; Eileen Neely,
Federal National Mortgage Association (Fannie Mae); Bonnie O'Dell,
Federal National Mortgage Association (Fannie Mae); Forest
Pafenberg, National Association of Realtors; Wendy Peca, Chicago
Title and Trust; Julie Reeves, National Council of State Housing
Agencies; Cheryl Regan, Federal Home Loan Mortgage Corporation
(Freddie Mac); Sharon Ridenour, Norwest Mortgage; Douglas
Robinson, Federal Home Loan Mortgage Corporation (Freddie
Mac); Vicki Rydell, Mortgage Bankers Association; Connie St. John,
Bank of America; Margot Saunders, National Consumer Law Center;
Michael Schlerf, Mortgage Bankers Association of America; Christine
Seltz, Hewitt Associates; Jay Shackford, National Association of

Home Builders; Adrian Skiles, Atlanta Mortgage Group; Dave Totaro, Dime Savings Bank; Rick Trilsch, Florida Public Interest Research Group (PIRG); John Tuccillo, National Association of Realtors; Robert Van Order, Federal Home Loan Mortgage Corporation (Freddie Mac); Andrea Waas, National Association of Mortgage Brokers; Margery Wasserman, National Association of Personal Financial Advisors; Sabrina White, Merrill Lynch & Company; William White, Department of Veterans Affairs; George Wilson, Department of Housing & Urban Development; Lemar Wooley, Federal Housing Authority; Jean Wussow, National Association of Realtors; Kris Yamamoto, Countrywide; Catherine Zimring, Countrywide Funding Corporation.

CHAPTER 8: INSURANCE

Roy Assad, RBA Insurance Strategies; Rich Bailey, Provident Life & Accident Insurance Company; Bob Barney, Compulife; Birny Birnbaum, Consumers Union and the Center for Economic Justice; Bob Bland, Quotesmith; Phyllis Bonfield, American Society of Chartered Life Underwriters; Joseph Bosnack, Sr., Arthur Rothlein Agency; Ann H. Brockmeyer, Hartmann & Associates; Bruce Bruscia, Golden State Insurance Services; Karen Burger, American Institute for Chartered Property & Casualty Underwriters; Anthony Burke, Internal Revenue Service; John Calagna, New York State Department of Insurance; Brenda Cargile, Federal Crime Insurance Program; Dee Caruso, Illinois Department of Insurance; Diane Coffey, American Council on Life Insurance; Mark Connor, Department of Labor; Richard Coorsh, Health Insurance Association of America; Sam Cunningham, Anderson & Anderson Benefits Insurance Brokers; Glenn Daily, fee-only insurance consultant; Dan Devine, EBRI; Jack Dolan, American Council of Life Insurers; Bill Dommasch, Geico; Henry Dowdle, Provident Life & Accident Insurance Company; Pam Drellow, Blue Cross & Blue Shield Association; Andrew Ede, MassMutual Life Insurance Company; Susan Farmer, American Society of Chartered Life Underwriters; Terrence Fergus, KPMG Peat Marwick; Anne Getz, Moody's Investors Services; Terrence Gordon, Avis Rent-a-Car System; Ed Graves, The American College; Gene

Grebowski, American Council on Life Insurance; Paul Gribbons, Paul Revere Life Insurance Company; Don Haas, Haas Financial Services; Karen Hamilton, American Institute for Chartered Property & Casualty Underwriters; Ed Hansen, Mercer; Judith Hill, The American College; Rick Hill, 20th Century Insurance Company; Katherine Hoffman, National Association of Professional Insurance Agents; Charles Horne, Amica Mutual Insurance Company; James Hunt, Consumer Federation of America; Robert Hunter, Consumer Federation of America; Ted Huntington, Professional Insurance Agents of California & Nevada; Amy Ingram, Termquote; Kenneth Ingram, Termquote; Linda Jackson, Department of Labor; Donald Jayne, Executive Financial Systems; James Johnson, Unum Provident; Peter Katt, independent life insurance advisor; Susan Keller, Golden Eagle Insurance Company; Dr. Peter Kensicki, East Kentucky University; Rick Koski, Buck Consultants; Amy Kraus, Mutual of Omaha Insurance Company; Arlene Lilly, American Council of Life Insurance; Eliot Lipson, independent insurance consultant; Dick Luedke, State Farm; Jim Marks, Society of Chartered Property & Casualty Underwriters; Greg Marsh, Geico; Brandi Marth, Fireman's Fund Insurance Company; Judith Maurer, Wholesale Insurance Network; Keith Maurer, Wholesale Insurance Network; Mike Mayers, Beall, Garner, Screen & Geare Company; Larry Mayewski, A. M. Best Company; Wayne McHargue, American United Life Insurance Company; Jennifer McInnis, Amica; Annalise McKean-Marcus, Hertz Corporation; Robert Miller, New York Life Insurance Company; Al Minor, Health Insurance Association of America; Tom Monson, State Farm; Rhonda Moritz, A. M. Best Company; Todd Muller, Independent Insurance Agents of America; Tim Murphy, Northwestern Mutual Life Insurance Company; Nan Nases, Illinois Department of Insurance; Haig Neville, Haig Neville Associates; Eric Nordman, National Association of Insurance Commissioners; Mike Norton, UNUM Life Insurance Company of America; Mike Odom, Blue Shield of California; Bill O'Neill, Standard & Poor's; Kendal Leigh O'Neill, Time Warner; John Paganelli, First Transamerica Life Insurance Company; Jerry Parsons, State Farm Insurance Company; Carolyn Pemberton, Employee Benefit Research Institute; Nancy Peskin, Metropolitan Life Insurance Company; Chris Petrocelli,

Petrocelli Group; Irving Pfeffer, insurance consultant; Tim Pfeifer, consulting actuary; Jerome Phillip, Mutual of Omaha Insurance Company; Stephanie Poe, William M. Mercer; Diana Reace, Hewitt Associates; Donna Reichle, National Automobile Dealers Association; John Roman, American Association of Preferred Provider Organizations; Fred Rumack, Buck Consultants; Walter Runkle, Consumer Credit Insurance Association; Jeanne Salvatore, Insurance Information Institute; Bob Sasser, State Farm Insurance Company; Paul Schattenberg, USAA; Tracy Schauer, IDEA; Iris Shaffer, Blue Cross & Blue Shield of Illinois; Craig P. Shanley, Amica Mutual Insurance Company; Tracy Sherman, UNUM Life Insurance Company of America; Dr. Harold Skipper, Department of Risk Management & Insurance Research, Georgia State University; Judy Snelson, Allied Insurance Agencies of America; Camille Sorosiak, American Hospital Association; Steve Stark, Selectquote; Dale Stephenson, National Conference of Insurance Guarantee Funds; Morey Stettner, insurance consultant; Mark Stevens, Federal Emergency Management Agency; Dottye Stewart, Wholesale Insurance Network; Jennie Storey, Provident Life & Accident Insurance Company; Ron Sunderman, Skogman Ralston Carlson; Phil Supple, State Farm; Doug Tillett, National Association of Life Underwriters; Julie Vokracka, American Express Company; Billy Watson, Anderson & Watson; Don White, The Group Health Association of America; Eric Wiening, American Institute for Chartered Property & Casualty Underwriters; Jim Woods, lowest-premium.com; Loretta Worters, Insurance Information Institute; Gay Yellen, Ameritas Life Insurance Company; Mark Zagaroli, State Farm; John Zarubnicky, First Transamerica Life Insurance Company.

CHAPTER 9: HOW TO MAKE YOUR LIFE LESS TAXING

Nancy Anderson, H&R Block; John Battaglia, Deloitte & Touche; Henri Bersoux, Ernst & Young; Andrea Bierstein, Kirby, McInerney, and Squire; Robert Blodgett, TurboTax; Anthony Burke, Internal Revenue Service; Joan Carroll, Coopers & Lybrand; William Church, Ernst & Young; John Collins, Investment Company Institute; Gary DuBoff, Ernst & Young; Ed Emerman, A. Foster

Higgins & Company; Wilson Fadely, Internal Revenue Service; David Fridling, Towers Perrin; Jerry Gattegno, Deloitte & Touche; Stephen Gold, Tax Foundation; Steven Gold, Center for the Study of the States; Jeffrey Gotlinger, Ernst & Young; Nadine Habousha, Arthur Andersen; Tom Hakala, KPMG Peat Marwick; David Hochstim, Bear Stearns; Ken Hubenak, Internal Revenue Service; Malin Jennings, Investment Company Institute; Judy Keisling, H&R Block; Sidney Kess, CPA; Stuart Kessler, Goldstein Golub Kessler & Company; Roger Kirby, Kirby, McInerney, and Squire; John Koegel, Grant Thornton; Dina Lee, Ernst & Young; Terry Lemons, Internal Revenue Service; L. Harold Levinson, Vanderbilt University; Glenn Liebman, Ernst & Young; Norm Magnuson, Associated Credit Bureaus; Tom Margenau, Social Security Administration; Brian Mattes, The Vanguard Group; Marilyn Morrison, Fidelity Investments; Colette Murphy, Ernst & Young; Tom Ochsenschlager, Grant Thornton; Maggie O'Donovan, Coopers & Lybrand; Glenn Pape, Ayco Company; Jodi Patterson, Internal Revenue Service; Sylvia Pozarnsky, Ernst & Young; Todd Ransom, H&R Block; Ellen Ringel, Price Waterhouse; Diane Rivers, tax attorney; Don Roberts, Internal Revenue Service; Jeff Saccacio, Coopers & Lybrand; Sherri Sankner, BDO Seidman; Bertram Schaeffer, Ernst & Young; Martin Shenkman, tax attorney; Susan Stawick, Internal Revenue Service; Ronald Stone, Stone & Associates; Richard Stricof, BDO Seidman; Peter L. Tashman, CPA; Susan Van Alstyne, H&R Block; James E. Velten, Coopers & Lybrand; Mary Vogel, H&R Block; Sidney Weinman, Research Institute of America; Craig Wolman, Ernst & Young; Paul Yurachek, Gurtz & Associates; John Ziegelbauer, Grant Thornton.

INDEX

ABOUT THE AUTHOR

Beth Kobliner has been writing and speaking on personal finance for over a decade. From 1988 through 1995, she was a staff writer at *Money* magazine, and more recently has contributed to *The New York Times*. A regular commentator on television and radio, Kobliner appears frequently on CNN, MSNBC, and public radio's *Marketplace,* and has been a repeated guest on *Today, This Morning,* and *Oprah*. She began her career researching and writing more than one hundred columns for the personal finance pioneer Sylvia Porter, whose syndicated column appeared in over 150 newspapers nationwide.

Kobliner has also been an active spokesperson for the financial concerns of Americans in their twenties and thirties. She currently sits on the board of the Women's Institute for a Secure Retirement (WISER) and in 1998 was appointed as one of sixteen honorary advisors to the National Academy of Social Insurance.

Kobliner graduated from Brown University, and lives with her husband and two children in New York City.